John Morrison Davidson

Eminent radicals in and out of Parliament

John Morrison Davidson

Eminent radicals in and out of Parliament

ISBN/EAN: 9783337152567

Printed in Europe, USA, Canada, Australia, Japan

Cover: Foto ©Suzi / pixelio.de

More available books at **www.hansebooks.com**

Eminent Radicals

in and out

of Parliament.

BY

J. MORRISON DAVIDSON
(OF THE MIDDLE TEMPLE),
BARRISTER-AT-LAW.

London:
W. STEWART & CO.,
THE HOLBORN VIADUCT STEPS, E.C.
1880.

COLSTON AND SON, PRINTERS, EDINBURGH.

TO THE READER.

THESE brief Sketches of Eminent Radicals were originally contributed to the *Weekly Dispatch.*

They were each written at a single spell, and it was not at first intended that they should be republished.

They, however, attracted an attention gratifying to me in proportion to its unexpectedness.

Many brother journalists and several distinguished members of the Legislature, whose judgment I was bound to respect, urged reproduction. Hence this volume, which owes much to the liberal enterprise of the publishers.

As regards the Sketches themselves, their chief merit, if they have any, consists in this, that they have not been "written to order," but, by the indulgence of the Editor of the *Dispatch,* express as nearly as possible the sentiments of the writer regarding twenty-four representative Radicals, with most of whom he is personally acquainted.

These "Men of the Left" I regard as the salt of our political world. Nevertheless, I can say with truth that, if I have set down nothing in malice, neither have I consciously extenuated in aught.

To complete the roll of Eminent Radicals, at least a score of other honourable names ought to be added. "There be of them that have left a name behind them, that their praises might be reported. And some there be that have no memorial; but these also were merciful men, whose righteousness shall not be forgotten; with their seed shall remain a good inheritance, and their glory shall not be blotted out. The people will tell of their wisdom, and the congregation will show forth their praise."

J. M. D.

6 PUMP COURT, TEMPLE,
   January 1880.

CONTENTS.

EMINENT RADICALS IN PARLIAMENT.

	PAGE
WILLIAM EWART GLADSTONE,	9
JOHN BRIGHT,	19
PETER ALFRED TAYLOR,	29
SIR CHARLES WENTWORTH DILKE,	38
JOSEPH COWEN,	50
SIR WILFRID LAWSON,	61
HENRY FAWCETT,	71
JOSEPH CHAMBERLAIN,	84
THOMAS BURT,	95
HENRY RICHARD,	105
LEONARD HENRY COURTNEY,	116
ANTHONY JOHN MUNDELLA,	125

EMINENT RADICALS OUT OF PARLIAMENT.

JOHN MORLEY,	137
ROBERT WILLIAM DALE,	147
JOSEPH ARCH,	158
EDWARD SPENCER BEESLY,	168

	PAGE
CHARLES HADDON SPURGEON,	179
JAMES BEAL, ...	191
MONCURE DANIEL CONWAY,	200
CHARLES BRADLAUGH, . .	210
JAMES ALLANSON PICTON, .	223
FREDERICK AUGUSTUS MAXSE,	231
THE HON. AUBERON HERBERT,	240
EDWARD AUGUSTUS FREEMAN,	251

EMINENT RADICALS
IN PARLIAMENT.

I.

WILLIAM EWART GLADSTONE.

> "His strength is as the strength of ten,
> Because his heart is pure."

MR. GLADSTONE has himself defined a Radical politician as one who "is in earnest." I thankfully accept the definition, and unhesitatingly place his honoured name at the head of this series of Biographical Sketches of Eminent Radicals. He is, and has ever been, pre-eminently in earnest —in earnest not for himself but for the commonweal. The addition, "for the commonweal," is essential to the definition for time was, of course, when Mr. Gladstone was not numbered with eminent Radicals, but with eminent Tories, whose characteristic it is, if they are in earnest at all, to be in earnest chiefly for themselves or the interests of their class. Of this latter reprehensible form of earnestness, I venture to affirm Mr. Gladstone has at no time been guilty. While yet in his misdirected youth among the Tories, he was never really of them—

> "He only in a general, honest thought,
> And common good to all, made one of them."

The circumstances of his birth and education almost necessarily determined that he should enter public life as "the rising hope" of Toryism. The strength, candour, generosity, and innate nobility of his nature have with equally irresistible force made his whole subsequent career a slow but sure process of repudiation of everything that Tories hold dear. Forty-six years ago, when he entered Parliament for Newark, as the nominee of the Duke of Newcastle, he was the hope of the High Tory party; to-day he is the hope of the undaunted Radicalism of England, which, despite Conservative reactions and Whig infidelities, knows nothing of defeat, but, like Milton—blind and fallen on evil times—"bates not a jot of heart or hope, but steers right onwards." Old as he is, his true place is at the helm of the Radical barque. Who can foresee himself?

William Ewart Gladstone is the fourth son of Sir John Gladstone of Fasque, Kincardineshire, first baronet. He was born on the 29th December 1809, at Liverpool, where his father, who had originally come from Leith, was then famous as a successful merchant, and as an influential friend and partisan of Canning. The name was originally spelt Gladstanes or Gledstanes, *gled* being Lowland Scottish for a hawk, and *stanes* meaning rocks. It is still not uncommon in many parts of rural Scotland to call a man by the place of his abode at the expense of his proper patronymic. In earlier times such local appellations often adhered permanently to individuals, and it is to this process that the Gladstone family is indebted for its name.

The ex-Premier's mother was the daughter of Mr. Andrew Robertson, Provost of Dingwall, whose descent the credulous Burke traces from Robert Bruce, the patriot King of Scotland. Be this as it may, Mr. Gladstone is of pure Scottish blood—a fact of which he has oftener than once expressed himself proud. Indeed, the *perfervidum ingenium Scotorum* is his in a remarkable degree, and it has its influence on public opinion across the Border, notwithstanding his English training and his antipathetic High-Churchism. However England may abase herself before the gorgeous Lord Benjingo, Scotland will never turn her back on the undecorated Gladstone. There lives not a Scotsman that is not inwardly proud of him, for blood is, after all, thicker than water. Evicted from one English constituency after another for his devotion to Liberal principles, there is a sort of "fitness of things" not without a certain pathos in the gallant effort which the country of his forefathers has made to seize a seat for him from between the teeth of the great feudal despot of the North, "the bold Buccleuch."

From a very tender age young Gladstone exhibited a wonderful aptitude for learning, and an almost superhuman industry, which age, instead of abating, seemingly increases. His daily autograph correspondence with high and low, rich and poor, conducted chiefly by the much-derided post-card, would afford ample employment for about six Somerset House clerks working at their usual pace. He possesses, I should say, without exception, the most omnivorous and untiring brain in England, possibly in the whole world. No wonder that his course at Eton and at Oxford was marked by the highest distinction. A student of Christ Church, he graduated "double first" in his twenty-second year, a superlative master of the language and literature of Greece and Rome. He availed himself of every advantage the university could bestow, and, unlike most other scholars who subsequently become politicians and men of the world, he has never ceased to add to the immense store of his academic acquirements. He has published Latin sacred verses not appreciably inferior in grace to those of Buchanan and Milton, and as a Homeric student his "Studies of Homer and the Homeric Age" entitle him to no mean place among scholarly critics.

Unfortunately, however, for him, the sciences of observation—chemistry, botany, geology, natural history, and the like—were in his day almost wholly neglected at Oxford, and in place thereof an incredible mind-distorting theology was in vogue, from the evil consequences of which the ex-Premier has not yet been able altogether to emancipate himself. It has laid him open to many false charges, and to some true ones. It made him for years a defender of the utterly indefensible Irish Establishment, and when at last "the slow and resistless force of conviction" brought him to a better frame of mind, the change was attributed by thousands who ought to have known better to a concealed conversion to Romansim. In vain has he striven in pamphlet and periodical to rebut the allegation, and to make intelligible to the English people his theological standpoint. Newman, Manning, Capel, the most redoubtable champions of Roman Catholicism in England, he has met, foot to foot, and hand to hand, on their own ground, and foiled with their own weapons. He has proved with amazing learning and ingenuity worthy of the Schoolmen that the Papacy has at last succeeded in "repudiating both science and history," and that his Holiness himself is next door to Antichrist.

He, a simple layman, has demonstrated that he is one of the greatest theologians of the age. Still, much as I admire learning in every department of human intelligence, I must confess that I should have liked Mr. Gladstone better had he been more of a Gallio in such matters. One would almost as soon see a noble intellect like his exercising itself about the exploded theories of the astrologists or alchemists as about the decisions of Church Councils, early or late.

His personal religion is, however, altogether another matter. It is the chief source of his overpowering sense of duty, of his righteous indignation, of his tender humanity. He is as much a Christian statesman as Pym, Sir Harry Vane, or Oliver Cromwell. His unaffected piety has opened up to him the hearts of his Nonconformist fellow-countrymen as nothing else could have done. Where he is best known he is most esteemed—viz., at his seat of Hawarden, a fine property, bought by his wife's ancestor Sergeant Glynne, Chief Justice to Oliver Cromwell, on the sequestration of the Stanley estates, after the execution of James, the seventh Earl of Derby.

Every morning, by eight o'clock, Mr. Gladstone may be seen wending his way to the village church of Hawarden to engage in matins as a prelude to the work of the day. Even when Prime Minister of England he has been found in the humblest homes reading to the sick or dying consolatory passages of Scripture in his own soft melodious tones.

The best controller of the national exchequer that the country has ever had, his personal charities are almost reckless. In the course of his long walks in the neighbourhood of Hawarden, his pockets have an astonishing knack of emptying themselves, and amusing stories are told of his having had to walk home inconvenient distances of ten and twelve miles in the dark because of his inability to raise so much as a third-class railway fare. As Prime Minister he refused an increase of salary, and when he quitted office he was so impoverished that his famous collection of china is said to have been sold in consequence.

All his known habits and recreations are of the most innocent and healthy kind. He has nothing either of the jockey or the gamekeeper in his composition—a fact which may account for a good deal of the antipathy exhibited towards him by the enlightened squirearchy of England. Yet Mr. Gladstone has none of the "lean and hungry look" of a Cassius about him. He is not a total abstainer, but he is next door. His is pre-eminently a *mens sana in corpore sano*. As is well known, he is one of the most stalwart tree-fellers in England. His skill with his axe would not disgrace a Canadian backwoodsman, and he has curious taste in carving and pottery which is almost scientific.

Never was there a public man whose private "record"— to use an Americanism—has been more blameless. In his zeal for domestic purity, he has not hesitated to rebuke the "conjugal infidelity" which, since the death of the Prince Consort, has developed itself in close proximity to the Throne. In a word, he is a Christian statesman with all the advantages and disadvantages which adhere to that character.

Let me now say a word of his renown as an orator. As a speaker I should be disposed to place him midway between Bright at his best and Beaconsfield at any time. For moral earnestness Mr. Bright is not his inferior, and in the command of pathos, humour, clear-cut thoughts, and chaste, limpid English, he is undoubtedly his superior. On the other hand, in versatility, in capacity for receiving new ideas, and of marshalling multitudinous details, Mr. Gladstone has no living equal. He is the orator of affairs. He has done what no one has ever done before him, made Budgets eloquent, and figures to possess a lofty moral significance.

Lord Beaconsfield unquestionably possesses in an eminent degree some of the first requisites of oratory. He is more witty, more ornate, and more audacious than his great rival, but all is spoiled by levity, hopeless inaccuracy, and, I fear, essential insincerity. "Can there be," Mr. Carlyle has asked, "a more horrid object in creation than an eloquent man not speaking the truth?" Was it "the cool conscious juggler," the "Miraculous Premier" of to-day, that the Prophet of Chelsea had in his mind's eye when, years ago, I heard him put this important interrogatory on the occasion of his Rectorial address to the students of Edinburgh University? Again, I fear, Yes.

Mr. Gladstone's oratory is marred by excessive copiousness of diction, yet there is a charm in this rare defect. He plunges right into a sea of words from which there seems no possible extrication, and when he emerges safe and sound his hearers feel like those who, "in the brave days of old," beheld Horatius "plunge headlong in the tide":—

> "And when above the surges
> They saw his crest appear,
> All Rome sent forth a rapturous cry,
> And even the ranks of Tuscany
> Could scarce forbear to cheer."

Mr. Gladstone's conduct as a Parliamentary leader has been severely censured by professed Liberals, and his resolution to dissolve Parliament in 1874 has been specially instanced as a proof of strategic unwisdom. I distinctly demur both to indictment and proof. Those who say that he is not a good leader are not "in earnest," and such men can never be expected to follow Mr. Gladstone with much comfort to themselves. He is the natural leader of the Advanced Liberals in the House. The Brights, Dilkes, Chamberlains, Taylors, and Courtneys would find no difficulty in following his lead. As for the dissolution of 1874, so much complained of, no Liberal Minister professing to govern, as every Liberal Minister is supposed to do, in accordance with the will of the people, could, in the face of the adverse bye-elections which had taken place, honestly refrain from directly appealing to the constitutent authority. Indeed, the pity is, it seems to me, that the appeal was not made sooner, for if that had been done, all might have been well. The Conservative reaction might have been nipped in the bud.

It remains to notice in very brief compass a few of the more important events in the ex-Premier's public life, giving preference to the more remote. In 1832 he was returned for Newark in the Conservative interest, and in 1834 Sir Robert Peel made him a Junior Lord of the Treasury. In 1835 he found himself Under-Secretary for the Colonies. Shortly after Sir Robert's Administration fell, and Mr. Gladstone, in the cool shade of Opposition, found leisure to write his oft-quoted works, "The State in its Relations with the Church," and "Church Principles considered in their Results." Lord Macaulay, in the *Edinburgh Review*, thus spoke the judgment of posterity:—"We dissent from his opinions, but we admire his talents; we respect his integrity and benevolence, and we hope that he will not suffer political avocations so entirely to engross him as to leave him no leisure for literature and philosophy."

In those days Mr. Gladstone held the untenable doctrine that it is the business of the State to uphold "the true religion." He ardently strove to find for the State Church a moral basis and justification which it can never have. In so doing he was "in earnest," but oblivious of the wisdom of one who understood the genius of Christianity better than himself: "My kingdom is not of this world." Since then "the slow and resistless force of conviction" has come to his aid.

In 1841 Sir Robert Peel came back to office, and Mr. Gladstone was made Vice-President of the Board of Trade. In 1843 he became President of the Board, and for the first time his wonderful genius for finance had full scope. In 1845 he resigned office rather than be a party to adding to the endowments of Maynooth, which he had condemned in his work on "Church and State." Shiel wittily remarked that "the statesman had been sacrificed to the author." In point of fact his resignation is a standing rebuke to those who have basely accused him of place-hunting.

From this time onwards Mr. Gladstone exhibited in increasing measure and in numerous ways his leaning towards Liberal opinions. Canningite and Oxford influences began to lose their hold over him. "I trace," he said at Oxford in December last, "in the education of Oxford of my own time one great defect. Perhaps the fault was mine, but I must admit that I did not learn when at Oxford that which I have learned since—viz., to set a due value on the imperishable and inestimable principles of human liberty." In the Budget of 1845 he defended a proposal to put slave-grown sugar on a less favourable footing than free, and when the Corn Law question became a "burning" one he resigned his seat for Newark because of the anti-repeal views of the Duke of Newcastle. His powerful pen was, however, at the service of the repealers, and when the battle was fought and won he was returned in 1847 for the University of Oxford. He was still, of course, nominally a Tory, but one of his first acts was to support the removal of Jewish disabilities, to the confusion of many of those whose "rising hope" he was still supposed to be.

In the session of 1849 he made a powerful speech in favour of the reform of our colonial policy, from which much benefit has indirectly flowed to the colonies.

In 1851 "circumstances purely domestic" took him to Naples, and there his humanity was stirred to its very core by the unheard-of brutalities of King Bomba. His passionate cry for redress sounded throughout the civilised world: "I have seen and heard the strong and true expression used, 'This is the negation of God erected into a system of government.'" For once Lord Palmerston was on the side of justice, and the sword of Garibaldi eventually wrought out for the Neapolitans the just vengeance which Mr. Gladstone had invoked on their tyrants.

In the Administration of 1859, Mr. Gladstone, as Chancellor of the Exchequer, was instrumental in the repeal of the paper duty and in contracting the commercial treaty with France. Of his remission of taxes and reductions of the National Debt it is unnecessary to speak. They are achievements engraved with an iron pen on the financial records of the country.

Two great questions, and two only, of his time has he completely misjudged, the Crimean war and the American war. Of the first he was, to some extent, *particeps criminis*, and with regard to the latter a singularly rash and hostile utterance numbered him with the friends of Secession. For the former he has atoned by his late almost superhuman efforts to prevent its recurrence; and for the latter there is ample compensation in our wisest international act, the Alabama arbitration.

Of the mighty impulse which he gave to the movement which ended in household suffrage being conferred on "our own flesh and blood," of the imperishable achievements of his late Ministry in passing the Ballot Act and the Education Act, in abolishing purchase in the army, and above all in disestablishing the Church of Ireland and reforming the land laws of that unhappy country, what need to speak? To no Englishman of our time has it been given to perform such eminent service to his country and to humanity. His Radicalism, commencing to meander more than forty years ago among the stony uplands of Toryism, is now, as the limit of life is approached, a majestic river, whose ample flood will never be stinted or stayed till it is lost in the ocean of eternity.

The times are fickle and out of joint. At the last general election the constituencies deliberately cried out, "Not this man, but Barabbas!" They have since given many signs that they have had quite enough of Barabbas. That the exceeding gravity of the times demands the return to office of the ex-Premier there can be no doubt. He is emphatically the man of the situation. In any case, if he has not done enough for humanity,—if he has still, as he says, a whole catalogue of "unredeemed pledges" to submit,—he has done enough and more than enough to enshrine his name imperishably in the hearts of all good men:—

> "His life was gentle ; and the elements
> So mixed in him, that Nature might stand up
> And say to all the world, *This was a Man!*"

II.

JOHN BRIGHT.

———◆———

"Thou art e'en as just a man
As e'er my conversation coped withal."

THERE is a quaint passage in "Ecclesiasticus" which expresses better than anything I can think of my conception of the way in which Mr. Bright will be regarded by a not distant posterity. "Let us praise famous men," it runs, "and our fathers that begat us. God hath wrought great glory by them through His great power from the beginning; men renowned for their power giving counsel by their understanding, and declaring prophecies; leaders of the people by their counsels and by their knowledge meet for the people, wise and eloquent in their instructions; rich men furnished with ability, living peaceably in their habitations." "All these," it is added, "were honoured in their generations, and were the glory of their times." And, assuredly, if characteristics such as these appertain to any man of our day and generation, it is to John Bright. What leader of the people has given wiser counsel, more eloquent instruction—nay, declared more prophecies? As applied to him the title of Right Honourable is, for a wonder, fully deserved. It fits like a glove. From the beginning of his career until now "great glory has been wrought by him," and that, too, "through His great power," Mr. Bright would be the first to postulate.

Least of all our public men is the illustrious Tribune of the People an adventurer, self-seeker, or demagogue. I do not know that he can be described as a "rich" man. Riches is a specially comparative term in this aristocracy-ridden land, but certainly the Anti-Corn Law agitation found him a well-to-do man, "furnished with ability, living peaceably in his habitation" at Rochdale, where he might have remained to this day hardly distinguishable from the mass of his fellow citizens, had he not had what, in the phraseology of Puritanism, is named a "call." He was at the mill, as Elisha was at the plough, when the divine messenger laid hold of him in the guise of a gaunt, starving multitude, for whose wrongs he was imperatively commanded to seek redress at the hands of a heartless and stupid Legislature. The Corn Laws repealed, the horizon of his public duties widened, but the spirit in which he has continued to act has remained the same. He is the great Puritan statesman of England, ever consciously living, as did his favourite poet Milton, "in his great Taskmaster's eye." This is the key to his simple but grand character, as it is to that of the much more complex Gladstone—a singular fact, certainly, in view of the grave doubts now entertained in so many not incompetent quarters with respect to the objective reality of all religious beliefs.

Mr. Bright has completed his sixty-eighth year, having been born in 1811, in his father's house at Greenbank, near Rochdale. Needless to say his ancestors did *not* "come over at the Conquest." So far as is known, there is not a single "de" among them. The first discoverable local habitation of the Brights is a place still called "Bright's Farm," near Lyncham, in Wiltshire. Here, in 1714, a certain Abraham Bright married Martha Jacobs, a handsome Jewess, and shortly afterwards the couple removed to Coventry, where Abraham begat William Bright, who begat Jacob, who begat Jacob junior, who, coming to Rochdale in 1796, was espoused to Martha Wood, the daughter of a respectable tradesman of Bolton-le-Moors, and became in due course the father of John the Great, the subject of this sketch.

Mr. Bright's ancestry abounds in Abrahams and Jacobs, Marthas and Marys. He has a sort of vested interest in Scriptural characters and Scriptural knowledge which comes as instinctively to him as fox-hunting to a squire of the county. He is a hereditary Nonconformist, nearly all his relatives, as is well known, being members of the Society of Friends. He may be said to have been born resisting church rates. His father, a most estimable man, could never be induced to pay them, and was, in consequence, as familiar with execution warrants as with the pages of his ledger. Not a bad example, assuredly, for a youthful People's Tribune! Bright the elder had started life as a poor but honest weaver, working, as his right honourable son has told all the world, for six shillings a week! In 1809 he took an old mill named Greenbank. Some Manchester friends who had confidence in his intelligence and integrity supplied the capital, and by the time that the ex-President of the Board of Trade had attained years of discretion, the family were in easy circumstances. The business has since been much developed, but the knowledge that Mr. Bright, from the first, possessed a substantial "stake in the country," has given a cogency to his more Radical and humanitarian opinions, in the eyes of the middle class, which no amount of mere argument could have ever supplied.

Was Mr. Bright equally happy in his education? The question is one of great difficulty, but, on the whole, I am disposed to think he was. True, he did not learn much at the Friends' schools which he frequented, but, on the other hand, unlike Mr. Gladstone, with his great academic acquirements, he learned nothing which it has been necessary for him by a painful process to unlearn. If, like Shakespeare, he "knows little Latin and less Greek," he knows uncommonly well how to do without them. At the Ackworth and York schools his heart was cultivated if his head was not crammed. The foundations were laid deep and strong of a placid, free, wise, and upright manhood. "Knowledge comes, but wisdom lingers." It was the educational aim of the Friends of Bright's childhood to instil wisdom first, and to leave knowledge pretty much to take care of itself. I do not like to contemplate what might have happened to Mr. Bright if he had gone to Eton and to Oxford with Mr. Gladstone and drunk in all the pernicious ecclesiastical and political nonsense which the ex-Premier imbibed in his misdirected youth. Mr. Gladstone has survived Oxford and come out clothed and in his right mind, but it is highly doubtful if Mr. Bright would have been equally fortunate. He is by temperament a Conservative, who has been singularly faithful to all the ideals with which he started life. What he is to-day he was forty-five years ago. His principles are far-reaching and susceptible of varied application, but I venture to affirm that if they were once realised, he would be about the last man in England to find new ones. He is the incarnation of Quakerism, summing up in his own person all its noble law and all its prophets. The sect which has been numerically so weak and morally so strong will never produce another such. Its theory of the public good, though perhaps the highest of any, is limited after all.

One part of Mr. Bright's education which was not neglected, and which has been to him from boyhood a source of real inspiration, I ought not to overlook—viz., his study of the great poets. He has a genius for appropriate quotation, and if I might give a hint to my young readers, let me recommend them to verify, as occasion offers, the sources from which he draws. They will be well repaid for the trouble.

Like most generous and humane natures, he is fond of the lower animals, more especially of dogs; but his canine, I am sorry to say, are not equal to his unerring poetic instincts. In this respect he is not much above the shockingly low average taste of Lancashire. In his youth he was a good football player, a smart cricketer, an expert swimmer, and during a period of convalescence, more than twenty years ago, he acquired the art of salmon fishing, which he has since, for recreative reasons chiefly, brought to considerable perfection. He is a total abstainer, and what with a steady hand, a quick eye, and indomitable patience, few better amateur anglers appear on the Spey.

He is a charming companion, with a weakness for strolling into billiard-rooms. Once at Llandudno, the story goes, he played in a public billiard-room with a stranger, who turned out to be a truculent Tory manufacturer from Yorkshire. While the game was proceeding, the Yorkshireman's wife chanced to ask some of the hotel attendants how her husband was engaged, and was beside herself with alarm on learning that he was in the company of one against whom she had so often heard him express the most bloodthirsty sentiments. "Are they fighting?" she asked, and could with difficulty be persuaded that no altercation was going on. About a couple of hours afterwards the husband turned up, rubbing his hands, and told his wife with much satisfaction that he had just been having a game at billiards with a most pleasant casual acquaintance, and that they had arranged for another trial of skill next day. "Why," exclaimed the lady, "it is John Bright you have been playing with!" The manufacturer's countenance fell, but speedily recovering himself he observed, in extenuation of his conduct, that the newspapers always told lies about people, and so thoroughly was he now satisfied of Mr. Bright's entire harmlessness that, in given circumstances, he should vote for him himself.

At home, at One Ash, Mr. Bright enjoys universal respect. His abode, though most unostentatious, is a model of comfort and good taste. His library is noteworthy, being specially rich in history, biography, and poetry. At the close of the Corn Law agitation upwards of £5000 were subscribed by his admirers, and 1200 volumes purchased therewith, as some slight acknowledgment of his powerful advocacy of the good cause. As of yore, he regularly attends the services at the humble meeting-house of the Friends, and as age advances the sources of his piety show no symptom of drying up. His charities, and—

> "That best portion of a good man's life,
> His little, nameless, unremembered acts
> Of kindness and of love,"

which are in reality numerous, are seldom recorded, because Mr. Bright, like his father before him, declines to blow a trumpet when he does a good deed. He acts on the principle of not letting his right hand know what his left hand doeth in such matters, and, as a consequence, his benefactions are better known to the beneficiaries than to the public.

As to Mr. Bright's relations with his work-people, many lying legends were at one time circulated by the Tory press. They practically, however, received their quietus on the 25th of January 1867, when the alleged victims of Mr. Bright's tyranny met and unanimously passed resolutions so complimentary to their employer that for shame's cause the Conservative organs had to look about for fresh subjects of vilification. At that time Mr. Bright was able to say, "From 1809 to 1867 is at least fifty-seven years, and I venture to affirm that with one single exception, and that not of long duration, there has been during that period uninterrupted harmony and confidence between my family and those who have assisted us and been employed in it." How few employers in this age of "strikes" can say as much!

With respect to Mr. Bright's oratory, I agree with all competent judges that it is as nearly as possible perfect. He is the prince of English speakers. I have been told by some authorities who have heard Wendell Phillips speak that he is equal to Mr. Bright, but from speeches by the celebrated American which I have read, I should very much doubt it. The heart, the conscience, the intellect, Mr. Bright can touch with equal ease. His speech is the natural expression of a mind at once beautiful and strong. The whole man speaks, and not, as is the case with most other speakers, only a part of him. His words glide like a pleasant brook, without haste and without rest. His rising in the House is always an event. I remember by chance being in the Speaker's Gallery on a Wednesday afternoon when he made his now celebrated speech on the Burials Bill. He had seldom spoken since his severe illness, and was not expected to address the House. The debate had been of the poorest select vestry stamp, without ability and without human interest of any kind, when suddenly a movement of expectation was visible on both sides of the House—

> "And hark! the cry is 'Astur!' and lo, the ranks divide,
> And the great lord of Luna comes with his stately stride.
> Upon his ample shoulders clangs loud the four-fold shield,
> And in his hand he shakes the brand which none save he can wield."

The effect was magical. Languid and recumbent legislators sat erect, and were all attention in a moment. It was curious to observe how the occupants of the Conservative benches, the majority of whom in the present Parliament look for all the world like a band of horse-jockeys and prize-fighters, were affected. Mr. Bright talked to them with all the simplicity and confidence of a good paterfamilias addressing his family circle with his back to his own mantelpiece. And such talk! No wonder that they listened with silent respect. The whole House was transformed by it, and began to feel something like a proper sense of its own duty and dignity. Before he had spoken five minutes, the level of the debate had been raised fifty degrees at least, and there was not an honourable, nor, for the matter of that, a dishonourable, member present who did not feel that the Government was morally and logically routed, whatever its numerical triumph might be.

Mr. Bright does one thing of which so many members are oblivious; he never in any of his speeches in Parliament forgets that he is in the Great Council of the nation; and however violent may be the supposition, he always assumes that his opponents are there to be convinced, if only the matter at issue is put in a proper light. The prevailing tone of his mind is one of hopefulness. He has large faith, and believes in the inevitable progress of humanity and the ultimate invincibility of truth. As he once said—"There is much shower and sunshine between the sowing of the seed and the reaping of the harvest, but the harvest *is* reaped after all."

But though his nature is large and forgiving, in solemn earnestness of rebuke he is unmatched. Once or twice Lord Palmerston, in the very height of his power and popularity, was made to wince like a convict under the sentence of a judge, and, if we except the unique moral insensibility of a Beaconsfield, it would be difficult to conceive of a more arduous undertaking than that of reaching the conscience of Lord Palmerston.

In the terrible struggle which threatened to rend the great American Republic to pieces, the innermost soul of the Tribune of the People was stirred within him, and he touched the limits of actual prophecy. In the darkest hour of the fortunes of the North he declared—"The Chancellor of the Exchequer (Mr. Gladstone) as a speaker is not surpassed by any man in England, and he is a great statesman; he believes the cause of the North to be hopeless; and that their enterprise cannot succeed. . . . . I have another and a far brighter vision before my gaze. It may be a vision, but I will cherish it. I see one vast confederation, stretching from the frozen North in unbroken line to the glowing South, and from the wild billows of the Atlantic westward to the calmer waters of the Pacific main; and I see one people and one language, and one law and one faith, and over all that wide continent the home of freedom and a refuge for the oppressed of every race and of every clime."

It remains to notice, however briefly, some of the more noticeable events of Mr. Bright's public life. They have not been so numerous as might, on first thoughts, be supposed, for he has all his days been a sower of seed and not a reaper, and of much that he has sown future generations will reap the fruit. His "record" will be best found in his collected speeches, which are, in my opinion, the finest in the language, whether as regards matter or diction. I know no politician who has been more uniformly in the right when others have been in the wrong, and I know no greater master of the English tongue.

His first public appearance was made at Rochdale in 1830, in his nineteenth year. It was in favour of temperance, and is said to have been a success. Like most young speakers, he commenced by committing to memory what he intended to utter on the platform, but soon abandoned so clumsy and exhaustive a method of address. Instead of *memoriter* reproductions he held impromptu rehearsals at odd hours in his father's mill before Mr. Nicholas Nuttall, an intelligent workman and unsparing critic; but even now his perorations are written out with the greatest care. In those days Mr. Bright was a diligent reader of the *Dispatch* newspaper, and I trust he is still addicted to a practice so laudable. Like most young men in easy circumstances, he had a desire for travel, which was gratified by a visit to Jerusalem. On coming within sight of the Holy City he was melted to tears.

In the month of October 1838, the Anti-Corn Law League had its insignificant and unpromising beginning. Five Scotsmen, W. A. Cunningham, Andrew Dalzell, James Leslie, Archibald Prentis, and Philip Thomson, residents in Manchester, along with William Rawson, a native of the town, met like the Apostles of old, in an "upper room," and decreed the orgin of the mammoth association. In the printed list of the members of the provisional committee Mr. Bright's name stands second. He had found his vocation, and in the course of the memorable campaign that followed, he and the late Mr. Cobden contracted a friendship which has justly become historic. In speaking in the House of Mr. Cobden's decease, the strong man, bowed down with the weight of his sorrow, was barely able to utter:—"After twenty years of most intimate and almost brotherly friendship with him, I little knew how much I loved him until I found that I had lost him."

In 1843, Mr. Bright first took his seat in Parliament for Durham, and in 1847 he was returned for Manchester without opposition. In 1852 he was re-elected after a contest, but at the subsequent general election of 1857 he lost his seat on account of his unbending opposition to the Crimean war and to the swagger of Palmerston in China. In the autumn of the same year, however, he was returned by Birmingham at a bye-election, and has continued to represent the great Radical Mecca in Parliament ever since.

His memorable defeat at Manchester was, for him, the greatest moral victory of his life, and he has had many. With a sublime courage which has never been surpassed, he strove almost single-handed to arrest in its mad career a whole nation in pursuit of a mischievous phantom. In the American war his services to his own country and to America were unrivalled, and happily more successful.

That he is one of the best and most intelligent friends of India, of Ireland, and of the unenfranchised and unprivileged masses of Englishmen and Scotsmen, will go without saying. As a member of Mr. Gladstone's Cabinet he was introduced at Court, and is said to be a favourite there. I should have liked him better had he continued—to use his own words —"to abide among his own people." Evil communications have a tendency to corrupt the best manners, and Mr. Bright has never been at his best since he made the acquaintance of royalty.

Latterly the brunt of the fighting has fallen on Gladstone, who, by an arduous heart-searching process, has, at seventy, reached conceptions of the public good which were familiar to Mr. Bright's mind at twenty. It is now Mr. Bright's turn to put his powerful hand to the plough. He looks vigorous as ever, and it has not been his wont to spare himself in great emergencies. Let him remember the wisdom of Ulysses addressed to the " great and god-like " Achilles :—

> " To have done,
> Is to hang quite out of fashion, like a rusty mail,
> In monumental mockery."

III.

PETER ALFRED TAYLOR.

———◆———

"And I have walked with Hampden and with Vane,
Names *once* so gracious in an English ear."

HAVING now portrayed, however imperfectly, our two most illustrious Radical statesmen, Mr. Gladstone and Mr. Bright, I come to deal with one who is not a statesman—who makes no pretension to statesmanship—but who as a politician has nevertheless "been fashioned unto much honour from the cradle." His name will not be found, I think, even among that multitude which no man can number, the "Men of the Times."

Nor is the omission so culpable as may at first sight appear, for Mr. P. A. Taylor belongs at once to the Radical past and the Radical future rather than to the imperialised present. He is the most unique figure in the House of Commons, a man who in the days of the Long Parliament would have been after gentle Lucy Hutchinson's own Republican heart, and who in those of Queen Victoria has been best appreciated by such gifted pioneers of progress as Mazzini and Mill. He has now represented Leicester in Parliament for seventeen years, and all that time he has neither led nor followed: neither been mislead by the leaders of his party nor been found following the multitude to do evil. If he has led at any time, it has been as the captain of forlorn hopes, the champion of forgotten rights, the redresser of unheeded wrongs. He is the Incorruptible of the House. In evil and in good report he has striven to subject every issue that has presented itself to the test of general principles of human well being.

I am not now considering whether he has been uniformly right in particular deductions from these principles. He may or he may not; all I say is that he has been uniformly true to his principles from his youth up. They alone have been his leaders. Of "doctrines fashioned to the varying hour" he has known nothing, and, from the constitution of his mind, will never know.

Mr. Taylor is generally considered an eccentric member, but his eccentricity is wholly on the surface. Once understand his principles, or rather solitary principle of action—viz., that liberty, liberty, liberty, is the best of all things in all things political, religious, social or commercial, and the course which the senior member for Leicester will pursue on any given question may be predicted almost with mathematical certainty.

I always remember a curiously instructive telegraphic summary of a speech delivered by Mr. Taylor to his constituents about the time of the Republican agitation. It was a model of compression, but it illustrates admirably what I have been saying It appeared among other items of "Election News," and ran thus:—"Mr. P. A. Taylor, the member for Leicester, addressed his constituents last night. He declared for the Republic and against the Permissive Bill." I don't know whether the intelligent reporter saw any irony in the juxtaposition into which the Republic and the Permissive Bill were thus brought, but sure I am that Mr. Taylor would have recognised none. According to his views, the one was in favour of, the other in opposition to, liberty. Hence his support and his antagonism. Both flowed naturally from the same source—a source at once of strong personal conviction and ancestral pride.

It may appear somewhat strange to attribute ancestral pride to an out-and-out Democrat like Mr. Taylor, but it is impossible fully to understand his character without taking the markedly Liberal tendencies of his forefathers, both in politics and religion, into account. Mr. Taylor may be described as a hereditary Radical of two and a half centuries' standing.

The pseudo-science of heraldry is coming to have an unexpected value as an aid to the study of the laws of heredity. Mental-like physical characteristics are shown to persist and recur from generation to generation, contrary to all our preconceived notions of the determining causes of the opinions of individuals and the way in which they are formed. The acquisition of riches is vulgarly supposed to make the best of Radicals Conservatives. Self-interest, it is held, induces them instinctively to throw in their lot with the privileged classes, but the history of some of the most respectable and well-to-do families in England proves the very opposite. The instinct in favour of progress may fail for a generation, but it soon reappears.

Mr. Taylor's genealogy is in itself a standing refutation of ordinarily accepted theories. The name is distinctly of plebeian origin; but, as early as the reign of Edward III., Mr. Taylor's progenitors possessed large estates in Huntingdonshire. They "bore arms" of course, and, evidently with the desire, if possible, to *aristocratise* their name, they called themselves Taylards. And this continued to be the spelling till the close of the sixteenth century, when the patronymic was restored to the more ancient plebeian form by an irate Taylard who considered that he had had enough of aristocracy. The head of the family had died leaving a pregnant wife behind him and a will which intentionally or otherwise omitted the normal word "male." A girl was born, and an astute gentleman, named Brudenell, who afterwards became Earl of Cardigan, married the heiress and her estates, in her fourteenth year. The Taylards took the matter into Chancery, but failed to secure the succession, and being greatly impoverished, their chief representative came to London and established himself on the spot where Messrs. Longmans' well-known publishing house now stands, as plain "Mr. Taylor, Haberdasher."

He prospered in business, and was a staunch supporter of the Commonwealth, which rewarded his zeal by several important appointments. He was a warm friend of the regicides, and added to his political misconduct religious heresy. He ably defended the noted Socinian preacher of the day, Goodwin.

At the Restoration, William Taylor, son of this Republican haberdasher, was pardoned by Charles II. for his father's manifold offences, on the payment of a heavy fine—pardoned (he was but fourteen!) "for all manners of treacheries, crimes, treasons, misprisons, . . . all and singular murders."

Passing rapidly down the stream of time, we come to the Rev. Henry Taylor, of Portsmouth, who matriculated at Cambridge University in 1729. He is better known as Ben Mordecai, from the production of a very clever book entitled "The Apology of Benjamin Ben Mordecai for embracing Christianity." He possessed all the family characteristics in an eminent degree. In religion he was an Arian and Universalist, and neither menace nor persuasion could ever induce him to read the Athanasian Creed from his pulpit. He tried hard to get the Prayer-Book reformed, and all but succeeded in procuring the objects for which Broad Churchmen still sigh. He denounced the Game Laws, and would not turn on his heel to be introduced to royalty when it came in his way. Albeit a Churchman he was in all respects the prototype of the honourable member for Leicester, Radical in politics as in religion, with a caustic vein of drollery, of which the following extract from a circular to the clergy, found among his papers, may serve as a specimen. It reminds one forcibly of Mr. Taylor's own very clever contribution to the "Pen and Pencil Club" styled "Realities." It is fittingly labelled "Impudent," and begins: "One hundred and fifty sermons, such as are greatly admired and are but little known, engraved in a masterly running hand, printed on stout writing paper, and made to resemble manuscript as nearly as possible; in length from twenty to twenty-five minutes, as pithy as possible, intelligible to every understanding, and as fit to be preached to a polite as to a country congregation," etc.

Nor is Mr. Taylor descended from a Radical stock on the paternal side alone. His maternal grandfather was George Courtauld, who travelled much on philanthropic missions in America, and was the fast friend of Dr. Priestley and Thomas Paine. The first of the Courtaulds is said in infancy to have been smuggled to England in a pannier by his Huguenot guardians, at the Revocation of the Edict of Nantes. Not only was George Courtauld a zealous Unitarian, but his political sympathies appear also to have been Republican. Writing from America to a relative in England, he shrewdly remarks, "I cannot but think with Mr. Paine that you have no Constitution. You have, indeed, a form of Government, but how you came by that it is very difficult to say—certainly it was not that form which, after mature deliberation, the people of England chose for themselves."

Within the last few years Lord Beaconsfield has demonstrated to all whom it may concern that Mr. Taylor's grandfather and Mr. Paine were not far wrong in divining that the English people have "no Constitution," only "a form of Government," which, in the hands of a despotic Minister, may be twisted into the most dangerous imperialistic shape. "Our glorious Constitution" is a political imposture and superstition which the member for Leicester, the descendant of such a clear-sighted race of iconoclasts, can hardly be expected to swallow without protest.

Mr. P. A. Taylor, M.P., was born in London, in 1819. He is the eldest son of Peter Alfred Taylor, of the old and highly respected firm of Courtauld, Taylor, & Courtauld, silk manufacturers, Bocking, Braintree, Halstead. He was educated in the first instance at the Unitarian School at Brighton, then taught by the Rev. J. P. Malleson. At fourteen years of age he was removed to London, and for a short time he attended University College.

Of the Unitarians, as a sect, it has been wittily said that if they can only see their way to believe in one God, they invariably pay twenty shillings in the pound. They are an eminently rational, upright, and progressive people; and politically their services to the country have been invaluable. In all respects, Mr. Taylor's educational and social advantages were of the most enviable kind. His father was an ardent opponent of the Corn Laws, of Church Rates, and of a limited franchise. The friends of Mr. Taylor's youth were reformers of the highest intellectual grasp, including Mill, Mazzini, Colonel Perronet Thomson, and Ebenezer Elliot, the Corn-Law Rhymer.

The man, however, to whom Mr. Taylor owed most was the celebrated W. J. Fox, the minister of South Place Chapel, Finsbury, where the Taylors, father and son, attended for many years. Mr. Fox was a preacher of extraordinary talent and energy. From being the "Norwich Weaver Boy" he became simultaneously minister of the most intellectual congregation in the metropolis, member of Parliament for Oldham, and last, not least, he wielded the powerful pen of "Publicola" in the *Weekly Dispatch*. After his death, Mr. Taylor, in one of the best speeches he ever delivered, said of him with much truth: "His political principles were not so weakly based that he feared to trace the result in the history of various kinds of government; nor his religion so poorly grounded as to fear scientific inquiry. He searched after truth, and followed wherever it might lead him." In portraying Fox's virtues, Mr. Taylor described the leading features of his own mind.

Very early in life Mr. Taylor entered his father's business, for which he showed aptitude of the highest order, and by 1866 he was able to retire from the firm with a handsome competency. This fact is all the more gratifying that for upwards of twenty years previously he had been giving up much of his time to the public service.

In quitting connection with the firm, Mr. Taylor addressed a characteristic circular to all the *employés*. "My friends," it said among other things, "with the close of the old year has ceased, as you all probably are aware, my connection with the business, and therefore with you. I cannot let such a connection cease without just one word of kindly farewell, of hearty good wishes. In wishing you farewell, I reflect with satisfaction that the name of Taylor will still be represented in the house by my brother. Finally, let me say that should my name ever reach you in connection with any question of public interest, I can promise beforehand that it will only be on the side ever upheld by my father before me —that, viz., of justice for all, and of political enfranchisement for the working classes."

In Parliament, Mr. Taylor is rapt and solitary, living in the world of his own ideas. Nevertheless, his singleness of purpose, accuracy of statement, genuine humour, originality of ideas, and clear, effective speaking never fail to secure for him a respectful hearing, however distasteful may be the subject of his address.

At home he is a delightful host, an inveterate joker of jokes. His wife, a lady of great accomplishments, is hardly behind him in zeal for the public good. Every post brings heaps of letters from aggrieved subjects of her Majesty in all parts of the world. They are all carefully considered, and parliamentary or extra-parliamentary redress invoked, according to circumstances. In his capacity of redresser-general of unheeded wrongs and oppressions, Mr. Taylor has quite a business to attend to; and in this character have some of his greatest senatorial successes been achieved.

He is the terror of the "great unpaid," whose cruel antics throughout rural England he has done much to curb. Every day justices' justice is more of a byword and a reproach. He has striven hard to remove the inequalities of Sunday legislation, and the poor of London in particular owe him a debt of gratitude for taking the sting out of the great harasser of their lives, that too "busy bee," Bee Wright. It is but the other day that Mr. Taylor, at a cost of more than £2000, presented the working men of Brighton with a People's Club which will secure to them on Sundays something like the advantages of a local Carlton or Reform.

In the attempt to bring General Eyre to justice he was hardly less active than Mr. Mill.

The "cat" he has satisfied all humane minds is twice accursed, cursing him that administers and him to whom it is administered.

The Game Laws he has had the courage to expose in all their naked infamy to a country still held tight in the vice of feudalism.

He has been one of three in resisting the spoliation of the Exchequer by Royal princes and princesses, and the most important perhaps of all future Parliamentary reforms, the payment of members, he has made peculiarly his own. His speech on the latter subject is one of the most convincing ever delivered by him or any other living member of the House.

As President of the "People's International League," Mr. Taylor in his younger days was untiring in his endeavours to liberate Poland, Hungary, and Italy from the oppressor's grasp. By voice, pen, and purse, he did his best for the popular cause.

The only conspicuous blunder of his life was his advocacy of the Crimean war in opposition to Cobden and Bright. The wrongs of Poland rankled in his breast and blinded his judgment, as it fatally darkened the understanding of so many other true friends of freedom. In the American Civil War, needless to say, his sympathies were entirely with the North and the policy of abolition, of which he had long been a strenuous advocate.

In America the name of P. A. Taylor is perhaps better known than in England, and it will be better known to posterity than to his contemporaries. Nor is this to be wondered at, for in this royalty and aristocracy ridden land the member for Leicester is a "rare" figure, and precious as he is rare. He is, in a sense, "a survival" from the great era of the Commonwealth—a mind of the type of Vane, Ludlow, Hutchinson, Scott, and Hazelrig—an idealist in politics, but withal a practical idealist. He is more human than English, his principles being more or less applicable to all times and to all places. Having embraced a principle, he holds by it with the tenacity of a bull-dog, fearlessly pushing it to its remotest consequences.

This was the distinguishing mental characteristic of all the great Republicans of the seventeenth century. Since then an extraordinary blight has fallen on the political intelligence of Englishmen. They waste their best intellect in the defence of palpable anomalies and pernicious compromises. Even Gladstone and Bright have not escaped the contagion of compromise. They go to Court and are caught in the net of "Society," which sticks to them like a Nessus shirt. Peter Alfred Taylor has never been caught. He has gone to no Court but that of the Sovereign People. I honour the man and the constituency which has so long honoured itself by honouring him.

> "Stainless soldier on the walls,
>   Knowing this and knows no more—
> Whoever fights, whoever falls,
>   Justice conquers ever more:
> And he who battles on her side,
>   God, if he were ten times slain,
> Crowns him victor glorified—
>   Victor over death and pain."

IV.

SIR CHARLES W. DILKE.

> "A greyhound ever on the stretch
> To run for honour still."

IN treating of Gladstone, Bright, and Taylor, who have preceded the senior member for Chelsea in this series, I have in some measure felt on sure ground—the ground of history or accomplished fact. The youngest of the above trio is sixty, and had entered the arena of public life ere the subject of this memoir had well left his cradle. One could, consequently, speak of them almost with as much confidence as of the dead. Their lengthened past was a clear index to their necessarily briefer future. In due course they will pass over to the majority, and their works will follow them. With Sir Charles Wentworth Dilke it is altogether different. He belongs exclusively to the immediate present. It will take him thirty-five more years to attain the venerable age of the woodcutter of Hawarden. He is emphatically a contemporary, as fine an example as can well be found of the culture and aspirations of this generation. It is his future that is most important, and it is full of promise.

As Mr. Gladstone in his youth was pronounced "the rising hope of Toryism," so Sir Charles W. Dilke may with better assurance be hailed as the rising hope of Radicalism—of all that is sincere, capable, and of good repute in English politics. The odds are heavily in his favour. He has youth, health, wealth, birth, strength, talent, industry, firmness of character, special training, and moral courage of a very high order on his side. Such a combination of advantages seldom fails. If he is spared to his country for the next twenty years he will almost certainly be able to say with regard to her fortunes, whatever these may be, *Magna pars fui.*

"Never prophesy," said the wise Quaker, "unless thou knowest!" Nevertheless, I venture to predict that, sooner or later, Charles Wentworth Dilke will be called upon by the people of England to take a very high place, and he will succeed too, by the right of the fittest. Like his friend Gambetta, he has been tried in the fiery furnace of political calumny and social hate, and has not been found wanting. "Society" undertook to put him down, and he has put down Society. Of the two he has proved himself the stronger, and a better proof of capacity to serve the nation it would be impossible to adduce.

"That which is bred in the bone," says the proverb, "will come out in the flesh." The anti-monarchical sympathies of the Dilkes, like those of the Taylors, are at least as much inherited as acquired. No fewer than three of the Dilke ancestry were among the judges of Charles I., viz., the resolute Bradshaw, who presided over the High Court of Justice, Sir Peter Wentworth, and Cawley. All were stern foes of "one-man government," whether that one man were the "divine right" Charles Stuart, or the Puritan Bonaparte, Oliver Cromwell. "For what king's majesty," asks the immortal defender of the regicides, Milton, "sitting on an exalted throne ever shone so brightly as that of the people of England then did, when, shaking off that old superstition which had prevailed a long time, they gave judgment on the king himself, or rather upon an enemy who had been their king, caught, as it were, in a net by his own laws, and scrupled not to inflict on him, being guilty, the same punishment which he would have inflicted on any other?" . . . "This is the God," he continues, "who uses to throw down proud and unruly kings . . . and utterly to extirpate them and their family. By his manifest impulse being set at work to recover our almost lost liberty, we went on in no obscure but an illustrious passage pointed out and made plain to us by God Himself."

At his trial Charles vainly declined to recognise the authority of the Court, on the silly pretext that he himself was "the fountain of all law." "If you are the fountain of all law," curtly observed Bradshaw, "the people are the source of all rights." When the Cromwellian *coup d'état* took place, Sir Peter Wentworth was, I think, the last man in the House to protest against the violence offered to the representatives of the people, and Bradshaw afterwards told the military usurper to his face, "We have heard what you did, and all England shall know it. Sir, you are mistaken in thinking Parliament is dissolved. No power under Heaven can dissolve them but themselves. Take you notice of that."

One sister of Sir Peter Wentworth's was married to Bradshaw's brother, while another, Sybil Wentworth, became the wife of Fisher Dilke, from which union the distinguished representative of Chelsea in Parliament is lineally descended.

The Dilkes were probably of Danish origin, and are to be found settled at Kirby Mallory, in Leicestershire, as early as the middle of the sixteenth century.

Fisher Dilke was a Puritan of the Puritans, much given to angling and piety of an extravagant kind. He was a Fifth Monarchy man, and like his sect would have prepared the ways of King Christ and made the paths of his speedy return straight by first abolishing all existing authority and cancelling all bonds of human allegiance. He was doomed to sore disappointment. His co-secretaries mustered strong in Barebone's Parliament, but in the eyes of the pious Lord Protector did no good whatever, though they never deliberated without meanwhile setting apart a committee of eight of their number to seek the Lord in prayer. Their *mittimus* came speedily from the Protector in the memorable words, "You may go elsewhere to seek the Lord, for to my certain knowledge he has not been here for many years."

At the restoration of the Monarchy Fisher Dilke is said to have died of sheer grief, having first dug his own grave.

Of all Sir Charles's ancestors, however, the most remarkable was Peter Wentworth, the grandfather of Sybil, wife of Fisher Dilke, leader of the Puritan Opposition in Parliament in the reign of Queen Elizabeth, and brother-in-law to the famous Secretary of State, Sir Francis Walsingham. This Peter and his brother Paul were seldom out of trouble. Hallam calls them "the bold, plain-spoken and honest, but not very judicious Wentworths, the most undaunted assertors of civil liberty in this reign."

In the Parliament of 1575, Peter made a stiff speech in defence of the rights and privileges of the Commons. It is on record. "I find," said he, "within a little volume these words in effect: 'Sweet is the name of liberty, but the thing itself a value beyond all estimable treasure.' So much the more it behooveth us to take great care lest we, contenting ourselves with the sweetness of the name, lose and forego the thing." "Two things do great hurt in this place. The one is a rumour which runneth about saying, 'Take heed what you do, the Queen liketh not such a matter; whoso preferreth it she will be offended with him.' The other, a message is brought into the House either commanding or inhibiting, very injurious to the freedom of speech and consultation. I would to God these rumours and messages were buried in hell, for wicked they are; the Devil was the first author of them, from whom proceedeth nothing but wickedness."

And so on he went reprobating the venal flatterers of royalty who "make traitorous sugared speeches," "send to Her Majesty a melting heart that will not stand for reason," and who blindly follow their leaders instead of voting "as the matter giveth cause."

Peter was not permitted to finish his speech, but was given into the custody of the Sergeant-at-Arms, pending an examination of the delinquent by a Committee of the House."

His apology is recorded: "I heartily repent me that I have hitherto held my peace in these causes, and I do promise you all, if God forsake me not, that I will never during my life hold my tongue if any message is sent in wherein the liberties of Parliament are impeached; and every one of you ought to repent you of these faults and amend them."

He was, of course, sent to the Tower, where he remained over a month, when "Her Majesty was graciously pleased to remit her justly occasioned displeasances."

He returned to the House, but in the following session he was re-committed for a similar offence. Indeed, he appears latterly to have spent more of his time in the Tower than at St. Stephen's, and in the Tower the stout-hearted, liberty-loving man is believed ultimately to have perished.

His plainness of speech had aroused against him more than royal ire. He and Paul were both at constant feud with the prelates. On one occasion the Archbishop of Canterbury announced, in the hearing of Peter, that it was the function of Parliament to pass Articles of Religion approved of by the clergy without note or comment. "No," said the indomitable iconoclast, "by the faith we bear to God we will pass nothing before we understand what it is; for that were but to make you Popes. Make you Popes who list, we will make you none."

Through the member for Chelsea Elizabethan Peter yet speaketh. And how modern is it all! How little real progress have the English people made in liberty since these indignant words were uttered three centuries ago! Nay, may it not even be doubted whether in some respects we have not even lost ground? Have we not still bishops thrusting down our throats articles of religion which neither they nor we can understand? Have we not likewise our royal "messages" respecting manifold dowries and annuities, duly heralded by sinister "rumours" of royal "displeasance" which incontinently convert honourable members into a troop of Court flunkeys, and make even Liberal Ministers deliver themselves of "traitorous sugared speeches" enough to make Peter and Paul Wentworth turn in their coffins?—

> "Age, thou art shamed!
> Rome, thou hast lost the breed of noble bloods!
> Oh! you and I have heard our fathers say
> There was a Brutus once, that would have brook'd
> The eternal devil to keep his state in Rome
> As easily as a king."

Sir Charles Wentworth Dilke, M.P., is the oldest son of Sir Charles Wentworth Dilke, first baronet, and grandson of Charles Wentworth Dilke, the celebrated critic, whose literary judgment and administrative talent were the chief stock in trade both of the *Athenæum* and the *Daily News* in their younger days.

Sir Charles's father, as is well known, was much devoted to matters affecting Art and Industry, and was a leading promoter of the Great Exhibition of 1851. As some acknowledgment of his eminent services he was offered, and accepted, contrary to the advice of his father, the critic, a baronetcy. The old gentleman was an inflexible Radical, and Sir Charles may be said in all his mental and moral characteristics to be the son of his grandfather rather than of his father. He was the preceptor and companion of Dilke's youth. He was an antiquary as well as a critic, and loved to trace the descent of grandson "Charley's" mother from the gentle and unselfish regicide Cawley as a noble pattern for her to set before her son.

The future member for Chelsea was born in the borough which he now represents in September 1843. He is consequently in his thirty-sixth year. At the second of two private schools which he attended in the Metropolis, he displayed mathematical talent, and in due course he matriculated at Trinity Hall, Cambridge, with the intention of pursuing with assiduity his favourite study, in which he obtained a Scholarship. He soon, however, changed his mind, and betook himself to law, as calculated to bear more directly on a Parliamentary career, for which he very early determined to qualify himself. He worked hard, and was easily senior in the Law Tripos for 1865.

In 1866 he was called to the Bar by the Honourable Society of the Middle Temple. Shortly afterwards he started on a "round the world" journey of two years' duration. The trip bore excellent fruit in the well-known work "Greater Britain," which, in the first year of its publication, ran through four editions.

In 1868 he was returned to Parliament for Chelsea by a majority of nearly two to one, and again in 1874 he headed the poll, notwithstanding an opposition of unexampled violence.

Sprung from a race of journalists and *littérateurs*, his pen is never long idle. Since the publication of "Greater Britain" he had found time to publish the "Fall of Prince Florestan of Monaco," and to edit, under the title "Papers of a Critic," his grandfather's chief contributions to the pages of the *Athenæum*, which paper he also occasionally supervises in person.

As, however, his name has been at times connected with the *Dispatch*, I may take this opportunity of mentioning that he has not now, and never has had, any connection with that paper.

Since his former travels, he has been "round the world" a second time, his chief object being to acquaint himself with the state and prospects of Japan. He has visited every English-speaking corner of the globe, is thoroughly conversant with the condition of our Indian Empire, and is better acquainted with the language, literature, people, and government of Russia than any man in the House.

He is perhaps the first thoroughly competent Englishman who has ever seen and described the men, manners, and institutions of the United States as they really are, and not as they are wont to appear to the jaundiced eye of national jealousy and aristocratic aversion. The American Republic is substantially Sir Charles's "Greater Britain," to which he foresees the hegemony of the English-speaking race is ultimately destined to fall. He believes in the possibility of one omnipotent all-embracing federation of English-speaking men, of which the United States shall at once supply both the nucleus and the model.

In the study of foreign affairs he has taken nothing for granted. Everything he has examined on the spot and verified with his own eyes. He would make an incomparably well-informed Foreign Secretary, and it is not improbable, nay it would be gratifying to the whole Liberal party, that in the next Liberal Administration he should be offered and should accept office in that department of State.

Like Mr. Gladstone, he is an untiring toiler, and from the first he has worked on the most profitable lines. Whether as law-student, traveller, author, journalist, or politician, whatever he has done he has done faithfully and well.

Every recess he shuns delights and spends laborious holidays at his romantic provincial retreat at La Sainte Campagne, near Toulon, in digesting materials for a *magnum opus*, "The History of the Present Century."

He is personally a total abstainer, though opposed to the Permissive Bill, and is in all things a pattern of method and regularity of habits.

At Cambridge he was a finished oarsman. He is likewise a vigorous long-distance walker, a good marksman, and a deft fencer.

In nothing has he shown such marked improvement as in his style of public speaking. Though twice president of the Union Debating Society at Cambridge, he was at first a most unimpressive speaker—I hesitate to use his own term, "lugubrious." But now it is not so. He is fluent, easy, and agreeable; one of the best level business speakers in Parliament. As for the matter, *that* has at all times been such as to redeem the worst faults of manner. Just a little too much of it at a time, perhaps—more, at least, than can be well digested by a mass meeting even of Chelsea electors—but not one word in bad taste, "nothing extenuated, nothing set down in malice."

When he has been reviled—and who ever was more villainously overwhelmed by a hurricane of abuse?—he reviled not again. Like the soul of honour that he is, he has never stooped to personal invective. Under the severest provocation he has said nothing to wound the susceptibilities of the most sensitive. In this respect he has set an example to some of our foremost public men. Comes this extraordinary forbearance of grace or of nature, it may be asked. By nature, I should say. To him opposition from men or things is of exactly the same character. It is something to be overcome by patience and pressure in the line of the least resistance. In other words, the member for Chelsea is lacking in sympathy. He is fitted to become a great parliamentary leader rather than a Democratic agitator. His political aims, it is true, are much the same as were those of passionate old Peter Wentworth, his ancestor; but it would never for a moment occur to him to wish that the most impudent of royal begging messages should be incontinently buried in hell. Indeed, if insisting on some explanations being given with respect to the monstrous abuses of the Civil List, and if in affirming his preference for a Constitutional Republic based on merit to a Monarchy, however limited, founded on birth, he had shown more anger and less reason, sneers would have been regarded as the only weapon necessary to employ against him. It was the very fact that he used arguments which every snob in England knew to be unanswerable that the Royalist tempest—what I may call the "white terror"—was evoked.

It may here be convenient to consider the Republican episode in his career. There can be no doubt that Royalty was alarmed, that its numerous hangers-on were alarmed, and that the privileged classes generally, whose own existence depends on the maintenance of the Monarchical superstition as an article of the popular faith, were thoroughly alarmed.

"Kings most commonly," says Milton, "though strong in legions are but weak at argument, as they who have ever been accustomed from their cradle to use their will only as their right hand, their reason always as their left. Whence, unexpectedly constrained to that kind of combat, they prove but weak and puny adversaries." The Royalists made up for the weakness of their arguments by the weight of their brick-bats. At Bolton, while Sir Charles was addressing a large audience admitted by ticket, the place of meeting was assailed by a furious mob of Royalists, who succeeded in murdering one peaceable Radical, William Scofield, a working man, and wounding several others. The magistrates and the police both scandalously failed in their duty on the occasion, and to this day their conduct has never been adequately explained.

If the blood of an innocent man had been shed by Republican hands, what a howl for vengeance would there not have been heard! At Reading, the late Mr. George Odger, than whom a more able and upright politician never lived, was within an ace of meeting the fate of Scofield.

The leading organ of the "party of order," the *Standard*, threatened the representative of Chelsea with physical violence. "The attachment of Englishmen for the Royal Family," it said, "may take an unpleasantly practical form if Sir Charles Dilke should ever insult a party of gentlemen by repeating in their presence calumnies such as he was permitted to utter with impunity before the 'roughs' of Newcastle."

It is here worth putting on record the worst that Sir Charles did say in the famous address alluded to. The meeting was held in November 1871, Mr. Joseph Cowen in the chair. This was the head and front of his offending: "There is a widespread belief that a Republic here is only a matter of education and time. It is said that some day a Commonwealth will be our form of Government. Now, history and experience show that you cannot have a Republic without you possess at the same time the Republican virtues; but you answer, Have we not public spirit? Have we not the practice of self-government? Are not we gaining general education? Well, if you can show me a fair chance that a Republic here will be free from the political corruption that hangs about a Monarchy, I say for my part—and I believe that the middle classes in general will say—Let it come."

The answer should have been, We Englishmen have *not* public spirit; we have *not* the practice of self-government; we do *not* possess the Republican virtues of independence and self-respect, without which there can be no genuine Republic. We love to deceive both ourselves and others. It is the "name" of liberty that we affect; the "thing" itself is unknown to us.

Is it to be wondered at that Sir Charles Dilke, fresh from brighter countries like the United States and our colonial possessions, where self-government is a reality, should have misconstrued the reply of an oracle so ambiguous and untrustworthy? But no harm has been done by his miscalculation—rather much good. The country has been made to know that it has at least one public man of first-rate ability and dauntless courage, who is not afraid to reconcile administrative practice with the best political theory whenever the people are prepared to abandon their unworthy idols and to look the facts of history, experience, and common sense straight in the face.

And as for Sir Charles, he is an imperturbable, good-natured man, who doubtless considers that he took ample revenge on all his unscrupulous calumniators when he published anonymously his clever *brochure*, the "Fall of Prince Florestan of Monaco." Several leading Tory journals advised him to lay the lessons taught by the Radical Prince of Monaco to heart! How he must have chuckled! It is only natures of the largest and healthiest mould that are thus capable of looking amusedly at the comical aspect of their own doings.

In the domain of current domestic legislation, Sir Charles has played no unimportant part. It is to him we owe the popular constitution of our School Boards, it having been Mr. Forster's original intention to entrust the duties of school management to committees of Boards of Guardians.

His also was the clause which conferred the municipal franchise on female ratepayers. He procured for the working men of London a most desirable boon in the extension of the hours of polling, and in everything appertaining to the better representation of the people in Parliament he has taken a leading part. On the all-important question of the redistribution of political power in particular he is, it is not too much to say, the greatest authority in the House. Like John Bright, he loves the big constituencies, and would, as far as possible, make them all numerically equal.

He is not ordinarily an amusing speaker, but one of his speeches on the unreformed corporations will rank among the wittiest delivered by any member since he entered the House. His collected speeches on electoral reform, the Civil List, free trade, free land, and free schools are a ready repertory of trustworthy facts, which ought to be in the hands of every reformer. With respect to the Zulu war, in the session of 1879, with the approbation of Lord Hartington, he took the lead in opposition to the Government policy, a sufficient indication of the respect entertained for his judgment in colonial affairs.

In every department he is a friend of economy. In Parliament he is ever vigilant and never fussy. When he speaks it is always to contribute some new fact or unused argument to the debate, and he never fails to catch the ear of the House, which admires his straightforwardness, manly bearing, and unremitting attention to his parliamentary duties.

He is well versed in the forms of the House. Above all, he has honesty and excellent common sense to guide his steps aright.

If, with all these endowments, he should fail in the not distant future to achieve great things for his country, both I and many other observant sympathisers "whose judgment cries i' the top of mine" will feel just cause for sore disappointment.

V.

JOSEPH COWEN.

"Like one of the simple great ones
Gone for ever and ever by."

I SHALL never forget one delightful forenoon I spent with Mr. Cowen since his entrance into Parliament. Previous to his coming to St. Stephen's, he had been well known to me by reputation, but by reputation only.

As the disciple whom Mazzini, the prophet and high priest of modern Democracy, loved, I was curious to know what manner of man the great Northumbrian Radical really was. I arrived early, and found him in his library in the act of finishing his morning correspondence. I had just time to glance at his books before engaging with him in conversation. A man may be known by his books as by the company he keeps. They were almost exclusively composed of the most recent productions of the Democratic Press, such as one would expect to find on the shelves of an intelligent artisan politician rather than on those of the possessor of a residence in Onslow Square. And the appearance of Mr. Cowen himself was exactly in keeping. His features bore no trace whatever of having been imported "at the Conquest." There he sat, a genuine workman from Tyneside, the descendant of generations of honest toilers—plain and homely to a degree. Nothing but the lofty dome of brow betrayed the mental superiority of the man, and when subsequently he put on the never-failing slouched hat, even that not infallible sign of greatness was remorselessly hidden away.

Presently we began to talk as freely as if we had been acquainted for years. The villainous Northumbrian intonation was at first somewhat of an impediment in my way. I had never learned Northumbrian, and being a fair linguist, did not like to acknowledge my ignorance.

One or two proper names he was good enough to spell for me. As, however, he gradually became more animated his English became better and better, until at last he was one of the most articulate-speaking of Englishmen I had ever met.

It was a lovely day, and we decided on a stroll in the direction, as it turned out, of the modest house where Mazzini conspired against the crowned heads of Europe for so many years. On the way he spoke of that gifted friend of his youth and manhood—the greatest man, Mr. Cowen thinks, and I am half inclined to accept his estimate, that Europe has produced for centuries—of Garibaldi and Orsini, of Kossuth, of Herzen and Bakounin, of Ledru Rollin and Louis Blanc, but above all of the Polish revolutionary leaders Worcell, Darasz, Microslawski, Dombrowski, and Langiewicz.

I inquired why, of all the Continental exiles, he appeared to have been most drawn towards the Poles. He replied with profound feeling, "Because they seemed the most forlorn." There was no getting over this answer, which throws a flood of light on the deplorable action which Mr. Cowen has seen fit to take with regard to the Eastern question.

For years his house at Blaydon Burn, near Newcastle, had been an asylum for the victims of Russian tyranny. For years he had spent two-thirds of an ample income in keeping alive the patriotism of the Polish insurgents and other enemies of the White Tsar. To him Poland was and is a land of heroes and martyrs; Russia everything that is the reverse. So thoroughly identified was Mr. Cowen with the anti-Russian sentiments of the Polish and Hungarian exiles, that orders were issued by all the despotic Powers of Europe, by Russia, Prussia, France, Spain, and Italy, for his arrest, should he venture to set foot on their soil.

Not able to catch the son the police twice arrested his father, the late Sir Joseph Cowen, in his stead. His home at Blaydon Burn was incessantly watched by the spies of Continental Governments.

When Cowen and Mazzini met it was neither in Newcastle nor London, but generally in some quiet midway town or village, where they could not readily be subjected to espionage.

The despots of the Continent had, in point of fact, very good reason to regard Mr. Cowen as a dangerous personage. He was not merely a wealthy Englishman who gave of his substance freely in order that the axe might be laid by others to the root of the upas tree of their authority, but one who did not scruple when occasion offered to levy war against the oppressors, so to speak, on his own account.

During the last rising in Poland he fitted out, at his own charges, a vessel which it was intended should hoist the Polish flag, and, like another Alabama, sweep Russian commerce off the seas. She escaped from the Tyne without much difficulty, and reached Barcelona in safety. Her next destination was the coast of the little island of Elba, where a Polish commodore of experience, who had come all the way from the Russian naval station at Kamchatka—on French leave, of course—was waiting with a full complement of marines, to take possession in the name of the Provisional Government at Warsaw.

They waited in vain. The drunken ravings and cowardice of the English crew brought about the seizure and confiscation of the vessel by the Spanish authorities almost in spite of themselves. The chief naval authority of the port was at that time a brother of General Prim, himself a revolutionary. He winked hard, and it so happened, curiously enough, that the only Spanish man-of-war available for seizing her was under the command of an Englishman, formerly a Newcastle engineer, who, on being sent to inspect the ship and her papers, winked harder still. With reasonable promptitude she might have got clear off, but did not, to the great grief of Mr. Cowen and the Provisional Government of Poland.

The above is but one out of scores of daring enterprises with a similar object in which Mr. Cowen has been engaged. Once he had a wonderful box constructed and well lined with notes suitable for issue by the Secret Committee of Government over which Langiewicz presided. It was given in charge to a faithful messenger, with instructions to seek the headquarters of the insurgents by a somewhat devious route. No sooner did he set foot on the Continent, however, than he was seized by the police and put in prison. He was never tried, and never told his offence, but the contents of the well-filled purse with which he had started from England were weekly disbursed to pay his board for the space of a whole year. At the end of that time he was put on board a ship bound for London, and landed penniless.

Regarding the adventures, misadventures, and hair-breadth escapes of proscribed Poles, Italians, and Hungarians, Mr. Cowen has many a curious and pathetic tale to tell. He was the chief banker and general agent in this country of the European revolutionaries. Nearly all their more important correspondence passed through his hands on its way to and from the Continent, and for long his commanding position as a British manufacturer and shipowner, doing business in all parts of Europe, effectually baffled the most vigilant espionage of the despotic Powers.

Having seen the abode of the great Italian, we turned into Hyde Park, and under the shadow of Albert the Gilt conversed of current politics and living Radical politicians. He was very candid, and I remarked with interest how similar were his judgments of men and things to those which I could readily suppose Mazzini would have formed in similar circumstances.

One able member of Parliament was an Atheist to the backbone, and why such a one should be a Radical rather than a Tory, or why, indeed, being a wealthy man, he should care to trouble himself about politics at all, was a mystery to the member for Newcastle. Another was lacking in anything like genuine sympathy for the people, and had fallen into the abyss of wire-pulling and political beadledom. All unconsciously he had become as earnestly eloquent as if he were addressing a considerable audience, his usually homely features admirably mirroring the thoughts which rose spontaneously to his lips.

Mr. Cowen's abhorrence of atheistic or unbelieving politicians was to me all the more impressive that his own mind was evidently not untinged by sadness—had not altogether escaped the influence of that great despair with respect to the supernatural which has in our day overtaken the bravest and the best.

On taking leave of Mr. Cowen I had no hesitation in concluding that I had never met a more singular combination of simplicity of manner, business-like shrewdness, intellectual vigour, comprehensive sympathy, and powerful imagination. These qualities appear to me to mingle in disproportionate measure, but their co-existence in his mind affords a clue to the surprising splendour of his imagery, which, if the House had had a few more samples of it, might almost justify me in ranking him next to Bright as a master of senatorial eloquence.

If great poets are born, not made, so likewise are great orators, and sure enough Mr. Cowen is one of the few really great orators in the House. His style is neither that of Bright, Gladstone, nor Beaconsfield. His best periods have an antique, Roman-like stateliness which is to me peculiarly attractive. In their majestic roll they are more like those of the late Ledru Rollin than of any modern speaker.

Mr. Cowen was born at Blaydon Burn, near Newcastle, in the month of July 1831. His father, Sir Joseph Cowen, knight, who preceded him in the representation of Newcastle, was originally a working blacksmith. He was of an inventive turn of mind, and when the discovery of gas began to be utilised he hit on several ingenious contrivances for facilitating its manufacture. Before long he was a wealthy man, and one of the most respected and public-spirited citizens of Newcastle. It is to his untiring exertions and foresight that Newcastle in a great measure owes its mercantile prosperity.

He found the Tyne a shallow stream, up which vessels of the smallest draught could with difficulty sail. He left it so deepened that it is now one of the most navigable of rivers. The merit of this great achievement was publicly recognised by Mr. Gladstone, who in consequence had him dubbed knight—a distinction, however, to which he was indifferent. From the beginning to the end of his career he was a Radical reformer.

The Cowens are a somewhat numerous family, and have been settled in and around Blaydon Burn for about three centuries. They came originally from Lindisfarne, or Holy Isle, of which the stock had been denizens from a remote antiquity. The Cowens were among the first genuine English co-operators on record—co-operators in production as well as in distribution. They were for generations members of a singular society, instituted about the middle of the seventeenth century by an enterprising manufacturer, Crowley—the "Sir John Anvil" of Addison's *Spectator*—whose members worshipped in common, fed in common, and shared equally in the common profits of their industry. This society was not disrupted till 1814, in the lifetime of Mr. Cowen's grandfather. Since then, it may be worth remarking, co-operation has again, under Mr. Cowen's fostering care, taken a firm hold on Blaydon-on-Tyne.

Though Blaydon is a mere village, Mr. Holyoake, in his "History of Co-operation," declares that next to Rochdale it has the most remarkable store in England. It has grown from a house to a street. The library contains upwards of 1500 volumes of new books. The profits for 1876 amounted to £16,886. The society has an Education Fund of £400 per annum.

When the Co-operative Congress met at Newcastle in 1873, Mr. Cowen, not then M.P., was elected president, and delivered an address the remembrance of which still lives in co-operative circles.

Mr. Cowen's early education was received at a good local school, whence he proceeded to the University of Edinburgh, which then, by reason of the renown of its professors, enjoyed something like European fame. Russell, Palmerston, Lansdowne, had been there before him. Christopher North still lectured, and Lord Macaulay represented the city in Parliament.

With no professional object in view, young Cowen sought simply culture, and that he found to more purpose, perhaps, than it would have been possible for him to do elsewhere. He studied what subjects he pleased, preferring the time-honoured classics, became president of the University Debating Society, and entered heartily into the political and social life of the citizens.

His chief extra-mural instructor was the Rev. Dr. John Ritchie—a really great man in a small community. Though a preacher, and a Scottish preacher too, he was above sophistry, an intrepid Radical, and a first-rate platform speaker.

About this time also Mr. Cowen, while yet an Edinburgh student, made the acquaintance of Mazzini, who subsequently exercised over him an influence so remarkable. Young as he was Mr. Cowen had entered an indignant public protest against the infamous and, till it was proved, incredible violation of the illustrious exile's letters by Sir James Graham and the Post-Office officials. Mazzini was interested in his youthful defender, thanked him by letter, and to Mr. Cowen were addressed the dying patriot's last written words.

On returning to Blaydon, Mr. Cowen engaged actively in his father's business of fire-proof brick and retort manufacture, the firm normally employing as many as a thousand men. At the Blaydon works there have been no strikes, for the very good reason that Mr. Cowen, though an employer of labour, has always been regarded as an intelligent exponent of trades union views—in short, as a trusted trades union leader. His support of the nine hours' movement was from first to last of a most decided character, and such as everywhere to evoke the warmest feelings of gratitude among workmen.

His persistent efforts, too, to found, improve, and federate mechanics' institutes all over the populous Tyneside district ought not to be forgotten. For many years he personally discharged the duties of a teacher in one of these institutions, which owe so much of their success to his enthusiasm and talent as organising secretary.

Nor has Mr. Cowen been less active in the domain of pure politics, whether local or imperial. He is now president of the Northern Reform League—an organisation which has been in existence in one form or another for more than twenty years. He was present at its inception, and acted as its first treasurer. In the Reform demonstrations of 1867 the League played an important part, calling out an array of supporters which the Metropolis itself could hardly match.

As a member of the Town Council Mr. Cowen on several occasions declined the dignity of the mayoralty. This did not, however, prevent his brother councillors from getting a local Act of Parliament passed to enable them to make him an alderman when, by becoming a parliamentary representative, he had ceased to be a member of the municipal body.

To add to all these manifold activities, Mr. Cowen has for twenty years been the proprietor and political director of the *Newcastle Chronicle*, one of the most influential and aggressively Radical journals in provincial England. The *Chronicle* is what, alas! so few newspapers now-a-days are, a real political instructor within the area of its circulation. It has writers, among whom I may mention two well-known journalists, Mr. Thomas Brown and Mr. Adams, who for range of political knowledge and absolute fidelity to principle have no superiors in or out of London. The result was seen at the last general election. When the Conservative reaction ran high everywhere else, the Northumbrian Liberals smote their Tory opponents hip and thigh all along the line.

D

Twelve Liberals to one Tory were, if my memory serves me, the Durham returns.

There is one other noticeable but well-nigh forgotten publication with which the member for Newcastle was intimately connected which deserves to be recalled. In 1852 he purchased the small estate of Brantwood, Coniston, Lancashire, now, I believe, the property of Mr. Ruskin, as a local habitation for the *English Republic*, which consisted of a series of Republican tracts in prose and verse, pitched in a very lofty key. They were issued for five or six years, and Mr. Cowen, if I mistake not, united in his own person the somewhat incongruous, but in his case by no means incompatible, functions of poet laureate and treasurer of a movement symbolised by a beautiful tricolour of blue, white, and green, designed by the accomplished artist-editor, Mr. W. J. Linton. In those days Mr. Cowen was in fact, I presume, what he now is only in *theory*, a staunch Republican.

With regard to Mr. Cowen's parliamentary career, it is hard to speak with impartiality. His fervid Jingoism has affected with profound regret his warmest admirers, myself among the rest. There have not even been wanting some base enough to attribute his support of the wicked and disastrous foreign policy of the Beaconsfield Government to motives other than disinterested. The true explanation of his aberration is quite otherwise. He is still a Hungarian—a Polish insurgent. Nothing is changed. Russia is his mortal foe. Like a true Bourbon, he has neither learned nor forgotten. Any stick is good enough to beat the Muscovite dog with. He advocated the Crimean war in the hope that something might "turn up" for his exiled clients. Nothing came of it; but a fig for experience. Mr. Cowen is, like the great author and finisher of his faith, Mazzini, essentially an idealist—a poet with intense sympathy and vivid imagination. His sympathy and imagination have temporarily overwhelmed his reason. That is all. Nothing better, nothing worse. If I were to have the making of two perfect Radical politicians, I should mix Dilke and Cowen together. The one is two-thirds reason and one-third imagination, the other two-thirds imagination and one-third reason. Give C. one-third of D.'s reason, and D. one-third of C.'s sympathetic fancy, and then you would have a correct balance of powers.

Bright's is the only powerful intellect in the House in which reason and imagination are blended in just and equal proportions, the imagination acting as a stimulus to the reason, but never as a controlling power.

I will illustrate what I mean by a passage from Mr. Cowen's magnificently unwise Jingo speech in the House on the occasion of the supposed Russian advance on Constantinople:—

"I ask English Liberals if they have ever seriously considered the political consequences of an imperial despotism bestriding Europe—reaching, indeed, from the waters of the Neva to those of the Amour—of the Head of the Greek Church, the Eastern Pope, the master of many legions, having one foot on the Baltic, planting another on the Bosphorus. When icebergs float into southern latitudes, they freeze the air for miles around. Will not this political iceberg, when it descends upon the genial shores of the Mediterranean, wither the young shoots of liberty that are springing up between the crevices of the worn-out fabrics of despotism?"

Now, all this is very striking—nay, appalling; but John Bright, I am sure, knowing that icebergs have a habit of melting long before they reach the shores of the Mediterranean, would never have been guilty of bringing any berg of his so far South. As it is, the political iceberg from the North has liberated Bulgaria, while that from the South, pushed on by English Jingoes, has ineffectually striven to roll its icy mass over the young shoots of Roumelian liberty.

Apart, however, from this deplorable Jingo infatuation, Mr. Cowen's parliamentary achievements have in no way belied the high hopes that his friends reposed in his great abilities and immense experience. His speeches on the Friendly Societies Bill, on the County Suffrage Bill, on Mr.

Plimsoll's bill, on the County Courts Bill, the Licensing Boards Bill, and, above all, on the Royal Titles Bill, have given evidence of a varied capacity for legislative work which has not been equalled by any member of his own standing in the House.

During the parliamentary contest in Newcastle occasioned by the death of his father, Mr. Cowen delivered a series of speeches on political questions and public policy which justly arrested national attention. They have been collected, and will abundantly repay perusal. They are without exception as fine electioneering speeches as I ever read, and if he had never opened his lips again would have entitled him to no mean place among English orators and statesmen.

On one point only did he show a disposition to lower the Radical flag, to be unfaithful to himself and his glorious antecedents. He was repeatedly taxed with being a Republican, and his explanation was that he held the Republican form of government to be in theory the highest known to man, but that in practice he was devoted to the British Monarchy. Now, to my mind this is wholly illogical, and not altogether honest. Having discovered a true or best theory, it is the duty of every honest man to act on it, whether it be in the domain of politics or mathematics. If there is a better way, we have no right to fold our hands and content ourselves with the worse. "Ye cannot serve God and Mammon." To the sincere mind all compromise in such circumstances is impossible. It will not do to say, "Well, no doubt in theory the worship of God is the correct thing, but for all practical purposes the service of Mammon is perferable." Least of all living English politicians could I have conceived of Mr. Joseph Cowen appearing on a public platform with such an impotent formula in his mouth. In the case of others "thrift might follow fawning," but with Mr. Cowen it was not, and is not so. That he should not have been able to say to this contemptible spirit of subterfuge, "Get thee behind me, Satan," is to me a mystery even unto this day.

VI.

SIR WILFRID LAWSON.

> "And though that he was *witty* he was wise,
> And of his port as meke as is a mayde:
> He never yet no vilanie ne sayde
> In alle his lif, unto no manere wight—
> He was a vary parfit gentil knight."

I BELIEVE with all sound Christian people, our mendicant archbishops and bishops included, that it is as impossible for a rich man to enter the kingdom of heaven as for a camel to go through the eye of a needle. My experience has likewise agreed with that of the Pagan Fronto, who Marcus Antoninus says told him "that the so-called high born are for the most part heartless." But, as is generally admitted, there are exceptions to all rules, and Sir Wilfrid Lawson is an exceptional man. He is a baronet, and so wealthy that I am almost afraid to particularise with regard to his income. Having never suffered the least inconvenience from the deceitfulness of riches myself—my experience, alas! has been chiefly the other way—I prefer to speak of matter more within the scope of my knowledge. With respect to Sir Wilfrid Lawson, however, I am sure of two things. In spite of his baronetcy he is a "jolly good fellow," and in spite of his riches he may reasonably hope to enter in at the celestial gates, unless they are barred by John Calvin himself—a contingency which there is less and less reason to apprehend.

In any case there would be very little good of sending him

to "the other place." Like Monk Basil of the old church legend, he would almost certainly, if ordered down stairs, make a little heaven of mirth in his own more immediate neighbourhood, and so disturb general arrangements that it would speedily be found necessary to have him removed to more comfortable quarters. For not only is he witty in himself, but the cause that wit is in other men. It is impossible to converse with him for five minutes running without becoming in some measure affected by his irresistible spirit of "gay wisdom," as the Premier has felicitously designated his peculiar humour.

It is a total mistake to suppose that Sir Wilfrid's jokes are mere platform reproductions. He is even more witty in private than in public, and you never meet him that he has not the air of a man who has just experienced some extraordinary piece of good luck, in which you are called upon, if you are not an absolute churl, to participate. He is brimful and running over with sprightly sallies and clever epigrams. Indeed, they seem to come as naturally to him as dulness to most of us. And his wit is of the best kind. It is never used to wound the feelings of any, but to laugh men out of their follies, pretences, and insincerities. His keenest shafts are never envenomed, and are never sped except with a moral purpose. Were it otherwise he might be classed with the humorous light horsemen of debate—of whom Mr. Bernal Osborne was a favourite specimen—in which case he would, of course, be entitled to no place in this series.

As it is, I believe Sir Wilfrid Lawson to be one of the most earnest and trustworthy Radicals in the House of Commons. Some there are, doubtless, who hold that true moral earnestness is never to be found clothed in quasi-comical attire—that facetiousness and Radicalism are incompatible. My reply is that the honourable member for Carlisle finds genial satire to be by far the most effective weapon in his intellectual armoury, and that, like a wise man, he puts his special talent to the best use he can. In skilful hands the scimitar of Saladin will strike home as surely as the battle-axe of King Richard.

After some consideration of the matter, I have arrived at the conclusion that great Radicals, like great poets, are born, not made. They inherit rather than acquire the qualities of intellect and heart which enable them to point the path of human progress. Radicalism is a rare and generous fruit, which it takes generations to grow in anything like perfection.

Sir Wilfrid's grandfather, jovial old Mr. Wybergh, was the counterpart of his grandson in wit and in politics, except that he required the aid of something stronger than either tea or cold water in order to keep in good form. An obituary notice of him, not long since unearthed by Mr. George Augustus Sala, credits him with an " uninterrupted *gaieté de cœur*, which not even pain or sickness had power to subdue." When Lord Brougham made his historic descent on Cumberland in the Liberal interest, the old gentleman was one of his most active supporters, and much harm did he do to the Tories by the inimitable raillery with which he assailed them. On one occasion, observing that the Conservative side of the hustings was crowded with clergymen, he stretched out his hand towards them and prefaced a spirited onslaught with the text, " The Lord gave the word, and great was the company of the preachers."

He was not a Lawson at all, but the representative of an old Yorkshire family who had become connected with the county of Cumberland through marriage with Miss Hartley, whose sister was the wife of the then owner of Brayton. Old Wilfrid Lawson having no descendants, left his estates and name to his godson and nephew by affinity, the father of the present baronet. He, the late Sir Wilfrid, married a Miss Graham of Netherby, the sister of Sir James Graham, the well-known Minister of State—who was consequently the member for Carlisle's uncle. Sir Wilfrid senior was a staunch Liberal, who did not permit family connections to hamper him in the discharge of his public duties. When Sir James

Graham vacillated in his allegiance to Liberalism, his brother-in-law, who was universally esteemed for his many virtues, set an example to the constituency of fidelity to principle, by being among the first to record his vote against him. The poll was then open, and of two days' duration, and the consequence was that the Minister lost his seat. On repentance only was he permitted to resume it.

The witty champion of the Permissive Bill was born in the year 1829, at Brayton Hall, Aspatria, Cumberland. He succeeded to the family estates and the baronetcy, which has existed, with a break, for about two centuries, on the death of his father in 1867. His education was for a youth of his social status of a very limited kind. He was never either at a public school or at college; and if you ask him what instruction he received, he replies, with evident satisfaction, that he never had any. His father was a very "Low" or Evangelical Churchman—a teetotaller, too, for many years—who dreaded the contaminating influences of University life on his boys more than he coveted for them academic distinctions. What happened, accordingly, I cannot better describe than in the words of Sir Wilfrid's brother William, the author of "Ten Years of Gentleman Farming," a singularly candid and interesting book. "I had the advantage," he says, "of being the son of parents who were more anxious that their children should be happy and good than that they should be learned or great. My father had my education conducted—in a religious manner—at home, where I acquired a little Latin and Greek, and a few other things; and where, as is the case with many other youths, anything in the shape of lessons was not attractive to me, and I learned as little as possible. I had, before I was eighteen, travelled several times on the Continent of Europe, and had visited Egypt and Palestine; but circumstances never brought me in contact with rich or great people, and I had not much of what is called 'knowledge of the world;' nor, as I always had the prospect of enough wealth to enable me to live without working, did I form what are called 'business habits.'

Trained as a shooter of animals, a hunter of Cumberland beasts with hounds, and a trapper of vermin, I found myself, in the spring of 1861, in my twenty-fifth year, without an occupation, without many acquaintances—except among the poor, whom I had not learned to despise because they spoke bad grammar, and took their coats off too work—and without the reputation of having been successful in any undertaking except that of the mastership and huntsmanship of my brother's foxhounds."

As a consequence of this sort of training, Sir Wilfrid Lawson is almost entirely devoid of personal ambition. Goodness, not greatness, is the object at which he aims. He is rich, but his sympathies with the poor are as fresh and keen as if he were one of them. He has not been deluded by the deceitfulness of riches, nor is "rank" to him other than the poor "guinea stamp" in comparison with the pure gold of genuine manhood. I know no one in any station of life who seems to me to realise more fully that

> "Kind hearts are more than coronets,
> And simple faith than Norman blood."

For fifteen or sixteen years he has been a total abstainer, simply from a sense of duty towards his fellows, and not from any personal or physical antipathy to stimulants. While the world standeth he will do nothing to cause his brother to offend; nay, more, he will do his utmost to remove stumbling-blocks from his brother's path. In so acting he may be right or he may be wrong, but at all events the motive is eminently respectable.

In 1859, in his father's lifetime, he entered Parliament as member for Carlisle, and found a more useful and honourable occupation than that of "a hunter of Cumberland beasts with hounds." In March 1864, he first brought in a bill, since known as the Permissive Bill, "to enable owners and occupiers of property in certain districts to prevent the sale of intoxicating liquors within such districts." He lost his seat in consequence, and from 1865 to 1868 he was out of Parliament. Then the tide turned, and the cathedral city reversed its verdict, many publicans and sinners doubtless repenting them of the evil they had done.

Like most places blessed with a dean and chapter, the Carlisle electors are in truth anything but a model constituency. It is but lately that an obnoxious ex-mayor of the city petitioned against the return of two municipal councillors, on the ground of bribery and treating, and had them duly unseated, the joke of the affair being that among the more systematic treaters figured some of the most active members of Sir Wilfrid's committee. Altogether the trial revealed a state of social habits and political practices so reprehensible, that one can only be thankful that so questionable a constituency should elect to be represented in Parliament by so unquestionable a member as Sir Wilfrid Lawson. It is one of the advantages of virtue that vice is always compelled to pay it a certain unwilling homage.

It remains to speak of Sir Wilfrid's legislative career, and of certain conceptions of the common weal with which his name has become indissolubly associated in the public mind. Two interests of transcendent importance, one social, the other political, he has made peculiarly his own, viz., those of temperance and peace. He is the sworn foe of publicans and soldiers. He regards both as *hostes humani generis*, whom it is the duty of all good citizens to unite to extirpate. In place of strong drink he offers us cold water, and in place of war a court of arbitration. Was there ever such a visionary? Why, since the dawn of human history till now, these are the twin Molochs to which countless generations have sacrificed their first-born. Who are we that we should depart from the wisdom of our ancestors? Did not the son of man himself come eating and drinking? Are not the princes and potentates of the earth—our "sovereigns and statesmen"—they who set armies in motion? And do not all manner of priests, whether Protestant or Romanist, fervently thank God when the bloody work has been effectually accomplished? David going out with sling and stone against Goliath of Gath did not require to possess one-twentieth part of the sublime faith of him who undertakes to rout a combined array of publicans and Jingoes.

A wide survey of history seems to show that the essential habits of individuals and of nations are ineradicable. The asceticism of the Commonwealth was followed by the unbridled licence of the Restoration; the austere virtues of the Roman Republic by the unlimited vices of the Empire. Human nature is so imperfect that there is an undoubted danger in being "righteous overmuch." What, then, is the true motto of the temperance reformer? It is to be found in the words of Goethe, "*Without haste and without rest.*" The drinking habits of the people must be eradicated gradually, one branch of the upas tree being lopped off here, and another there, till at last the time may come when it will be safe to strike at the trunk itself.

I do not for a moment mean to affirm that Sir Wilfrid Lawson is so ignorant of human nature as to be likely to dash his head incontinently against it; but he has many intemperately temperate followers who habitually do so, to the great detriment of the cause which they and all well-intentioned citizens have at heart. Enthusiastic temperance reformers are so apt to under-estimate the warping influence of social customs and of early acquired habits, even on the healthiest consciences. I, for example, through force of association, am not an abstainer, though I often feel that it would be right I should be so; yet I am Pharisee enough to thank Heaven as often as opportunity offers that I am not like that inhuman "hunter of Cumberland beasts with hounds," Sir Wilfrid Lawson, Bart., the apostle of temperance, whose devotion to the public weal and domestic purity of life I so greatly admire. I would rather get hopelessly drunk every day in the week than even for once

"Blend my pleasure or my pride
With sorrow of the meanest thing that lives."

Howbeit, had I been born a fox-hunting squire like the baronet of Brayton, there are ten chances to one that I should have been as arrant a Nimrod as he. "That monster custom which all sense doth eat of habit's devil," is too much for us all, if not in one particular, then in another.

Like all friends of temperance who aim at possible reforms, I rejoice that Sir Wilfred, during the session of 1879, saw fit to substitute "Local Option" for the Permissive Bill. The latter had a detestable plebiscitary and imperialist flavour about it which made it stink in the nostrils of every man who believes that representative institutions afford the safest guarantees at once for liberty of the citizen and efficiency of administration. From this objection Local Option is free, and a flag is now unfurled around which may rally every one who is not the blind partisan of a "trade" which openly boasts of preferring its own small and not over-creditable "interest" to every consideration of national welfare.

For years the publicans have openly identified themselves with every reactionary "cry," and they will have themselves to blame if at last they find themselves at deadly feud with the whole Liberal party. It is perfectly intolerable that such a body of licensed monopolists should be permitted longer to make and unmake Governments. To this conclusion has Sir Wilfrid Lawson's persistent efforts brought us, and who shall say it is not a long way?

With regard to Sir Wilfrid's enlightened advocacy of peace principles, no exception whatever need be taken. He is not, so far as I know, a "peace at any price man," but he is the very incarnation of the righteous spirit of anti-Jingoism. Historically Jingoism is a ghastly recrudescence of all the brutal, bloodthirsty passions of bygone generations. Sir Wilfrid was one of the few members of the House who, at the moment that we seemed on the very brink of committing the incalculable folly and unforgivable crime of rushing into a second Crimean war, most clearly apprehended the true character of the impending calamity, and courageously pointed it out to Parliament and the country. It is in such crises that true Radicals, genuine patriots, come to the surface. It is not every man who, when such tried friends of freedom and national rectitude as Mr. Joseph Cowen are found fervently preaching the immoral and parochial doctrine of "my country right or my country wrong," has the fidelity to affirm, "I have a mightier country than you, and a larger interest to protect. The globe is my country, and its entire inhabitants are my countrymen. Eternal justice is the interest which I desire to see conserved."

This was the spirit in which Sir Wilfrid spoke when nearly everyone else feared to utter words of truth and soberness; and his constancy ought not to be forgotten. His cause, the cause of international arbitration, is a growing one. In spite of appearances, the day-dream of Mazzini will yet be realised. There will be a United States of Europe, as of America, and the sad Italian,

> "Who, rowing hard against the stream,
> Saw distant gates of Eden gleam,
> And did not dream it was a dream,"

will be numbered among the world's greatest seers.

Sir Wilfrid has likewise, in the matter of the royal grants, along with Sir Charles Dilke and Mr. P. A. Taylor, done all that one faithful representative could to rescue the people's hardly-earned money from the devouring maw of useless princes and princesses.

For the rest, the member for Carlisle, on subjects with which he is less familiar, always follows the best lead, and his vote will never be found recorded among the *ayes* when it should be among the *noes*.

He is not what can be called an orator, but his style of speaking is admirably adapted to the matter, which is no less closely reasoned than wittily conceived. He is the readiest and perhaps the most pungent writer of satirical verses I ever met. If he were setting himself to it, he could fill columns of *Punch* every week, to the great advantage of the proprietors. He is almost as good a writer of verse as I am of prose—which is saying a good deal. I subjoin a very recent specimen, consisting of a paraphrase of the Ministerial reply to Mr. Samuelson's question regarding the language officially used in Cyprus:—

> " About Cyprus we scarce know what language to speak,
> Whether English, or Turkish, or Russian, or Greek ;
> There's only one language we can't speak, forsooth—
> When Cyprus is mentioned we never speak truth."

VII.

HENRY FAWCETT.

"This is he who, felled by foes,
Sprang harmless up, refreshed by blows."

FOR twenty-one years the brightness of noonday has been to Henry Fawcett, "member for Hackney and Hindostan," as the blackness of midnight. As is well known, he has been stone blind during the whole period of his public life. The fact is a most painful one, which I allude to thus early, not for the purpose of exciting sympathy, but because it is impossible to estimate aright the magnitude of Mr. Fawcett's achievements if the heaviness of the odds against which he has had to contend is not duly taken into account.

There are always clever people ready to demonstrate that untoward calamities, which do not happen to themselves, are somehow blessings in disguise. Are you lamed for life? So much the better for *you*. Is there not thus effected an immense saving of shoe-leather? For the future you are independent of shoemakers. Are you deprived of sight? Good for you again; for is it not a fact that the blind have a marvellous gift of groping their way in the dark? Do not, for example, the excavations of Herculaneum and Pompeii testify that in their last agony the doomed inhabitants sought the aid of sightless guides to direct their flight?

Most true, there *is* generally some compensation for the heaviest misfortune, but it is, alas, as a rule, are too small for the loss sustained. And such, no doubt, has been the experience of the eminent politician and economist, Henry Fawcett.

Bereft of sight, he has achieved much; with sight, he would beyond question have achieved still more. For his is an exceedingly strong and healthy nature, as little prone to succumb to the enervating influences of prosperity as to the prostrating blows of adversity—a true Samson Agonistes, whose locks, however closely shorn by unlucky chance, were bound to grow some day and somehow.

His intellect is characterised by a vigour that is almost redundant, a tenacity of purpose that turns not back, and a personal courage curiously combined with caution which it would be exceedingly difficult to match inside or outside of Parliament.

Physically he is a picture of health and strength, one of the tallest men in the House, with long sinewy limbs and that peculiar poise about the shoulders suggestive of a leonine bound, which is generally observable in persons of extraordinary intrepidity of character. As might be expected of one in such fine animal condition, Mr. Fawcett's habitual mood is cheerful, even to mirthfulness. He has escaped being a mere athlete by becoming a scholar, and it is pretty certain that, if he had not been a philosopher, he would have been a demagogue.

He has strong natural affinities for the "unwashed" multitude. "March without the people," he would say with Ledru Rollin, "and you march into night; their instincts are a finger-pointing of Providence, always turned towards real benefit."

Men cast in such a big mould as Mr. Fawcett are almost inevitably democrats. The mere *gaudium certaminis* of politics is life for them. With culture and honesty of purpose such as the Cambridge Professor possesses, robust, hearty natures of this stamp make the most trustworthy Radical politicians. They have what is so necessary for political life, "staying power." They do not despair of progress because for a time there is an ebb in the popular tide. They know that high-water mark will again be reached before long, and if they cannot do better they are content to wait the event.

Henry Fawcett, M.P., was born in the neighbourhood of Salisbury, in the year 1833. His father, Alderman Fawcett, of Salisbury, was born at Kirby Lonsdale in 1793. He is now consequently in his eighty-sixth year, and a haler old gentleman or more resolute Radical it would be difficult to find in all England. He came to Wiltshire from Westmoreland in his youth, and after engaging for some time in trade, betook himself to the more congenial occupation of a gentleman-farmer. His energy and intelligence as an agriculturist were conspicuous, and when the Anti-Corn Law agitation was initiated both were heartily enlisted on behalf of the League. Even yet he is an effective public speaker, and is a personal friend and warm admirer of Mr. Bright.

Mr. Fawcett's mother is no less remarkable. Like her husband, the alderman, she is a sort of *semper eadem* no less in mind than in body. She is a keen politician—on the right side, of course—and to her does Mr. Fawcett attribute, in no small measure, the strength of his own Radical convictions.

Thus happy in his parentage, the member for Hackney was no less so in other essential particulars affecting his childhood and youth. He was country bred—and such a country, too—imbibing no taste that was not equally good for head, heart, and body. Health, the essential condition of all great achievements, he stored up abundantly, while at the same time the discipline of his mind was by no means neglected.

His family were neither rich nor poor, but in that "just middle" state which neither suggests to the youth that exertion is superfluous, nor inflicts on him the labour of acquirement as an unavoidable drudgery. Till his fourteenth year he attended a local school in the vicinity of Salisbury, whence he was removed to Queenwood College, Hants, where he remained for two years. There he had the good luck to benefit by the teaching of Professors Tyndall and Frankland. He next attended King's College, London, and in 1852 he was duly entered as a student of Trinity Hall, Cambridge. To Cambridge young Fawcett brought with him an unquenchable love of all manner of rural pursuits, the frame of an athlete, the ringing voice of a huntsman, and a tolerable store of learning.

He did not neglect his opportunities at the University. He was an adept at boating, skating, riding, angling, walking, racquets, cricketing, and prizetaking. In 1856 he graduated Seventh Wrangler, and was subsequently elected a Fellow of his college.

From a very early age he had displayed premonitory symptoms of a more than ordinary devotion to politics. While still an undergraduate the writings of the late John Stuart Mill made a deep impression on his mind, and partly determined him to seek an entrance into Parliament by the time-honoured avenue of the Bar. He accordingly commenced to "keep terms" at Lincoln's Inn, where he would have been duly "called" had not the terrible calamity to which I have already alluded intervened.

In the autumn of 1858 he was one day out with a small party engaged in partridge shooting. A covey rose and flew over a slight elevation, on the remote side of which Mr. Fawcett had momentarily disappeared. A companion unfortunately fired at the instant his head topped the rising ground, and two pellets, with something like diabolic precision, neatly perforating the spectacles he was wearing, lodged themselves in the retina of the eyes, and "at one stride came the dark." From that day to this,

> "Those eyes, though clear,
> To outward view, of blemish or of spot,
> Bereft of light, their seeing have forgot;
> Nor to their idle orbs doth sight appear
> Of sun, or moon, or star throughout the year,
> Or man or woman."

The pain of the accident was soon over, and it remained for Mr. Fawcett to consider how far so irreparable a mischance had necessarily affected his habits of life and future prospects. His invincible pluck did not desert him for a moment. Luckily his academic training was completed, and the benchers of Lincoln's Inn, on hearing the sad facts of the case, considerately offered to "call" him to the Bar without further to do. He might succeed as a counsel in spite of his blindness. Armed with logic, imperturbability, and physical endurance such as his, one might undoubtedly accomplish much. Still, the drawbacks to a successful professional career were undeniable, and Mr. Fawcett wisely, it seems to me, resolved not to encounter them, but to take a straighter cut to Parliament.

Except in this particular, however, he determined that his blindness should make "no difference," and it is wonderful how little it has actually affected his habits and intentions. In the very heart of London he has contrived to secure a modest house with a garden one-tenth of a mile long, where he can promenade all alone to his heart's content. He is never so happy as in the open air, and in his native Wiltshire his pedestrian feats have become almost proverbial. His topographical knowlege is so minute, that when his guides are at fault he not unfrequently directs them—from early recollections of natural objects, of course.

He religiously frequents the University Boat-race on the Thames, and is as heartily interested in the proceedings of the day as the keenest-eyed observer. At Cambridge he is stroke-oar of the "Ancient Mariners'" boat, and a better stroke no crew of "mariners," ancient and modern, need desire.

He is a good swimmer. When the Fens are frozen he takes to his skates as naturally as a duck in the water takes to her webs. On such occasions his daughter, a graceful maiden of eleven winters, precedes, her father whistling playfully.

He is likewise an ardent equestrian, and when in residence at the University, seldom a day elapses that the Professor of Political Economy may not be seen, accompanied by some one of his numerous friends, cantering fearlessly on Newmarket Heath or Across Flat. He occasionally even follows the hounds on a well-trained steed, and so hard a rider is he said to be that the livery-stable keepers have two tariffs, one ordinary for those who have *not* been seen in the society of Professor Fawcett, and one extraordinary for those that have.

Add to this that Mr. Fawcett is one of the best and most indefatigable amateur salmon and trout fishers that can well be imagined, and it will readily be admitted that no great "difference" has overtaken him with regard to outdoor recreations.

But if this is the case with respect to his personal habits, it is none the less true of his political intentions. He had hoped to enter the House as a successful counsel. As it was, he had to seek admission without the aid of that quasi-passport, without fame, and without what is even still more indispensable to a parliamentary candidate, money. Not that he was by any means a poor man, in the strict sense of the word. He has always been in comfortable circumstances, thanks to a provident father and his own exertions; but rather in the sense that his wants have been few and legitimate rather than that his income has been large. But he has had no superfluous thousands with which to oil the electoral wheels of any constituency. He has, however, invariably got over this difficulty with characteristic boldness and commendable candour.

His first venture was with the electors of Southwark in 1861, on the death of Sir Charles Napier, "Black Charlie." He did not know a soul in the borough, which he invaded with his secretary in a cab. They went straight to a printer's, and ordered a number of bills to be issued announcing the candidature of Henry Fawcett in the Radical interest.

He had previously spoken in public, once in Exeter Hall on trades unionism, and once at Glasgow, at the Social Science Congress, with considerable acceptance; but to all except the merest fraction of the electors, his very name was unknown; and worse and worse, when they came to meet him he was blind, and they soon had it from his own lips that he was not rich, and would employ neither paid agent nor canvasser.

Was there ever such a madman? Howbeit, the great ability and striking gallantry of the blind candidate soon began to tell with the constituency, and there is no saying what might have happened if Mr. Fawcett had not been over-persuaded to retire before the poll to avoid the charge of creating a division in the Liberal ranks. The experience he had gained, however, was of the most valuable kind. It went to prove, incredible as it may appear, that the portals of the "rich man's club" at Westminster may be successfully forced at the cost of a few hundreds by candidates at once poor and honest, if only they have the requisite faith and ability to make the venture.

In 1863, Mr. Fawcett contested the borough of Cambridge on the same principles that he had found to answer so unexpectedly well in Southwark. He was defeated, but by an insignificant majority.

He next contested Brighton in 1864, warmly espousing the cause of the North in its struggle with the slave-holding States of the American Union. Again he was unsuccessful, but the following year, nothing daunted, he returned to the charge, and was elected by a large majority.

In 1868 he was once more victorious, but at the general election of 1874, the *annus mirabilis* of Tory reaction, both he and his Liberal colleagues in the representation were thrown out, and replaced by Conservative nobodies.

Besides the general wave of reaction, which ran high nearly everywhere, there were special objections to Mr. Fawcett. He was not a rich resident, whose patronage benefited the shopkeepers, and he was, rightly or wrongly, opposed to the Permissive Bill without having the smallest hope of support from the publicans. But he lost his seat, to the deep regret of the most reflecting electors of Brighton, and of earnest and intelligent Radicals throughout the country.

It was impossible, however, that such a man should long be excluded from the Legislature. In two months' time a vacany occurred in the representation of the vast Metropolitan constituency of Hackney, and the eyes of the Liberal electors were at once turned with one accord towards Mr. Fawcett. He was elected without difficulty, his great services to India, and his persistent opposition to all encroachments on Epping Forest and the New Forest weighing heavily in his favour in the electoral balance.

In Parliament, Mr. Fawcett's career has been one of no ordinary success. He is recognised by all parties in the House as a speaker of decided mark, and his vote is always to be weighed as well as counted. He entered the Legislature with a body of well-defined principles, and he has stuck to them manfully through evil and through good report. His political conceptions are in a great measure those of his friend, the late Mr. John Stuart Mill. Unlike Goethe, for example, it was the special function of that great and generous thinker to fertilise, not sterilise, the minds of other men;

> "And methinks the work is nobler
> And a mark of greater might;
> Better far to make a thinker
> Than to make a proselyte.
> Nobler for the sake of manhood,
> Better for the cause of truth.
> Though your thinker be but rugged
> And your proselyte is smooth."

Mr. Fawcett's ideas may be described as ultra-individualist in their tendency. He is an "administrative Nihilist," who believes that government is at best a necessary evil, and that the less the people have of it, and the more they are left to seek their own happiness in their own way, the better for them.

In a country like Germany, with its Autocracy on the one

hand and its Socialism on the other, he would be between the upper and the nether millstone, and would assuredly, politically speaking, be speedily pounded to atoms. Here and in the United States the tendency is decidedly towards a more and more comprehensive individualism; but it is very doubtful whether in several instances Mr. Fawcett has not given us somewhat "too much of a good thing." His opposition, for example, to Mr. Mundella's Factory Acts Amendment Bill, limiting the labour of women in factories to nine hours, was, to say the least, an attitude of doubtful wisdom. If women could protect themselves from oppressive toil, then, of course, Mr. Fawcett was right; if the evidence was the other way, then he was wrong. The question is one of evidence solely, and I for one am of opinion that Mr. Fawcett's judgment was not in accordance with the evidence, He was willing, nay, has exerted himself manfully, to extend the benefits of factory legislation to the children of agricultural labourers, on the ground that they could not help themselves. How much better off were the majority of those for whose benefit the Nine Hours Bill was introduced? In reality hardly any.

Again, with respect to the licensing question, Mr. Fawcett's position has somewhat too much of the *non possumus* about it. The problem is one, doubtless, of very great difficulty, and certainly the Permissive Bill was a crude attempt to deal with it. But to tell us that Local Option is as objectionable as the Permissive Bill, or even more so, is to affirm one of two things—either that the present licensing system is perfect and inviolable, or that free trade in liquor is the true remedy for the monstrous evils of intemperance to which society is on all hands admitted to be a prey. If no remedy is the true remedy, then we ought to know it.

On the Republican question, too, I am free to admit Mr. Fawcett's conduct has been unsatisfactory. *In principle* he has declared himself a Republican, while *in practice* remaining a Royalist. Such an attitude is untenable, illogical, and altogether unworthy both of the man and the cause.

More I need not say. These positions, however, which the member for Hackney defends with so much gallantry and so little regard for his own popularity, are, generally speaking, virtues in excess, and cannot for a moment be permitted to weigh with any rational mind in judging of his career as a legislator.

Who can ever forget the evening when the blind member was the only representative of the people who *saw* his way into the lobby where Sir Charles Dilke and Mr. P. A. Taylor were tellers against the dowry to the Princess Louise? What Londoner can ever be too grateful to him for preserving from imminent alienation the ancient rights of the people in Epping Forest? If he had been member for Hackney at the time he was fighting so doggedly against the threatened enclosures, there might have been some suspicion that it was done merely to gratify his constituents. As it was, not even that pardonable kind of self-interest can be laid to his charge.

It will likewise be long remembered by the skilled artisans of London with what courage and devotion he acted as chairman of the late Mr. George Odger's committee in Southwark, when that Republican artisan statesman was so near obtaining a well-merited seat in the Legislature of his country.

But it is as the "member for India" that Mr. Fawcett's name will be handed down to posterity. He has the largest constituency of any man in the world, and his responsibilities have become as real as if they were imposed by law. He is the true Minister for India; Lord Cranbrook and Mr. Stanhope are but clerks by comparison, accomplishing like hirelings their official day. It is not to Lord Cranbrook but to Henry Fawcett that millions of Indians look for redress of grievances, for words of sympathy and comfort.

It is to be hoped that when the next Liberal Administration comes into power, the unique position which the member for Hackney holds in the hearts of the Indian people will not be overlooked. His presence at the India Office would do more to secure India than twenty Afghan expeditions. Mr. Fawcett has been at enormous pains to acquaint himself with the actual state of India, and yet his first application to the subject was more like an accident than anything else. He happened to oppose as a gross and shameful injustice the proposal of the Goverment of the day to saddle the Indian Exchequer with the cost of a particular entertainment given to the Sultan of Turkey. Bit by bit his knowledge of the systematic manner in which India is "exploited" by England grew, and he at last resolved to subject the whole question of Indian finance and Indian administration to a patient and searching analysis. For years he worked four hours every day at the tangled skein as one would for an examination, and when data failed him he had influence enough to secure the appointment of a Parliamentary Committee on Indian Finance, which sat for three whole sessions.

At the end of the investigation he had as fully mastered the subject as it was possible to do. He has all the more important figures by heart, and can hurl them with crushing effect at the head of whoever takes it upon him to unfold the Indian Budget.

It is one of the beneficial effects, if I may so speak, of Mr. Fawcett's blindness that he speaks, and does not read, his figures to the House. These, through his youthful but smart secretary, he selects so appropriately and uses so sparingly that his financial statements are singularly lucid and unencumbered, each set of figures being the evidence of some solid argument.

By dint of great perseverance the country has at last, in some measure, been got to realise that India is as near as possible a sucked orange, and that if we do not retrace our steps and repent us of the evil we have been doing, the "brightest gem in her Majesty's diadem" will speedily be in pawn. At this moment an Indian bankruptcy stares us in the face with all its terrible consequences. The limit of taxation has been reached, while the expenditure of the Administration is unlimited as ever.

To Mr. Fawcett more than to any other man or half-dozen of men do we owe our knowledge of the appalling condition of the "brightest gem," which, if one could imagine a gem being so ill-behaved, may explode any day with such violence as to shake to its foundations the throne not merely of the "Empress of India," but that of the Queen of England also. In this grave relation the voice of Henry Fawcett has been as the voice of one crying in the wilderness. If the British people have not made their paths straight, it has not been his fault.

The Indian people are frequently taxed by Anglo-Indians with ingratitude. I may mention, by the way, that Mr. Fawcett has not found it so. It is now some time since a great number of very poor Hindoos subscribed a sum sufficient to defray the cost of his next election for Hackney. The fund has been invested for the purpose in the names of Sir Charles Dilke, Professor Cowell, and Mr. Dacosta.

Mr. Fawcett is not merely an excellent platform speaker and a trenchant parliamentary debater, but he is a political economist of no mean order. His "Manual of Political Economy" has run through five editions, and ought to be in the hands of every youthful student of economic science. The "Economic Position of the British Labourer" is likewise a valuable contribution towards the elucidation of a painful subject; while "Pauperism: its Causes and Remedies," though in my opinion mistaken in some of its conclusions, is yet an eminently suggestive book.

In addition to the above works, Mr. Fawcett published in June 1879 "Free Trade and Protection," one entire edition of which was shipped for Australia and the United States, while another was taken up by the Cobden Club. There is besides a goodly volume of his collected "Speeches," which will well repay perusal, and another of "Essays," the conjoint production of Mrs. Fawcett and himself.

In conclusion, I cannot mention the name of this accomplished lady without according her my small meed of praise. If it was passing sad that Mr. Fawcett should lose the use of his own eyes, it was passing fortunate that he should obtain the aid of such another pair. When I think of this, it almost repents me that I should have spoken so slightingly of the compensation theorists in the first paragraph of this sketch.

VIII.

JOSEPH CHAMBERLAIN.

> "I am your Mayor.
> Few things have failed to which I set my will;
> I do my most and best."

SIR JOHN FALSTAFF, in his days of rotundity, could recollect a time when he was slim enough to "creep through an alderman's thumb-ring." But there are aldermen and aldermen. The Cockney type, with which Shakespeare and we Londoners, alas, are but too familliar, is an ignorant, obese, pompous being, "who struts and stares and a' that"—a glutton and a wine-bibber, an inveterate jobber, and a Jingo.

The subject of this sketch, Alderman Chamberlain, M.P., the renowned ex-Mayor of Birmingham, is the exact reverse of this picture. Of all living Englishmen he has deservedly earned the highest reputation as a municipal administrator, and he remains a pre-eminently courteous and cultivated gentleman—a lover of books, of paintings, and of flowers. Indeed I have heard an excellent judge say of the ex-Dictator of Birmingham, with his lithe limbs and classical features, that he is perhaps the best bred man in Parliament; and if he is not the most learned, he is certainly one of the most studious members of the House. There is a certain "pale cast of thought" on Mr. Chamberlain's youthful handsome face which gives an added interest to his charm of manner.

Democracy, it has been alleged, both produces, and is

partial to, coarseness in its representatives. The reverse is nearer the truth. Really good manners—the happy way of doing things—can never be acquired in an exclusive or aristocratic society, by reason of the paucity and uniformity of the models; and it is an indisputable fact that Radical constituencies *cæteris paribus* prefer to be represented by men of culture and refinement. Witness the choice by Paris of such representatives as Victor Hugo, Ledru Rollin, and Louis Blanc, and by Massachusetts of Webster, Adams, Charles Sumner, and many others such. If in England the union of culture and Radicalism is less observable, the reason is not far to seek. Excepting Birmingham, which returns Bright and Chamberlain to Parliament, there are scarcely any genuinely Democratic constituencies in this country. We are aristocratic, and therefore coarse in our preferences.

But this does not help me with the ex-Mayor, who is not merely a thoughtful political student, but one with whom it is impossible to converse, however briefly, without discerning that he is a man of genuine good feeling, strict integrity, resolute purpose, and unquestioning belief in the people as the only legitimate source of authority. If he is admired by the men of Birmingham, the admiration is at least mutual.

He is a singular example of a prophet who *is* honoured in his own country, and who makes no concealment of his conviction that that country is "the hub of the universe."

His remarkable self-possession his detractors in Parliament have been pleased to call overweening self-confidence. It is really nothing of the kind. There are more Parliaments than that mongrel thing which assembles at St. Stephen's to do little but mischief. Is there not the Town Council of Birmingham—the threshold of which it is as difficult for a Tory to pass as for a rich man to enter the kingdom of heaven; and has not Mr. Chamberlain for years sat *princeps inter pares* in that Radical Witanagemot, playing the part of a terrestrial Providence to an entire community? If

Parliament could be constituted as the Town Council of Birmingham is constituted, then Mr. Chamberlain might begin to respect it. As it is, he feels that it is below rather than above the level of his experience.

The parliamentary machine is vaster than the municipal, but its mechanism is less perfect and the results are every way less satisfactory. If he were asked whether the Town Council of Birmingham could not manage the affairs of the nation better than the entire paraphernalia of Queen, Lords, and Commons, I have little doubt what his answer would be, and I am not at all sure that he would be wrong.

Parliament has, in fact, reached an unparalleled state of incompetency and inertia, and it is only men like Mr. Chamberlain, who come to it with fresh eyes and with an undoubted capacity for the conduct of affairs, that are able to estimate its performances at their true value. Mr. Chamberlain has shown himself to be what I may call a great municipal statesman, and being so, he has perpetually before him a valuable standard of comparison, such as is not possessed in an equal degree by any other member of Parliament. No one else stands exactly on the same political plane, and no one in so brief a space—it is scarcely ten years since he made his first speech in support of Mr. Dixon's candidature for Birmingham—ever contrived to attach to himself a more numerous and respectable following in the country.

Mr. Chamberlain was born in London, in July 1836. He is consequently in his forty-third year, but in appearance he is more like a man of thirty-three than of forty-three.

The Chamberlains were originally a family of Wiltshire yeomanry, settled at Shrivenham, but for a hundred years previous to the removal of the late Mr. Chamberlain to Birmingham they had carried on, from father to son, on the same spot in Milk Street, Cheapside, and under the same name, an extensive business as leather merchants and shoe manufacturers.

In religion the family was Unitarian, and almost as a

matter of course Radical in politics. "Take a thorn bush," said the once renowned Abd-el-Kader, "and sprinkle it for a whole year with water; it will yield nothing but thorns. Take a date tree, leave it without culture, and it will always produce dates." And so it was with Mr. Chamberlain. He was not left without culture, for a Unitarian upbringing is generally an education in itself; but for one that has since evinced so marked a capacity for literary expression, both spoken and written, his scholastic training appears to have been but meagre. He was, indeed, a pupil of University College School for some time, but at the early age of sixteen he was put to business.

In his eighteenth year his father became one of the partners of the great screw manufacturing firm of Nettlefold & Chamberlain at Birmingham, and thither the future Mayor went with the family. There he devoted himself assiduously to the development of the paternal industry, which ultimately assumed gigantic proportions, the firm employing as many as two thousand "hands."

Throughout, employers and employed were on the best of terms, and when, in 1875, Mr. Chamberlain, after his father's death, finally retired from the business in order to devote himself exclusively to the public service, he did so with an ample fortune and the best wishes of the numerous operatives of the firm, who embraced the opportunity to bestow on him a handsome token of their regard in the shape of a valuable piece of plate.

Mr. Chamberlain has oftener than once acted as an arbitrator in labour disputes, and always with the utmost fairness and good sense, his most notable award, perhaps, being one which substituted a sliding scale for a fixed rate in the memorable coal-mining strike in Staffordshire in 1873-4.

Mr. Chamberlain was thirty-two years of age before he ever addressed his fellow-citizens, and he at once made his mark as a singularly clear, articulate, methodical speaker. The fact is peculiar, but not altogether inexplicable. For years before he had been a diligent reader, utilising all his spare time in his library, the shelves of which are filled with some three thousand well-selected volumes. He had thus acquired much knowledge, and what with a ready tongue and rare nerve, he felt fully equipped for the brilliant public career on which he entered in 1868.

Onerous and honourable duties were at once thrust on him. In 1868 he accepted the chairmanship of the famous Education League, and in the same year he became a member of the Town Council. In 1870 he was returned as one of the members of the School Board of Birmingham, and in 1873, when the Secularists, so called, secured a majority on the Board, he was elected chairman. In 1873 he was likewise unanimously elected Mayor, and in 1874 and 1875 a similar honour awaited him.

At the general election in 1874 he contested Sheffield in the Radical interest, but the town of Roebuck, Broadhead, and the *Sheffield Telegraph* knew itself better than to seek the services of so reputable a representative. He was at the bottom of the poll, the "frightful example" to all Radicals, Roebuck being at the top. An army of one thousand five hundred publicans worked night and day for this result. The whole town was given over to indescribable riot, and Mr. Chamberlain, who exhibited the greatest personal intrepidity and good humour, was oftener than once exposed to serious risks. Roebuck, singularly enough, was supported by the *Daily News*. Not many months elapsed, however, before Mr. Dixon retired from the representation of Birmingham, and the Mayor took his place in Parliament unopposed.

One event that occurred in Mr. Chamberlain's mayoralty I must not forget. In November 1874, the Prince of Wales practically invited himself to Birmingham, and much curiosity was felt as to the manner in which the Mayor would receive the Heir-Apparent. Mr. Chamberlain has never concealed his preference for Republican institutions, and the visit was necessarily of a somewhat embarrassing character. Nay, more, the Court party probably intended it to embarrass. They had scored an immense triumph, and they were determined to follow it up by bearding Radicalism at headquarters. They had succeeded in cementing the shattered reputation of his Royal Highness with surprising cunning. After the theatrical and almost blasphemous apotheosis of the Prince at St. Paul's on the occasion of his recovery from an illness which it would take a great deal to convince me was not purposely exaggerated, it was evidently felt that almost anything might be attempted in the way of humbugging the people. *Vult populus decipi et decipiatur.*

The Republican Mayor was to be put on his mettle, and what he did was this. He agreed to receive the Prince as the guest of the town, but he voted against defraying any portion of the expenses of the royal visit out of the public rates. Rather than that he would be host himself. For the rest, to have received the young man at all Mr. Chamberlain could not have gone through the performance with less offence to Republican feeling. His language was a miracle of dexterous steering between loyalty to the People and loyalty to the Prince—two interests for ever incompatible.

All the same, his Royal Highness had the best of it. What royalty wanted was a big gratis advertisement at the expense of the Radical Mecca, and it got it. The British Monarchy exists, as quack medicines exist, by dint of wholesome "puffing," the only difference being that the first is gratuitously advertised by its dupes, while notices of the latter are paid for by the parties directly interested. Now the Mayor unquestionably placed himself among the dupes of royalty, but I am free to admit he was in a strait place.

But Mr. Chamberlain's mayoralty was distinguished by more useful if less ornamental work than that of entertaining worthless princes. In the successive years during which he presided over the Town Council with consummate tact and administrative talent, he courageously grappled with three great questions affecting the welfare of the borough. Unlike most towns of more ancient date, Birmingham possessed no revenue but the rates when Mr. Chamberlain took office.

F

He looked about, and he soon found another source of civic income. He resolved that Birmingham should no longer be at the mercy of private companies for its gas supply. He made up his mind that the Corporation should possess itself of the undertakings of the Birmingham Gas Light and Coke Company, and of the Birmingham and Staffordshire Gas Light Company, and he was manfully backed by the Council. And with what result? In three years' time £80,000 have been appropriated in aid of the rates, £50,000 allocated as a reserve fund, £40,000 as a sinking fund; while the cost of gas to the consumers has been reduced 6d. per 1000 cubic feet, being equivalent to a saving of £60,000 per annum.

Having thus disposed of the two gas companies' undertakings, Mr. Chamberlain next resolved to deal with that of the Birmingham Waterworks Company. It also, after the inevitable calculations, negotiations, and parliamentary action, became the property of the Corporation, and though it has not been deemed advisable to raise revenue out of such a primary necessary of life as water, a good reserve fund has been laid past and a thoroughly efficient supply secured to the community.

Like other towns, Birmingham is not without its "slums," and to these the Mayor next turned his attention. Taking advantage of the provisions of the Artisans' Dwellings Improvement Act, and borrowing at the $3\frac{1}{2}$ per cent. rate, the Corporation has already purchased for the sum of £1,500,000 the area covered by all the vilest habitations in the borough. The Act empowers the municipal authorities to pull down, but not to re-erect. The private individuals, however, to whom the Corporation may convey a title will have to rebuild under conditions conformable to the health of the community and to the special convenience of the working class. It need surprise no one if Mr. Chamberlain be yet found to have been a better sort of Haussman to Birmingham.

Nor are the daring schemes of this municipal innovator

yet exhausted. Not content with giving the people light, water, and wholesome dwellings, he proposes shortly to make them the proprietors of their own public-houses; and from the favourable manner in which the Lords' Committee on Intemperance have spoken of his proposals, it is not at all unlikely that Parliament will permit the capital of the Midlands to make the experiment which her ex-Mayor desires.

What he proposes is that the Corporation should possess itself of all the public-houses in Birmingham—some 1800 in number—the owners having first been expropriated on a scale of compensation fixed by the Legislature. Thereupon 1000 are to be abolished at a stroke, and the remainder equipped in such a manner as to supply all the legitimate wants of the community. And the scheme, he calculates, will pay, and pay well.

It has several obvious advantages. The servants of the Corporation would, unlike the publicans, have no interest either in the insobriety of their customers or the adulteration of the liquor sold. The poor man's drink would be as good as the rich man's, which is far from being the case at present; the political power of the publican would be annihilated; and last, not least, the necessity for police espionage would be almost at an end. There is no one cure for drunkenness, but this seems as feasible as any for a great community; and if the ratepayers of Birmingham are willing to risk their money in giving so bold an application of the Gothenburg system a fair trial, there can be no reason in the world why they should be restrained. It may be that Birmingham is destined to initiate a public-house reform as contagious as has been the example which she has set to other places in respect, for example, of education and Liberal organisation.

As chairman of the School Board of Birmingham, and as president of the National Education League, Mr. Chamberlain has achieved nearly as great things in the educational as in the municipal world. Under his chairmanship of the

Birmingham Board a complete separation was effected between secular and religious instruction, while 14,500 children were added to the Board schools, and 9700 to the denominational. The League, of course, was not able to embody its ideal of a free, universal, compulsory, and secular system of education, but all the same it did a world of good in curbing the vagaries of Mr. Forster and the insolent pretensions of Churchmen.

In 1876 the League was dissolved, but its spirit yet liveth, and may perchance before long take unto itself a new body. Should this not be so, its programme is nevertheless as certain to be ultimately realised as has been the case with the "points" of the "People's Charter."

It is unnecessary to enlarge further on Mr. Chamberlain's local achievements. He has a manifest genius for everything affecting the work of corporate bodies, and would make a heaven-born President of the Local Government Board. His speeches in Parliament on the County Boards Bill and the Prisons Bill would alone have stamped him as a master of everything that pertains to a "spirited domestic policy," of which the country stands so much in need, and of which it hears so little.

Mr. Chamberlain, however, has greater claims on the Liberal party than any that I have yet adduced, and these are of a special and most important character. When our spirits have failed us, and the majority have seemed disposed to be "led"—whither our "leaders" would not or could not tell us—he has always come cheerily up in the pages of the *Fortnightly* with a new "programme" to put in our hands. He has rallied us to the cry of Free Land, Free Church, Free Schools, and Free Labour; and when that was not enough, he has set himself to "reorganise" and put us in marching order with our faces to the foe. Like all true men and brave spirits he is greatest and most helpful in adversity. For why? Is he not the father of the much derided, much denounced "caucus," which is yet destined to be such an important factor in the political life of the country?

Mr. Chamberlain, however, claims no special credit in connection with the caucus. He simply regards it as in some form inevitable, and therefore he tries to make the most of it. With the old restricted franchise, when the electors were a select and privileged class, no such party discipline was required. A caucus is simply an elected committee. Sixty voters may require no such committee to prepare their business for them, simply because they are practically a committee already. It is quite another matter when the numbers rise to 600, or 6000 or 16,000, as the case may be. Then some understanding must be come to, some suitable machinery must be devised to give effect to the general desires. In such circumstances the English race naturally and instinctively have recourse to popular election to rectify matters, and this, after all, is the worst sin that can be laid at the door of the "caucus."

The great matter, Mr. Chamberlain insists, is to ensure that your Hundred, Three Hundred, or Six Hundred be truly representative of the party voters. If that is secured all is well; if not, not. Whoever distrusts the caucus honestly worked distrusts the people as the true source of power. The party vote need not be one whit less honestly recorded because it is informal. Such, as I understand it, is Mr. Chamberlain's position, and it seems well-nigh unanswerable.

What then are the advantages of such an organisation of the Liberal forces? They are various. One is, and it is perhaps the most obvious, that it tends to put a strong check on what Scotsmen call "divisive courses" at elections. At the last general election twenty-six votes on a division were lost to the Liberal cause through a suicidal multiplication of Liberal candidates at the polls!

There is, however, it must be admitted, another and a much more certain method of preventing such disasters—viz., the French method of compelling by law a second ballot where no candidate has secured a clear majority of the voters.

It is perhaps too much to expect that any such sensible

rule will ever be adopted by the British Legislature, but Mr. Chamberlain admits that it is the true remedy, although that provided by the caucus is, of course, not inconsistent with it.

But it is not on this ground so much that Mr. Chamberlain justifies the caucus. He regards it as an invaluable school for political instruction. Nor is that all. The National Liberal Federation, of which Mr. Chamberlain is president, has in more than one sudden emergency shown a promptitude in bringing pressure to bear on the Government, by means of powerful deputations and concerted public meetings, that never could have been rivalled by any conceivable isolated action. Mr. Bright, in introducing to Lords Hartington and Granville the great national deputation in favour of peace, summoned by the Federation and the National Reform Union, pointedly described it as "a remarkable deputation—such a one as I have not seen before in my political experience."

Of course, with a more constitutional premier than Beaconsfield at the helm of the State, the occasions on which the Federation would thus require to review its forces would be few and far between, but certainly for the present the Liberal party owes the president of the Federation a deep debt of gratitude for the disinterested sagacity he has displayed in striving to furnish it with such a potent weapon of defence ready to its hand.

The National Liberal Federation was constituted at Birmingham in May 1877, and Mr. Gladstone, it will be remembered, was one of its sponsors. It then numbered forty-six associations; it has now risen to over a hundred, and every week adds to its strength and efficiency. It combines in a marvellous manner complete local autonomy with a capacity for concerted action something like that which existed amongst the Hanse Towns of the Middle Ages. Mr. Chamberlain has done surprising things as a party organiser, but this is distinctly his masterpiece.

IX.

THOMAS BURT.

> " Go far and go sparing,
> For you'll find it certain,
> The poorer and baser you appear,
> The more you'll look through still."

THE results of the general election of 1874 were surprising in many respects, and to many persons; but probably to none more so than Mr. Thomas Burt, M.P. While other prospective legislators were studying or wassailing at Oxford and Cambridge, the honourable member for Morpeth was laboriously ransacking the bowels of the earth in grimy Northumberland for coals wherewith to supply the complex wants of the British public. Like Goldsmith's village preacher. " he ne'er had changed, nor wished to change his place," and when his fellows first advised him of their intention to bring him forward as a candidate for Parliamentary honours, he replied in the words of the anti-Utopian:—

> " Oh, brothers, speak of possibilities,
> And do not break into these wild extremes,"

But elected he was to take his seat among his "betters"—among lordlings and millionaires—in the choicest of West-end metropolitan clubs, and that, too, with an ease which contrasted sharply with the ill-success in other constituencies of more widely-known "labour candidates."

This effect, however, was not without an efficient cause.

Apart from the fact that the Morpeth register was in a condition exceptionally favourable to the return of a genuine working man, Mr. Burt was in reality, with all his seeming diffidence and meagre presence, an exceedingly formidable candidate.

He is able and "canny" to a degree, and conspicuously devoid of those faults that do more easily beset trades-union leaders. He never, for example, speaks on any subject with which he is not thoroughly conversant, and his range of topics is by no means limited. He never tells you on the first occasion that you are alone with him, that every other exponent of the claims of labour, except himself, is a fool or a knave; and when he makes an engagement he keeps it, with all the punctuality of a good middle-class man of business who knows the value of time.

He is, in truth, a singularly fair-minded man, as capable of looking at any issue arising in the labour market from the point of view of the employer as of the employed. From contact and observation he has learned to combine, in a great measure, the characteristic virtues of both classes, while discarding their special vices. His sympathies are, of course, entirely with the working man, but the impartiality of his judgment saves him from anything like indiscriminate partisanship.

His workingmanism, too, is of such a catholic kind as practically to obliterate the hateful distinctions of class altogether. It does not stop at handworkers, but embraces all honest brain-workers as well. It is only with the monstrous army of royal and aristocratic Do-nothings and Eat-alls, which in this England of ours is permitted to such an unparalleled extent to lay waste the harvest of honest industry, that Mr. Burt is at war.

In politics he is a very intelligent English Radical, and nothing more. He is actuated by no Socialistic or subversive passions, and if he gives the best portion of his legislative attention to the interests of his own class, it is simply because he thinks, and thinks justly, that these are the most neglected at St. Stephen's. We hear of "officers and gentlemen." If he is a workman, he is likewise a gentleman. Like the late Mr. Odger, he has succeeded in completely emancipating himself from the warping influences of class-feeling, and by dint of a severe course of reading and reflection he has arrived at conceptions of the public good which may be truly called statesmanlike. There are not many men in Parliament regarding whom it would be honest to aver as much. But the politics of the pit are manifestly more enlightened, more national in scope, than those of church or castle, bar or barrack-room; and if Mr. Thomas Burt be a fair specimen of "pitmen" politicians, I have no hesitation in saying that it is a misfortune for the country that there are so few of them in the House.

Wonderful to relate, he represents his constituents in Parliament, not himself. If the truth were told, "log-rolling" is an art as well understood at Westminster as at Washington, and, to my certain knowledge, Mr. Burt has, on more occasions than one, resisted the machinations of the tempter with scrupulous fidelity.

Mr. Burt was born at Murton Row, a small hamlet about two miles from North Shields, Northumberland, in November 1837. His ancestors, needless to say, did not "come over at the Conquest." The fact is not recorded, but I believe they were in England long before that great national calamity. His father, Peter Burt, was an upright, hard-working miner, much addicted in his spare hours, if he may be said to have enjoyed such, to Primitive Methodism, trades unionism, and reading. He was a "local preacher," and his literary tastes, as may be readily imagined, had a strong theological bias. But he was distinctly a superior man, and no mere narrow-minded sectarian. The truly apostolic Channing was among his treasured authors, an insignificant fact perhaps in itself, but one which helped materially to stimulate the youthful intelligence of his son, and to cast his character in a noble mould.

Thomas Burt's mother was likewise no ordinary person.

She possessed a solid judgment and a tender heart, and while she lived she was the angel of the lowly household, which saw many ups and downs before the member for Morpeth reached man's estate.

When Burt was but seven years of age, the great Northumberland strike began, and he thus early tasted something of the bitter fruit of these labour struggles, which he has since exerted himself so strenuously to avert. Burt senior being a prominent striker, his family, with many others, was evicted from its humble abode, and might have perished from exposure but for the benevolent intervention of a neighbouring farmer, who contrived to accommodate no fewer than three households in two small rooms.

At the end of the strike, Burt's father, being a "marked man," and regarding discretion as the better part of valour, retreated to Helton, in the county of Durham, where he found employment for about a year. Subsequently, the family moved to Haswell Blue House, a hamlet midway between Haswell and Sholton Collieries, and in the former of these mines, Thomas Burt, M.P., commenced work as a "trapper" on his tenth birthday. His schooling had necessarily been of an irregular kind, and though not without

> "The gleams and glooms that dart
> Across the schoolboy's brain,
> The song and the silence in the heart,
> That in part are prophecies, and in part
> Are longings wild and vain,"

Burt entered the Inferno of Haswell Colliery without having exhibited any conspicuous talent, and to all appearance the gates of night closed remorselessly behind him.

It may be of interest to those, if there be any such, who still believe in the luxurious miner of the newspaper legend, with his curious taste in champagne, pianos, and greyhounds, to know something of the honourable member's underground experiences, and these, I may premise, were by no means exceptional. He commenced as a "trapper," at 10d. per day of twelve hours. A "trapper" is a doorkeeper who sat, or sits, in utter darkness, peering wistfully into the "palpable obscure" for the approach of any mortal with a lamp. Such occupation might suit a notorious criminal of a philosophical turn of mind, but none other.

Promotion, however, soon came Mr. Burt's way. He became a subterranean "donkey-driver," and his wages rose 4d. per diem. Then followed "management of an inclined plane" at Sherburn House Pit, between Durham and Thornley, wages from 1s. 4d. to 1s. 6d.; and later, two years' "putting," or pony driving at Dalton Colliery, wages from 1s. 6d. to 2s. per diem.

In 1851 the family ceased to sojourn in Durham and returned to its native Northumberland, settling ultimately for a period of eight or nine years at Seaton Delaval. Here further promotion awaited young Burt. He became a "water-leader," and his wages varied from 2s. 6d. to 3s. 6d. per day. "Water-leading" is not a specially amusing occupation. Before you know where you are, you are frequently up to the waist in the subterranean liquid, which has about as much fancy for being "led" as a Tipperary pig. Add to this that the hours of labour, though nominally twelve, were practically thirteen "from bank to bank," and that the distance to and from home was a good two miles' walk, and it will readily be granted that the honourable member for Morpeth's opportunities for self-culture were in no way enviable.

At fifteen years of age he had besides recklessly cut himself off from the consolation of champagne by becoming a total abstainer, and somewhat later he had to cure an inherited weakness for the cultivation of music simply because he had no time to spare. In his eighteenth year, however, he graduated as a pitman. He became a "hewer," and his wages rose to from 4s. to 5s. per diem, the hours of labour sensibly diminishing at the same time.

And so on Mr. Burt went "toiling, rejoicing, sorrowing," till the autumn of 1865, when he was elected by his brother workmen general secretary of the Northumberland Miners'

Association. Then, after eighteen years of unremitting underground toil, and the usual miners' hairbreadth escapes with his life, Mr. Burt got permanently to the surface, and eight years later his apparition startled the "rich men" at St. Stephen's.

From pit to Parliament is assuredly a long way and an arduous. It may not be a very great or even desirable distinction to be able to write M.P. after one's name, but nobody will deny that to earn the right, as matters stand, is an achievement of almost fabulous difficulty for a man that has neither birth nor wealth to recommend him. In Mr. Burt's case both these passports to electoral influence were conspicuous only by their absence; yet here he is with perhaps as attached a constituency as any in England behind him. Other members pay vast sums for the honour of being permitted to represent their constituents in Parliament. Here, on the contrary, you have a body of electors who voluntarily tax themselves in order to pay their member a salary of £500 a year for representing them. Was there ever a more daring outrage on constitutional propriety? And, what is stranger still, this phenomenal member, whose praises are alike in the mouths of Ministerialists and Opposition, is an avowed foe of royalty and aristocracy, of "Beer and the Bible." There is scarcely an "ism," from Republicanism downwards, that he cannot swallow without so much as making a wry face. Since Andrew Marvell's time there has been no such marvel in Parliament as Thomas Burt, the chosen of Morpeth.

At about fifteen years of age he began, all unconsciously of course, to educate himself for the discharge of his present responsible duties. And he educated himself to some purpose. While "his companions slept" this physically feeble but mentally strong Northumbrian miner "was toiling upwards in the night." He eschewed the public-house and kept the very best society—the society of Channing, Milton, Emerson, and Carlyle; of Shakespeare, Tennyson, Longfellow, Wordsworth, Shelley, and Burns; of Burke, Grattan, and

Curran; of Macaulay, Gibbon, and Hume; of Scott, Thackeray, Dickens, and George Eliot; of Adam Smith, John Stuart Mill, Bastiat, Fawcett, Thornton, and other illustrious intellects. Latin and French he hammered out as best he could from the pages of "Cassell's Popular Educator," while Euclid and shorthand received no inconsiderable share of his attention. And whatever he read he mastered and assimilated with a rare appreciation of all that he found true and beautiful.

Then came the application of all this acquirement—a true and beneficent application. He did not wrap his talents in a napkin, but devoted them ungrudgingly to the elevation of his fellow-workmen. He lectured on temperance, trades unionism, arbitration, co-operation, education, the advantages of Mechanics' Institutes, politics, and gradually became a clear, judicious, and convincing public speaker.

He was a Sunday-school teacher, a day-school secretary, and an organiser of temperance societies. He came to read men as he had read books, with intelligence and sympathy, and the miners on their part were quick and generous to discern that they had found in their fellow-workman a true friend and able counsellor.

In 1860 the Burts left Seaton Delaval and settled at Choppington, now a portion of the parliamentary borough of Morpeth, and here it was that the great administrative talents of the honourable member first displayed themselves. He speedily became the delegate of the Choppington men, and ultimately, in 1865, General Secretary of the Northumberland Miners' Mutual Confident Association.

The union was then under a heavy cloud. There was but £23 in the exchequer, and an extensive strike—the Cramlington—was proceeding. The new secretary was bitterly attacked by a "A Coalowner" in the columns of the *Newcastle Chronicle*. He replied with characteristic dignity and spirit. "I was chosen agent for this association," he wrote, "for the purpose of doing the best I could to aid the workmen in securing justice. I did not force myself on the men; they urged me to take the office; and as soon as they can dispense with my services I am prepared to resign. But so long as I am in office I will do my best to serve my employers. Four months since I was a hewer at Choppington Colliery. As a working man, I was in comfortable circumstances, serving employers whom I respected, and who, I believe, respected me. I had been at that colliery nearly six years, and during that time I had never a wrong word with an official of the colliery. 'A Coalowner' may ask there whether I was a 'demagogue' or an 'agitator.' I left the colliery honourably, and I have no doubt I can get my work again at that place if I want it. If not, I can get work, I doubt not, elsewhere, and under good employers too, for I long since made up my mind not to work for a tyrant. I say this merely to let your readers know that the position I hold is not degrading either to myself or the men who employ me."

Largely as the result of this rare combination of moderation and firmness on the part of the secretary, external aid flowed freely into the coffers of the association. When the strike ended a surplus of £700 remained over.

By Mr. Burt's advice this sum, instead of being divided among the several collieries in the union, was made the nucleus of a central fund, which in a few years increased to £16,000, while the membership of the union was quadrupled.

Though in Parliament, Mr. Burt is still the adviser-general and appellant-judge of the association, whose solidarity and wise counsels have done so much to inspire both employers and employed in Northumberland with feelings of amity and mutual respect. Recently there has been a sensible decline in the membership of the union, owing chiefly to the wholesale depopulation of certain districts consequent on the prolonged depression of trade and the enforced stoppage of the less remunerative pits. Within the last three and a half years the miners of Northumberland, to their credit be it recorded, have expended nearly £17,000 in support of brethren thus thrown out of employment. Indeed, that they should have hitherto been able to face the crisis so manfully and efficiently can only be regarded as another miracle of thrift and self-sacrifice worthy of the men who, by returning Mr. Burt to Parliament as their "paid member," were the pioneers of one of the most necessary and important political reforms of the future.

The circumstances attending the return of the member for Morpeth to Parliament have never yet received the general attention and commendation they deserve. They were most remarkable. Two pitmen, Mr. Robert Elliot (a poet of no mean merit) and Mr. Thomas Glassey, along with two brothers, Drs. James and Robert Trotter, local medical practitioners, did the heaviest portion of the electioneering, which, at the height of the Tory reaction, resulted in 3332 votes being recorded for Mr. Burt, against 585 for his amiable Tory opponent, Major Duncan.

Never was there such unbounded enthusiasm. The prophet of Choppington was indeed honoured in his own country. His election expenses were defrayed by public subscription. He had nothing to do but address the electors and prepare to draw his parliamentary salary, which if not large is perhaps amply sufficient for his modest wants and limited desires.

Well may Morpeth, the borough of the derided "Howkies," with their short lives—computed to reach an average of only twenty-eight years—their sore toil and pitiable pay, say to the most virtuous constituency in the kingdom, "Go thou and do likewise."

> "Go on until this land revokes
> The old and chartered lie,
> The feudal curse whose whips and yokes
> Insult humanity."

And as for the fortunate member for Morpeth, he has in Parliament, I think, redeemed all the legitimate expectations that were formed of him. His speeches on the County Franchise Bill, on the Employers' Liability for Injury Bill, on the grants to Wales and Connaught, and, above all, his hearty denunciation of the Afghan war, leave nothing to be desired.

With regard to the Medical Bill, he showed somewhat too great a confidence in quack doctors and unlicensed bone-setters, but that is a small matter.

For the rest, as I have said before, his conduct in the House has evoked the praise of all parties. The worst of Tories admit that he is "fair," and herein perhaps lurks a danger for the member for Morpeth. Reformers of great wrongs cannot afford to cultivate this spirit of fairness to excess. Be fair, be fair, be not too fair! "Beware ye when all men speak well of you, for so did they of the false prophets that were before you."

X.

HENRY RICHARD.

───◆───

"And evermore beside him on his way
The unseen Christ shall move."

IN the House of Commons are to be found a good many members who profess the Christian religion—at all events in public—but excepting Mr. Henry Richard there are very few, so far as I know, who make the smallest pretence of literally squaring their politics by the precepts of the New Testament.

The politics of Rome and of Canterbury—of the Papal and Anglican priesthoods—are, of course, well represented at St. Stephen's, but their relation to Christianity proper is so remote, or indeed antagonistic, as to merit no recognition in this connection. They are merely ecclesiastical intrigues, and in no true sense Christian or even religious in their aim or tendency.

But Mr. Richard's position is different. He is distinctly a Christian politician, and herein lies his strength or weakness as a legislator. The estimable "Apostle of Peace" is, wonderful to relate, a Gospel Radical, and it is by that difficult standard that it will be necessary in some measure to try him. He believes that Christianity supplies the politician, as it does the individual, with a true, or rather *the* true, conduct-chart, and his pamphlet "On the Application of Christianity to Politics" leaves us in no doubt as to his canons of Biblical interpretation.

"I have no hope," he tells us, "for the future of this world that is not connected with Christianity."

When "every thought shall have been brought into captivity to the obedience of Christ," then only will Mr. Richard feel satisfied that we are politically on the right rail. There are not two moralities, he maintains—a private and a public, a personal and a political. Mr. Richard's method with the Jingoes is the shortest of any. Is it not written, "Thou shalt not kill?" Therefore is the occupation of the soldier for ever accursed, cursing alike conqueror and conquered.

According to this exegesis, such gallant Christians as Sir Henry Havelock and Captain Hedley Vicars, of pious memory, were little better than public cut-throats or licensed murderers. So be it. Mr. Richard will shrink from none of the consequences of his understanding of Holy Writ. The commandment is absolute. "Avenge not yourselves, but rather give place unto wrath, for it is written, vengeance is mine, I will repay it, saith the Lord." "Resist not evil." "See that none render evil for evil unto any man, but ever follow that which is good, both among yourselves and to all men." "If you do well and suffer for it, and ye take it patiently, this is acceptable unto God."

These are hard words for flesh and blood to apply literally, but Mr. Richard in his "Defensive War" makes it plain that he will, no more than Hosea Biglow, admit of any dodging :—

> "If ye take a sword and dror it
> And go stick a feller through,
> Guv'ment ain't to answer for it,
> God will send the bill to you."

If a robber assail you with murderous intent, there are "three courses" open to you. You may expostulate with him on the error of his ways, you may exert moderate force to restrain him from burdening his soul with a great crime, and, lastly, you may exhibit true moral courage by running away as fast as ever your legs will carry you; but on no account are you to lay the flattering unction to your soul that, under any circumstances, is there such a thing as "justifiable homicide" possible.

Similarly with regard to other questions of vital public interest, such as the support of religion by State, whether in Church or school, the member for Merthyr finds something like absolute prohibitions where the great majority of professing Christians appear to discover the reverse.

How wonderful is Mr. Richard in his exegesis! How wonderful are the majority of Christians in theirs! How marvellously malleable are the memorials of the Christian faith themselves! Humanly speaking one would say some of them must be at fault, but which, I am pleased to think, it is not my province to determine.

Infidel Radicals are in these days of general apostasy as thick as blackberries. It is refreshing occasionally, for the sake of variety if for nothing else, to encounter one who is thoroughly orthodox. "The stone which the builders rejected, the same is become the head of the corner." Nor am I unmindful of the warning—"And whosoever shall fall on this stone shall be broken; but on whomsoever it shall fall it will grind him to powder."

Suffice it for my purpose to postulate that Mr. Richard is as good a Radical as he is a Christian, and that with him the terms are in a great measure convertible. May Heaven multiply this particular school of Christians, for never were they more sorely needed than at present :—

> "Keep thou the child-like heart
> That shall his kingdom be,
> The soul pure-eyed that wisdom led
> E'en now His blessed face shall see."

Henry Richard, M.P., was born at the little town of Tregaron, Cardiganshire, in 1812. The locality is peculiarly Welsh in all its aspects, and the "member for Wales" is, as is befitting, of pure Welsh descent, his mother's maiden name having been Williams.

His father and grandfather were both ministers of the

Calvinistic Methodist persuasion, the latter for the long space of sixty years. In one of his addresses to his constituents at Merthyr, Mr. Richard told them, with manifest pride, "that he had come of a good stock who had served Wales well in days gone by." And so it was. His father, the Rev. Ebenezer Richard, of Tregaron, was no ordinary man. Welshmen, even more than Scotsmen, appear to benefit by the kind of instruction which is conveyed in "sermons," and Richard senior was a powerful preacher, the memory of whose pulpit oratory is still cherished in South Wales. Nor was he prominent only in spiritual things. For many years he was general secretary to his denomination, and along with the Rev. Thomas Charles, of Bala, he conferred on the Principality what was at the time an inestimable boon, viz., a thoroughly comprehensive system of Sunday-school education, which had regard to the wants of adults as well as of juveniles.

His home at Tregaron was the rallying point of much of the religious and philanthropic activity of South Wales. The chief actors concerned believed, and not without reason, that they were engaged in a work no less momentous than the regeneration of the Principality, and their earnestness, as might have been expected, made an indelible impression on the open mind of young Richard, whose earliest memories are of fervent "revivals," "seasons of refreshing," etc.

From the doctrines imbibed in his childhood he has never appreciably departed, yet the tenacity with which he sticks to his creed is not to be confounded with bigotry. In the sphere of civil action there is not in all England a more enlightened advocate of the broadest freedom. His human sympathies are as generous and keen as they were fifty years ago. In his case there has been none of that

> "Hardening of the heart that brings
> Irreverence for the dreams of youth"

such as, I am bound to say, it has been mine to observe in but too many victims of early Calvinistic training.

But it must not be supposed that his education was

altogether of a religious complexion. At an early age he was sent to Llangeitho Grammar School, and subsequently, when eighteen, he became a student of the Highbury Independent College, London, the Calvinistic Methodists having then no theological school of their own.

At both places the instruction was sound so far as it went, and Richard, as was to be expected from a youth of his conscientious disposition, did not fail fully to avail himself of his opportunities.

At the close of his theological curriculum he joined the Independent Communion, and became minister of Marlborough Chapel, Old Kent Road. The congregation was moribund, but the Rev. Henry Richard was equal to the occasion. In a short time the attendance greatly increased, a considerable debt was paid off, schools were built, and a literary institute was established.

It was not long, however, before Mr. Richard found a wider field for his talent, and perhaps a truer .vocation. In 1843 occurred in Cardiganshire and Carmarthenshire what were known as the "Rebecca Riots." The Welsh roads were then encumbered with turnpike gates to an unendurable extent, and some of the younger men among the tenant farmers, despairing of relief by more legitimate means, had recourse to nocturnal acts of demolition.

The Principality was overwhelmed with obloquy in consequence, and but for the courageous stand taken by Mr. Richard, who publicly explained the origin and narrow limits of the disturbances, there is no saying to what foolish acts of repression the Government of the day might not have been induced by the panic-stricken magistracy to have recourse.

But the matter did not end with the Rebecca Riots. In 1846 a Government Commission was sent into Wales to inquire into the state of education in the Principality. The Commissioners' report duly appeared in three formidable volumes, formidable alike for their contents and size. The Welsh were deliberately described as the most debased, ignorant, lewd, and vicious people under the sun. The misrepresentation, it cannot be doubted, was most vile. Something like a wail of anguish broke from the heart of the ancient Cymric race. The Commissioners had apparently listened to nothing but the calumnies poured into their ears by territorial justices of the peace and Anglican parsons with empty churches.

Again Mr. Richard came forward as the champion of his slandered countrymen, and in a masterly lecture which he delivered in Crosby Hall in the spring of 1848, he vindicated the character of the Welsh people, and succeeded in a great measure in rolling back the rising tide of English prejudice and calumny.

Further, in 1866 Mr. Richard contributed to the *Morning Star* an exhaustive series of letters on the "Social and Political Condition of Wales," the value of which Mr. Gladstone thus handsomely acknowledged in the speech which he delivered as President of the National Eisteddfod, held at Mold in 1873 :—" I will frankly own to you that I have shared at a former time, and before I had acquainted myself with the subject, the prejudices which obtain to some extent with respect to Wales, and I am come here to tell you how and why I have changed my opinion. It is only fair that I should say that a countryman of yours, a most excellent Welshman, Mr. Richard, M.P., did a great deal to open my eyes to the true state of the facts by a series of letters which, some years ago, he addressed to a morning journal, and subsequently published in a small volume, which I recommend to all persons who may be interested in the subject."

Not without reason has Mr. Richard been dubbed "member for Wales." He incarnates all the best characteristics of his race.

If he is trusted as a good Welshman he is none the less so as a staunch Nonconformist. Welshmen are born Dissenters, and it is natural that they should follow Mr. Richard in such matters; but it is a higher compliment to him to say that the confidence of his countrymen is heartily endorsed by the whole body of English and Scottish Nonconformists. There is not a better representative Nonconformist in Parliament than the member for Merthyr. His opposition to the obnoxious clauses of the Education Act of 1870 was as hearty as that of the most pronounced "Secularist" in the House, and went a long way to prove that Christianity properly understood and applied to politics means something far other than priestcraft and obscurantism.

The member for Merthyr spoke with all the more authority, that for years he had been one of the most active promoters of popular education in Wales. He was one of the first members of the Congregational Board of Education, and when that body ultimately showed too strong a partiality for denominational interests he joined the Voluntary School Association, founded on a broader and more unsectarian basis, and during the whole subsequent period of its useful existence he was its honorary secretary,—travelling, speaking, and writing on its behalf, and taking an active part in the establishment and control of its Normal Schools.

It is, however, neither as Welshman, Nonconformist, nor Educationist that Mr. Richard's name is destined to go down with honour to remote posterity. It is as the strenuous advocate of peace that he will be entitled to lasting remembrance.

In 1848 he was appointed secretary of the Peace Society; and in 1851 he finally abandoned the ministry in order to devote himself soul and body to the good cause. He felt that it was not enough to denounce the blood-guiltiness of war. Wars are but barbarous methods of settling international disputes. Let us urge on "sovereigns and statesmen," he reasoned, "a better way, one at least not a disgrace to civilisation and Christianity. Let us boldly bring forward in the Legislature a resolution in favour of arbitration as a substitute for the sword."

In 1848, Mr. Cobden was appealed to, and assented to

become the standard-bearer of the Peace Society, and to his intense gratification the resolution which he moved the following session was supported by no fewer than seventy-nine votes.

On the Continent, likewise, the work went bravely forward. From 1848 to 1852, International Peace Congresses, promoted by Mr. Richard and Mr. Elihu Burritt, were held at Brussels, Paris, Frankfort, London, Manchester, and Edinburgh. The Paris Congress was presided over by Victor Hugo, while the London Conference was attended by Garrison, Phillips, Lucretia Mott, and other distinguished Americans. Bright, Lamartine, Arago, Humboldt, Liebig, Suringar, Coquerel, Brewster, Cormentin, Girardin, Beckwith, Garnier, and many other illustrious persons, were among the foremost advocates of the movement.

But "Messieurs les Assassins" were not prepared to let slip their bloody pastime so easily. Louis Napoleon perpetrated his execrable *coup d'état*, and the war-spirit was again evoked with fourfold violence. The Crimean war followed, and the exertions of Mr. Richard and the Peace Society were perfectly paralysed. The Press ridiculed them; they became a byword.

At the close of the war in 1856, when the Plenipotentiaries were sitting in congress at Paris, negotiating terms of peace, it occurred to Mr. Richard and his friends that an effort ought to be made to get the principle of arbitration recognised in the treaty. Lord Palmerston was seen by an influential deputation, but held out no hope. Still Mr. Richard persevered.

No one, however, could be induced to accompany him to Paris. At last he addressed himself to the guileless Quaker, Joseph Sturge. "Thou art right," was the instant reply, "and if no one will go with thee, I will." They started accordingly, along with Mr. Hindley, the member for Ashton, and their faith was rewarded. Lord Clarendon earnestly pleaded their cause with the Plenipotentiaries, who unanimously declared in favour of recourse being had to the good offices of some friendly power before any appeal should be made to the arbitrament of the sword.

This formal sanction given to the principle of international arbitration has not been wholly inoperative. In the settlement of the Alabama claims, England and America set a memorable example of moderation and good sense to the entire family of nations—an example, alas, which has since then been but too seldom imitated. For why? Something more must be done to restrain the illimitable horrors of war, than to provide a feeble substitute for multitudinous homicide, after the causes have come to a head. The causes must themselves be eliminated. Could arbitration ever restrain a Napoleonic *coup d'état*, or influence for a moment such dynastic exigences and ambitions as brought France and Germany into their last terrible death grapple? The French and German peoples had no quarrel with each other. The quarrel was entirely one between their rulers, supported by the governing oligarchy of the two countries. In the same way the English people have had no cause of discontent with the poor Afghans or Zulus.

War is wholly the work—the infamous work—of "sovereigns and statesmen." Sovereigns *must* have wars. However peaceful their professions, they have a direct and overwhelming interest in the maintenance of division and discord among nations. Were it not for wars, the occupation of kings would be gone, and the credit of the kingly form of government would sink to zero. In other words, Europe must become a federated, self-governing Republic, before the world can hope to attain to a permanent peace. Until the People are Sovereign, until the "United States of Europe" have been established, "the ogre of war," as Bastiat has well said, "will cost as much for his digestion as for his meals." Till democracy has in every state put down all her enemies under her feet, there cannot, in the nature of things, be any genuine disarmament.

Let Mr. Richard ponder this matter, and prepare to deal less gently than he has been in the habit of doing with the causes of war—with the aforesaid sovereigns and statesmen. Does he want a text to warrant him in seeking to rid the world of these illustrious vultures? Here is one that ought to suit him: "Ye know that they which are accounted to rule over the Gentiles exercise lordship over them, and their great ones exercise authority upon them. But so shall it not be among you: but whosoever will be great among you shall be your minister. And whosoever shall be the chiefest shall be the servant of all."

They who exercise lordship over us tell us of patriotism. What is patriotism? I have seen some of the votaries of the patriotic goddess at their devotions. I witnessed the loathsome exploits of the Hyde Park Jingoes, and I saw the Cannon Street Hotel sacked by the unconvicted thieves of the Stock Exchange. I have had enough of patriotism for a lifetime. I agree with Dr. Johnson that "patriotism is the last refuge of the scoundrel." There is but one Fatherland—the World; and one body of Countrymen—the Human Race. I know of but one patriotism, that of the ancient Roman, "*Ubi bona ibi patria.*" Instead of a blessing it is often a misfortune to have been born in a particular locality or country:—

> "In what land the sun doth visit,
> We are brisk whate'er betide;
> To give space for wandering is it
> That the world was made so wide."

Mr. Richard first entered Parliament for Merthyr in 1868, under the most honourable circumstances. Nearly the whole of the available suffrages were recorded for him, the Hon. Mr. Bruce (now Lord Aberdare) and Mr. Fothergill dividing the second votes between them.

The Welsh landlords never received so sharp a lesson. They retaliated by evicting some two hundred of Mr. Richard's supporters. He shortly impeached the transgressors in one of the boldest speeches that had been heard at St. Stephen's for a very long time, and his fearless exposure of the delinquents had not a little to do with the passing of the Ballot Act.

In 1873 occurred perhaps the greatest triumph of his life. He proposed an address to Her Majesty, praying that she would instruct the Secretary of State for Foreign Affairs "to enter into communication with foreign Powers with a view to the establishment of a general and permanent system of international arbitration." Mr. Gladstone opposed the motion, but the Government was beaten by a majority of ten in a House of nearly 200 members. Addresses of congratulation poured in on Mr. Richard from all parts of the world, one from Italy being headed by General Garibaldi. Charles Sumner wrote from the Senate House at Washington, "It marks an epoch in a great cause. This speech alone with the signal result will make your life historic."

In the following September he visited nearly all the capitals and many of the chief cities of the Continent. Everywhere he was received with open arms and hailed as a sort of "Saviour of Society." More eloquent testimony to the unbearableness of the military yoke beneath which the nations of the Continent are groaning could not have been. His progress was converted by the grateful multitudes into something like a triumph in honour of the herald of that better time which shall be—

> "When the war drums throb no longer,
> And the battle flags are furled
> In the Parliament of Man,
> The Federation of the World."

XI.

LEONARD HENRY COURTNEY.

———◆———

"Can rules or tutors educate
The democrat whom we await?"

IN Mr. Thomas Burt, the member for Morpeth, we had an excellent example of what the mine and the trade union can do to form the mind and character of a legislator. Similarly, in Mr. Leonard Henry Courtney, member for Liskeard, we have an equally perfect sample of what an institution so far removed from the mine as the university, working at high pressure, can effect.

Mr. Courtney has been but a short time in Parliament, and I feel that it is consequently somewhat premature to take his political horoscope. He, however, entered the House so exceptionally well equipped for the discharge of his legislative duties, and has on the whole executed them so efficiently, that his claims to recognition as an Eminent Radical cannot be overlooked. He is beyond all question a very able man, whatever his critics in or out of the House may say to the contrary, and among the younger members of the Commons, I know no one whose future conduct will be better worth watching. He is one regarding whom it may be safely predicted that, to use a Scotch proverb, he will speedily "either make a spoon or spoil a horn." His detractors say that he has already spoiled the horn, chiefly by want of tact.

He is accused of the unpardonable parliamentary offence of "lecturing" the House instead of addressing it; and it must be admitted that the charge is not wholly groundless. Even those who are discerning enough to recognise his rare intellectual accomplishments and powers of close reasoning cannot endure this sort of thing. It is in human nature in such circumstances to call out—

> "If thou art great, be merciful,
> O woman of Three Cows!"

In the debate on Mr. Trevelyan's motion in favour of the county franchise, the member for Liskeard told the House, with very little circumlocution, that it had degenerated, and that the members generally were nobodies. The inference, of course, was unavoidable, that the speaker was somebody. Well, I readily admit both proposition and deduction, but "hold it not honesty to have it thus set down."

The great majority of Mr. Courtney's colleagues, it is true, are mere rule-of-thumb legislators, whereas his knowledge of politics is by comparison scientific. But the uninstructed are there to be persuaded, "educated," if you will, by the better disciplined intellects, and there is no surer test of genuine culture than the habitual exhibition of a tender regard for the feelings of the ignorant. Not that Mr. Courtney means it in the least. He is as little of a prig as any man I ever met—a downright hearty good fellow, as true as steel to his convictions of what is for the public good, and without any fundamental egotism of character. In private he has not a particle of the "Professor" about him, and as this fact comes to be commonly recognised, it may be hoped the memory of his public forwardness will be effaced and full justice done to his remarkable acquirements and good intentions.

Mr. Courtney, M.P., was born at Penzance, in July 1862. His father, John Sampson Courtney, of Alverton House, was a native of Ilfracombe, where his ancestors had been settled for two hundred years at least. Courtney senior, early in life, took to banking, and has for half a century been connected with the firm of Bolitho, Sons, & Co., bankers, Penzance.

Like his son Leonard, the eldest of a family of nine, he has always been mighty in figures, and is the author of several useful works, chiefly of local statistical utility—*e.g.*, "Statistics of Pilchard Fishery," "Transactions of the Royal Cornwall Polytechnic Society," "A Guide to Penzance," etc.

What the father accomplished on a local scale it has been the destiny of his son to amplify, as it were, to national dimension. At an early age he was sent to the Regent House Academy, the chief school in the neighbourhood, and from the first he displayed conspicuous talent. Latterly his studies were superintended privately by Dr. Willan. Then for a short time he was employed in the bank of Messrs. Bolitho, Sons, & Co., but finally, in his nineteenth year, it was recognised that a university career would best suit his strong love of study and remarkable powers of application. Accordingly, in 1851 he was entered as a student of St. John's College, Cambridge, and in 1855 he graduated with honours, which speak volumes in themselves. He was Second Wrangler and Smith's Prizeman.

Needless to say, such honourable achievements were not long without their reward. He became a Fellow of his college, and was speedily immersed in lucrative private tuition. His preliminary training had not been specially adapted to secure him such distinctions, and it is, therefore, impossible to withhold our admiration for the vigour of mind and body which enabled him to triumph so signally.

How far marked aptitude for mathematical studies is indicative of general intellectual superiority, has been the subject of much controversy. Lord Macaulay kept an exhaustive catalogue of senior wranglers who always remained juniors in everything but mathematics, and Sir William Hamilton estimated the disciplinary value of the study at a very low rate. The truth, however, seems to be that the gift or knack which enables one man to manipulate algebraic quantities so much more readily than another may or may not co-exist in the mind with other, it may be, greater endowments. One thing only is very certain, the process of intense ratiocinative specialisation to which wranglers must necessarily subject themselves cannot fail to seriously dwarf their other faculties. Off their special topics, the writings of great mathematicians have nearly always struck me as peculiarly bloodless and uninteresting, and it is no small praise to Mr. Courtney to say that he is an exception to this rule. In point both of reasoning and style, his contributions to the *Fortnightly*, for example, and his reported speeches, bear but few traces of the depletory process to which I have alluded. This exemption may, to some extent, be accounted for by the fact that on completing his university curriculum he broke vigorously into intellectual fields and pastures new.

In 1858 he was called to the Bar by the Honourable Society of Lincoln's Inn, and in 1872 he became Professor of Political Economy at University College, a post which he retained for nearly three years. During that time he acquainted himself with all the best writers on the subject, and became a warm advocate of the special views of John Stuart Mill. From Mill it is easy to see that he derived a great deal more than from the Alma Mater of which he is a Senior Fellow. With respect to the representation of minorities, and the female franchise more particularly, the mantle of the deceased philosopher has fallen on his shoulders. Mill was never at a university, yet it has been his part to fructify the intellects of such distinguished university *alumni* as Courtney and Fawcett. Without his influence there is no saying what they might not have been.

Oxford and Cambridge are in reality huge forcing houses for the production of young aristocrats, maintained at scandalous cost, in no sense national institutions, and about the last places in the world where one would dream of going in order to acquire the art of thinking. Such exceptionally intelligent and public-spirited emanations as the members for Hackney and Liskeard are in reality rather a misfortune than otherwise. Their "fellowship" is a snare:—

"The name of Cassius honours this corruption,
And Chastisement doth therefore hide his head."

It is hardly too much to say that if Oxford and Cambridge were erased from the map of England to-morrow, and the intellect of the country permitted to flow into freer channels, the political and general intelligence of the people would be elevated by the change many degrees.

Besides discharging the duties of the Political Economy Chair at University College, Mr. Courtney has held several other appointments which have necessarily extended the range of his intellectual vision. He has been an examiner in Literature and History for the Indian Civil Service, and examiner in the Constitutional History of England for the University of London. Since 1864 he has, moreover, been a *Times* leader writer, with all that that implies.

When he left his seat in the gallery to take his seat on the Opposition benches he entered the actual arena of politics armed, so to speak, *cap-à-pie*. In addition he had travelled much and examined on the spot the working of the political machinery of many lands. He had visited nearly every European country, the United States twice, as well as Canada, India, Turkey, and Egypt.

His first attempt to force the gates of St. Stephen's was made at the last general election, when he boldly threw down the gauntlet to that clever but unstable politician, the late Right Honourable Edward Horsman. Mr. Horsman won by the narrow majority of five votes. A somewhat acrimonious war of words followed, wherein Mr. Courtney had not the worst of it.

Towards the close of 1876 Mr. Horsman died, and Mr. Courtney and Lieutenant-Colonel Sterling entered the field, the former polling 388, and the latter 281 votes. Mr. Courtney's poll was the largest ever recorded for a candidate at Liskeard, and coming as it did when Liberal fortunes were very low, did a good deal to reinvigorate the party in Parliament.

It remains to consider, however inadequately, a few of the more prominent questions with which Mr. Courtney has identified himself. He is now the chief advocate in Parliament of the representation of minorities and of women, or to be more gallant, of women and minorities. Now, with regard to the question of minority representation much may be said *pro* and *con*. Mr. Mill undoubtedly regarded Mr. Hare's scheme of "proportional representation" as a political discovery of the most important character, and any such opinion of Mill's is, of course, entitled to respectful consideration. But Mr. Courtney is so enamoured of three-cornered constituencies" and "cumulative votes" that he positively refused to support Mr. Trevelyan's County Franchise Bill because it contained no provision for the realisation of a "principle which would re-create political life, raising it out of the degradation which overlaid it." Mr. Courtney tells us we are about to be overwhelmed by the billows of a tempestuous democratic ocean abounding in unknown terrors. There is but one escape, we must all put out to sea in tiny "three-cornered" boats, on pain of universal political shipwreck. Was there ever so great faith seen in or out of Israel? One recalls the exclamation of the Breton mariner, "How great, O Lord, is thy ocean, and how small is my skiff!" The danger to be apprehended is no less than the gradual extinction of the "independent member."

Now, apart from the fact that the independent member is generally a member who is not to be depended on, is it a fact that our experience of the actual working of the "cumulative vote" and of the "three-cornered constituency" has been so encouraging as to induce us to withhold the franchise from the county householder until the requisite number of "corners" and "cumulations" can be created? I chance to know the electoral circumstances, parliamentary and scholastic, of two important cities in the North, the one returning three members to Parliament by the three-cornered artifice, the other thirteen members to the School Board by the cumulative process. In the former case the Tories, at the last general election, managed to return their candidate simply because no human ingenuity could, with the secrecy of the ballot-box to contend against, so evenly apportion the two votes of each Liberal elector among the three Liberal candidates, as to keep the Conservative at the bottom of the poll. With an open vote, it was quite possible, though unnecessarily difficult, but under the ballot it was a preposterous game of blind man's buff—the veriest *ne plus ultra* of legislative folly. The minority succeeded with a vengeance.

In the other case three School Board elections have taken place. On the first occasion the Radical ("Secularist") minority put up too many candidates and returned none; next election they carried two, who found themselves powerless to influence the decisions of the ultra-orthodox majority. These two stood again, but as acquiescing in the ecclesiastico-educational policy favoured by the mass of the electors, and lost their seats, as they deserved to do. An intelligent and active minority with a just cause was thus effaced. It would be very unsafe to found any argument on such slender data, but it is quite possible that the ultimate effect of minority representation, at all events in its present shape, may be found to have the very opposite effect of what Mr. Courtney anticipates. Its tendency appears to be to confirm majorities in erroneous opinions, while hopelessly discouraging right-thinking minorities from further propaganda. When once we have obtained something like true electoral majorities it will be time enough to provide for the representation of minorities.

At the election of 1868, Lancashire, as Mr. Courtney has pointed out, with its included towns, returned twenty-two Conservative to eleven Liberal representatives, yet the Liberal vote was 104,000 strong, while the Conservative was only 102,000. Suppose the distinction of town and county were abolished once and for all, and each shire or aggregate of shires were permitted to vote for a group of candidates in proportion to its electorate, on something like the old French system of *scrutin de liste*, would not that give a fairer chance to "independent members" and candidates above "mediocrity" than thoroughly artificial corners and cumulations?

Let Mr. Courtney consider the matter, for certainly the minority representation craze has landed him in strange seeming contradictions.

On the one day he opposed the enfranchisement of the county householder, and on the next he proposed to remove the electoral disabilities of women. He would plead, doubtless by way of extenuation, that this was not a lowering, but an assimilation of the franchise, and that he was not consequently compelled by consistency to encumber his bill with any three-cornered contrivances. But the point is all too fine, and the House showed its sense of the incongruity of the situation by recording a majority of 114 votes against the measure, as compared with 80 the year before, and this notwithstanding the fact that the member for Liskeard's arguments were most cogent. It is hardly necessary to observe that, like all ardent advocates of female rights, Mr. Courtney is a bachelor.

But there is one question with respect to which the most captious Radical can have nothing but words of praise to bestow on Mr. Courtney. Since he first entered Parliament he has never ceased, in season and out of season, to oppose with rare foresight the disastrous policy of which the upshot has been the serious and discreditable war with the Zulus. His fidelity in this matter ought never to be forgotten.

On the 7th of August 1877, he moved the following resolution with respect to the annexation of the Transvaal:—
"That, in the opinion of this House, the annexation of the South African Republic is unjustifiable, and calculated to be injurious to the interests of the United Kingdom and of its colonies in South Africa." "We had formerly agreed," he said, "not to carry our arms into the middle of Africa, and to allow the Dutch Boers themselves to go into the interior. We had reversed that policy. We had taken on ourselves the immense burden of administering the affairs of the Transvaal. We had made ourselves responsible for what that Republic had done, *and would have to take up its quarrels with the native chiefs.* The cost would not be borne by the

colonies, and would have to be borne by us at home. The vote of to-night was the first symptom of the considerable expenditure which the country would have to bear for many years in connection with this matter."

Most true; "the pity is 'tis true." I reproduce these words from Hansard, because they are an imperishable monument of Mr. Courtney's sagacity as a counsellor of the nation in the conduct of difficult affairs. He demonstrated that Sir Theophilus Shepstone had, with a high hand, violated both the conditions by which the Colonial Office sought to bind him in his dealings with the Transvaal. He had issued his annexationist proclamation without the sanction of the High Commissioner, and against the wishes of the Boers, who publicly protested against the outrage in the proportion of twelve to one. The subjugation of the Transvaal was perhaps the most treacherous act, the basest manifestation of our "spirited foreign policy," and yet, alas, Lord Sandon, in the recent debate on Sir Charles Dilke's resolution, was able to say with truth :—"The honourable member for Liskeard has a right to raise the question of the Transvaal, but most of those opposite can scarcely do so with good grace. The annexation of the Transvaal was accepted generally by the two great political parties in the House."

Having done our best to restore the emancipated Roumelians to the hateful yoke of the Sultan, it was perhaps fitting that we should seek to subject these brave Dutch Republicans to that of the Empress of India. *O tempora, O mores!* I congratulate the member for Liskeard that in this infamous transaction his hands at least are clean.

XII.

ANTHONY JOHN MUNDELLA.

> " O heavens ! what some men do
> While some men leave to do ! "

THERE is no better example in Parliament of what is called a "self-made man" than Anthony John Mundella, the irrepressible representative of Sheffield Radicalism.

An apologist of the late Andrew Johnson, President of the United States, once urged, in the hearing of Thaddeus Stevens, that "Andy" was at least a "self-made man." The retort of that bitterest of politicians was crushing. " I am glad to hear it—it relieves Providence of a heavy responsibility." Now, one has at first a little of this sort of feeling with respect to Mr. Mundella. The edifice which this self-made man erects is apt to appear so much more elegant to the architect than to the public. Besides, the honourable member for Sheffield is a curious combination. His coat is one of many colours. He is half Italian, half English. He has been everything, from a "printer's devil" to a "captain of industry," and each avocation has left some traces of its influence on his character and sympathies. He is half workman, half employer. He is a Churchman and a warm advocate of religious equality ; a Radical and a supporter of the royal grants. He is a living illustration of the truth of a profound saying in Ecclesiasticus : "All things are double." Add to this that his energy is irrepressible ; that he is not afflicted, to put it mildly, with mock modesty; that he represents on pure principles a constituency which is preeminently the most rascally in England; that he is withal fundamentally an able and honest politician, justly regarded by the working class as one of its greatest benefactors, and it will readily be admitted that first impressions of such a man are apt to be erroneous.

Among so many seeming contradictions it is difficult to find the reconciling principle or central fact, but like all other men and politicians, Mr. Mundella may be known by the surest of all tests, by his "fruits."

I shall merely premise, before recounting the leading facts of his career, that it would have perhaps been better to classify the member for Sheffield as an Eminent Democrat rather than as an Eminent Radical. He is emphatically a man of the people, rightly or wrongly feeling as they feel, thinking as they think; and I doubt if there be in England, excepting Mr. Bradlaugh, a more effective out-of-door speaker, a more powerful haranguer of mass meetings. He is at home in a multitude, however vast or however rude. He is one of the very few members of the House of Commons who can beat down a refractory public meeting by unflinching resolution and sheer strength of lung. In the town of Broadhead such a qualification is simply invaluable, and but for the unsparing exercise of it at the election of 1874, the Liberalism of Sheffield would have showed but poorly indeed.

Anthony John Mundella, M.P., was born at Leicester, in March 1825, the eldest son in a family of five. Mundella senior was a Lombard refugee, a native of Como, who, taking part in the insurrectionary movement against the Austrians in 1820, was driven into exile. He landed in England almost penniless, and settled eventually in Leicester, where he endeavoured to earn a livelihood as a teacher of languages. Instruction in modern tongues was then a luxury in which but few indulged, and the luckless Antonio in consequence frequently broke the exile's bitter bread—endured what his immortal countryman Dante has called "the hell of exile." Educated for the Roman Church, he had no regular profession on which to rely. His income was consequently at all times precarious. He married, however, a remarkable woman, Rebecca Allsop, of Leicester, a lady richly endowed mentally, and possessed of some little property. She was an adept in lace-embroidery, then a remunerative art, and her skill and unremitting industry in the main supported the Mundella household for the first ten years of her married life.

Then there came a crisis. Her eyesight almost completely failed, and Anthony had in consequence to be removed from school in his ninth year, in order to put his childish shoulder to the wheel. So far his education had been carefully superintended. Mrs. Mundella had a wide knowledge of English literature, was a diligent Shakespearian scholar, and little Anthony had been as quick to learn as she had been apt to teach.

His acquirements accordingly secured him employment in a printing office, where he remained till his eleventh year. Thereupon he was apprenticed to the hosiery trade. He was most fortunate in his employer, a discriminating man, whose son, a member of Parliament, was the first to welcome Mr. Mundella to St. Stephen's on his return for Sheffield in 1868.

In his eighteenth year his apprenticeship was at an end. He had mastered his trade thoroughly, and contemporaneously he had learned all that could be acquired at the Mechanics' Institute of the town, and a great deal more. He was an indefatigable reader.

In his nineteenth year, so conspicuous was his business capacity that he was engaged as manager of a large enterprise in the cotton trade. At twenty-three he removed to Nottingham, to become junior partner in a firm which shortly transacted the largest hosiery business in the Midlands, Hone, Mundella, & Co., employing as many as 3000 "hands." Of this flourishing company Mr. Mundella is still a director, though not interfering very actively with the management. He is, moreover, chairman of the Commercial Union Insurance Company, and is a director of the National Bank and of the Bank of New Zealand.

To very few " printers' devils " or " stockingers " is it given thus to have a finger in the *grande commerce* of the country, but Mr. Mundella climbed the ladder steadily and skilfully, and it cannot be said of him that when he got to the summit he forgot the condition of the less fortunate toilers whom he left below. On the contrary, no working man in England has striven more earnestly or intelligently for the elevation of the mass than the member for Sheffield, as a bare enumeration of his political and legislative *res gestæ* will readily show.

Always precocious, Mundella's political career began in mere boyhood. The Austrian tyranny, which had driven his father from his native land, and the miserable condition of the " stockingers " among whom his lot was cast, naturally disposed him to become a partisan of the " Charter," which was at that time being earnestly advocated in Leicester by the well-known Thomas Cooper, author of the " Purgatory of Suicides," a work written in Leicester Gaol.

Cooper, in his interesting " Autobiography," published in 1872, gives us a vivid glimpse of the adolescent representative of Sheffield:—"I had been appealing strongly one evening to the patriotic feelings of young Englishmen, mentioning the names of Hampden, Sydney, and Marvell, and eulogising the grand spirit of disinterestedness and self-sacrifice which characterised so many of our brave forerunners, when a handsome young man sprang upon our little platform and declared himself on the people's side, and desired to be enrolled as a Chartist. He did not belong to the poorest ranks, and it was the consciousness that he was acting in the spirit of self-sacrifice, as well as his fervid eloquence, that caused a thrilling cheer from the ranks of the working men. He could not have been more than fifteen at the time; he passed away from us too soon, and

I have never seen him but once all these years. But the men of Sheffield have signalised their confidence in his patriotism by returning him to the House of Commons; and all England knows, if there be a man of energy, as well as uprightness in that House, it is Anthony John Mundella."

This picture is obviously somewhat overdrawn, but in the main it is doubtless correct. At Leicester, from 1840 to 1848, Mr. Mundella agitated by voice and pen for the "Charter," and had the satisfaction of hearing reform ballads of his own composition sung in the streets.

When he removed to Nottingham in 1848, new public duties awaited him. He was made successively Town Councillor, Sheriff, Alderman, Justice of the Peace, and President of the Chamber of Commerce. These local experiences were, of course, valuable to him as a legislator *in posse*, but it was in another and more original field that he first did signal and I might say inestimable service to the entire community.

He was the author in 1860, as he was the president for eleven years subsequently, of the Nottingham Board of Arbitration and Conciliation for the Hosiery Trade—the harbinger of so many others. Wearied with incessant "strikes" and "lock-outs," Mr. Mundella, after many weeks of fruitless negotiation, at last got employers and employed together.

After three days' discussion, the then existing strike was closed by mutual concession, and a resolution agreed to that in future all questions affecting wages should be authoritatively settled by a board consisting of nine duly elected representatives of the masters and nine of the men. The board held its first meeting on the 3d of December 1860. In an article on "Conciliation and Arbitration" in the *Contemporary Review* for 1870, ten years later, Mr. Mundella thus sums up the results of the experiment:—"Since the 27th of September 1860, there has not been a bill of any kind issued. Strikes are at an end also. Levies to sustain them are unknown; and one shilling a year from each member suffices to pay all expenses. This, not a farthing of which comes out of the pockets of their masters, is equivalent to a large advance of wages. I have inspected the balance-sheet of a trade union of 10,300 men, and I found the expenditure for thirteen months to amount to less than a hundred pounds."

It is against the operation of this beneficent principle—this proved success—that the Durham coalowners were the first, on a great scale, to attempt to lift impious hands. It is impossible for any impartial observer not to conclude that they preferred the darkness to the light, their deeds being evil. Mr. Mundella for one did not conceal that this was his view of the situation.

No sooner was the Nottingham method of settling trade disputes by arbitration recognised as feasible than Mr. Mundella, as its author, was invited by many towns, and among others by Sheffield, to give popular expositions of his system. Sheffield had suffered many things at the hands of Broadhead and his infamous crew, and so pleased was the cream of the working men with the prospect of escape from the vicious circle in which they were involved, that in 1868 they invited the chairman of the Nottingham Board to come forward as their candidate. He was returned at the head of the poll, notwithstanding the strenuous support given to Roebuck by the assassin Broadhead at trade union meetings.

On entering Parliament the honour of seconding the Address was conferred on him by Mr. Gladstone. Since then his efforts to benefit the working class have been unflagging, and, on the whole, most successful. His speech on the second reading of the Education Bill was pronounced by Mr. Gladstone to be the most important delivered on the occasion. He had examined into the educational systems of America, Germany, Switzerland, and Holland on the spot, and was therefore in a position to speak with authority on the all-important theme.

His persistent efforts to repeal the Criminal Law Amendment Act, that the equality of workmen before the law might be established, and to pass the Factory Nine Hours Bill in order that the hours of labour might be shortened to hapless women and children, have been rewarded. The Government has itself done what it would not permit him to do. All the same the credit must be accorded to Mr. Mundella, whose views on labour and factory legislation were at the last general election made test questions all over the North of England.

In 1878 he succeeded in carrying a useful bill for the Preservation of Fresh-water Fisheries, so as to increase the supply of food and give harmless sport to the poorer class of anglers. In the subsequent session his bill to abolish property qualifications in connection with all local government and municipal bodies was lost by only six votes.

To some, such legislative achievements may appear small and commonplace, but it should be recollected that this is the day of small things, and that in legislation, as in other matters, it is "the mean and common, the things of the eternal yesterday," that it is most desirable and least agreeable to tackle.

I have said that Mr. Mundella is a Democrat rather than a Radical, and I shall finally give an illustration of what I mean. On the vote to pay the cost of the Prince of Wales's mischievous jaunt to India he sided with the majority in favour of the royal subsidy, and he had the temerity to assign his reasons for so doing. "As long as we had a Monarchy we should be ashamed to have a cotton velvet or tinfoil sort of Monarchy; he did not believe in a cheap, shabby, Brummagem Monarchy; and he always would give his vote loyally and in consistency with those opinions which he believed to be the opinions of his constituents."

Now, it is impossible to say whether the Radicalism or the logic of this sentence is the worse; yet, I suppose, it must be admitted that such clap-trap is regarded by the *demos* of Sheffield—to use the language of our Democratic-Imperialist Premier—as "the voice of sense and truth." In the first place, apart from the fact that an advanced Radical might reasonably be expected to be ashamed of having a Monarchy of any kind, cheap or dear, Mr. Mundella knew, as every other member knew, that the reasons set forth for the Prince's trip were not the true reasons. In the second place, as a friend of the people, and knowing, as he so well knows, the sore privations of the masses, how could he, with a clear conscience, hint that a royal family, which directly costs the nation £1,000,000 per annum, is either cheap or shabby? The Presidency of the United States costs £10,000 a-year; and no impartial observer has ever yet affirmed that the simple courtesies and hospitalities of the White House compare unfavourably with the ridiculous tomfooleries of the Court of St. James's. In the third place, it is not the part of a good Radical, as Mr. Mundella seems to think, implicitly to follow the multitude, even if the multitude consist of one's constituents. There is a following of the multitude to do evil which the true Radical will resist, when necessary, at all hazards, in the interest of the people themselves. When great principles are at stake, the genuine Radical must ever be ready to go out into the wilderness, if need be, alone:—

> " Far in front the Cross stands ready,
> And the crackling faggots burn,
> While the hooting mob of yesterday
> In silent awe return
> To glean up the scattered ashes
> Into History's sacred urn."

Mr. Mundella has likewise a curious disposition to adorn his conversation with quite unnecessary allusions to the opinions of "lords" and other great people of his acquaintance, who are intellectually greatly his inferiors. In aristocracy-ridden England, this is nearly always a marked trait of the self-made man.

The fact is, the honourable member for Sheffield, with all his vigour of intellect and many virtues, has not altogether escaped the "society" contagion of which the Court is the centre, which has made so many strong men weak, and caused "the currents of so many enterprises of pith and moment to turn aside and lose the name of action."

>"O thou that sea walls sever
>   From lands unwalled by seas,
> Wilt thou endure for ever,
>   O Milton's England, these?
> Thou that wast his Republic,
>   Wilt thou clasp their knees?
> Those royalties rust-eaten,
>   Those worm-corroded lies
> That keep thy head storm-beaten
>   And sunlike strength of eyes
> From the open air and heaven
>   Of intercepted skies."

EMINENT RADICALS
OUT OF PARLIAMENT.

EMINENT RADICALS
OUT OF PARLIAMENT.

I.

JOHN MORLEY.

"He was a scholar, and a ripe and good one,
Exceeding wise, fair spoken, and persuading."

OF all Swift's bitter sayings, the bitterest perhaps was his observation that mankind are about as well fitted for flying as for thinking. If this be true—and it is not necessary to be much of a misanthrope to admit that generally speaking the human mind is a very imperfect instrument — nothing can be more deplorable than the slight esteem in which the ablest thinkers are held by the majority of English electors.

"Thirty millions of people, mostly fools," and without so much as the capacity to discern the importance of putting the helm of the State into the hands of the least foolish. Howbeit, the phenomenon is not new. "There was a little city, and few men within it, and there came a great king against it and besieged it, and built great bulwarks against it. Now there was found in it a poor wise man, and he by his wisdom delivered the city, yet no man remembered that same poor man." The true "saviours of society" are after all its original thinkers. Of these England has at no time been without her share, and in her treatment of them, politically speaking, she has walked with remarkable fidelity in the footsteps of the men of "the little city."

Witness Mill and Westminster. Westminster, in a moment of illumination, elected as her representative in Parliament the greatest political thinker in the kingdom, but soon felt the honour she had thus done herself more than she could bear, and returned in haste to her vomit. In no other civilised country except England could such a man have been excluded for any length of time from the national councils. In France, half-a-dozen signed articles would probably have brought him about as many offers of seats in the Legislature, while in the United States he would, to a certainty, have been made an ambassador of the first rank. Even Spain values her Castelars and Pi y Margalls— England alone keeps on, if not absolutely stoning the prophets, at least studiously neglecting them.

The result we see in the heavy arrears of domestic legislation, the helplessness and criminality of our diplomacy abroad, and, worse than all, the disgust with representative institutions which a Parliament of intellectual imbeciles is sure, sooner or later, to inspire.

I have been led to make the above remarks in consequence of its being intended to bring the subject of this sketch forward as a candidate for a metropolitan constituency at the next general election. I trust that no effort will be spared to secure the return of one who, in my opinion, has no superior out of Parliament in respect of those qualifications which go to make up real statesmanship.

That so distinguished an authority on nearly every one of the great questions, political and ethical, which agitate modern society should never yet have found a place at St. Stephen's, is a standing impeachment of the political sagacity of popular electorates. And it would be an additional cause for rejoicing if a scholar and a gentleman like Mr. Morley could be made to replace one or other of the corrupt ring of ignorant, vain-glorious, aldermanic gluttons who have taken so many of our metropolitan constituencies captive.

The contrast of political type would be sharp and salutary, and an important outpost of the City Tammany might thus be carried. Westminster, after discarding Mr. Mill, is hardly entitled to have it placed in her power to reject the greatest of his disciples.

As in the case of most speculative writers, the story of Mr. Morley's life is exceedingly simple, almost necessarily an *autour de ma chambre* affair. His life is in his books, which have influenced the thoughts of many who have never read them. He was born at Blackburn, in December 1838, the son of a physician in good practice. The father was pious without bigotry, somewhat eccentric, but, on the whole, a judicious parent. As might be expected in such circumstances, the future editor of the *Fortnightly* went the regular round of school, college, and bar. He was educated at Cheltenham College, whence he proceeded to Oxford, where he graduated in 1859. Subsequently he kept terms at Lincoln's Inn, and was duly "called" to the Bar by that Honourable Society, but never practised.

It is not a little remarkable that all this time Mr. Morley showed no particular aptitude or even liking for study. He who has since dug so sedulously about the very roots of the tree of knowledge, among the primary conceptions of the human race—he who is now in the very vanguard of "free thought"—was at college something of a mooning "Evangelical." Who in this mysterious world can foresee himself?

What a contrast, for example, is here to the experience of his friend Mill, whose old Pagan father, James, is credibly said to have imparted to him when an urchin the somewhat startling intelligence that there is no God, coupled with a prudent injunction to keep the information to himself.

Yet John Stuart Mill if he had lived much longer was apparently bidding fair to take a high place, not, certainly, among orthodox believers, but among the worthies of the

Unitarian calendar. Most powerful intellects are either religious or religiously anti-religious, superstitious or superstitiously anti-superstitious. Mr. Morley belongs to the latter category, and the fact is not inexplicable. At a certain period of youth, when the passions are strong and reflection is weak, religious emotions very frequently come in—and come in opportunely—to supply the restraining influence of reason. When they are no longer needed they die out, and if they have been very fervid the more ingenuous order of minds is but too apt to resent them as idle delusions and to rush into opposite extremes. Weaker and less ingenuous natures profess to feel them after they have ceased to influence, and so become religious hypocrites.

The transition is not easy to make, and I am not sure that Mr. Morley has been quite successful in the operation. Throughout his writings, with all their patient truthfulness and candour, I think I can discern a certain undercurrent of unconscious bias on the question of religion, as if the pendulum of reason had swung back with such violence as to become slightly overbalanced.

Unlike Mill, who approached the subject from a unique standpoint of impartiality, he makes at once too much and too little of the theme. But of this more anon.

In 1860 Mr. Morley commenced his career as a journalist and man of letters, and from the first he laid the hand of a master on whatever he touched. His earliest contributions were to the *Leader*, then an organ of advanced Liberalism, of which George Henry Lewes was the first editor. He worked with a will, and soon became known to those whose business it is to gauge intellectual capacity. In 1863 he joined the staff of the *Saturday Review*, on which he remained for five or six years. During that period he had for collaborateurs three of the most formidable intellectual gladiators in England— viz., Sir James Fitzjames Stephen, Sir William Vernon Harcourt, and Sir Henry Maine :—

"Tis heavy odds against the gods
When they will match with Myrmidons."

But Mr. Morley was equal to the occasion. Many of his *Saturday Review* articles were characterised by striking originality of thought and fearlessness of expression. One in particular, entitled "New Ideas," made so deep an impression on Mr. John Stuart Mill that he wrote to a friend anxiously inquiring who the author might be, and thus were laid the foundations of a life-long friendship of no ordinary intimacy and reciprocal esteem. I know hardly anything finer in prose than the reverence without obsequiousness which pervades Mr. Morley's article on the death of Mill. It is the very poetry of a manly sorrow.

"The nightingale which he longed for fills the darkness with music, but not for the ear of the dead master; he rests in the deeper darkness where the silence is unbroken for ever. We may console ourselves with the reflection offered by the dying Socrates to his sorrowful companions: he who has arrayed the soul in her own proper jewels of moderation and justice and courage and nobleness and truth, is ever ready for the journey when his time comes. We have lost a great teacher and example of knowledge and virtue, but men will long feel the presence of his character about them, making them ashamed of what is indolent or selfish, and encouraging them to all disinterested labour, both in trying to do good and in trying to find out what the good is—which is harder."—*Siste Viator*.

Ever ready to do battle in the front rank of Liberalism, Mr. Morley chivalrously undertook to edit the *Morning Star* at a time when, for reasons chiefly connected with the commercial management, success was no longer possible. Through no fault of his it was permitted to expire, and Radicalism thus lost a most faithful and competent advocate. To this day that loss remains unrepaired, and it has been one of no ordinary seriousness to the party and to the country, for since that time metropolitan Radicalism can hardly be said to have been represented in the daily press.

In 1867 Mr. Morley succeeded Mr. Lewes in the editorship

of the *Fortnightly*, and in his hands a hitherto colourless magazine soon became the recognised medium of all manner of new and not unfrequently very unpopular ideas. And this bold, uncompromising policy, I am glad to think, has met with a gratifying measure of success. The *Fortnightly* is a tower of strength to Radicalism in all its higher walks, and its editor is ever vigilant and resolute to "hold the fort" against all comers.

In the same year that Mr. Morley became the editor of the *Fortnightly*, he paid a short visit to the United States, and was introduced at the White House to the then President, Andrew Johnson. He did not, like certain weak-minded travellers with whom we are all acquainted, return professing to be cured for life of Republican ideals. On the contrary, he came back favourably impressed with the simplicity of American official life, and confirmed generally in his democratic sympathies.

In 1869, at a bye election, Mr. Morley contested his native Blackburn in the Radical interest, but without success. The "Conservative working man" was against him. In certain Lancashire constituencies it can no longer be doubted that this anomalous being exists, and exists in force. Conservatism implies that there is something to conserve, but in these God-forsaken regions you have the effect without the cause —men guarding rigorously what they never possessed. It is as if a slave with freedom within his grasp should cling tenaciously to his chains. Howbeit, Mr. Morley made a stubborn fight, and showed himself as cogent with his tongue on the platform as with his pen in the closet. He is a most skilful and persuasive speaker, with hardly a trace of those oratorical defects which generally mar the public utterances of great authors. He knows the difference between the written and the spoken linguistic mould, and can deftly cast his thoughts in either. Dissenting as he does even from the most heterodox Dissenters, I have yet heard him speak with rare acceptance on a Liberation Society's platform to the pink and flower of English Nonconformity. Such a spectacle of mutual toleration is among the most hopeful signs of English public life.

But it is at home in his literary workshop that the editor of the *Fortnightly* will be seen to most advantage. The appointments of Berkeley Lodge, Putney, are such as to make the mouths of more obscure journalists water. The ample library looks out on a beautifully-embowered lawn, while every domestic detail is perfect. A man who cannot write well with such happy surroundings has hopelessly mistaken his calling. And best of all is the frank, truthful, earnest conversation of the host himself. There is no evasion, no hedging. When I first met him we plunged right into the questions of Deity, of the immortality of the soul, of the Republic, of Robespierre, of Burke, of his friend Chamberlain, *et de omni scibili*, in an hour's time.

In reflecting he has a curious habit of listening as it were to the tones of some far-off voice. I could not agree with many of his positions, but felt the greatest difficulty in maintaining my own. His religious scepticism is very deep and subtle. He might, I dare say, if hard pressed, admit that there are evidences of divine arrangement in the universe amounting to a low degree of probability; and as regards a life beyond the grave he might go the length of dreading with Hamlet "what dreams may come in that sleep of death." But in any case he would turn away from such conjectural speculations, and substitute social for religious duties. This at once raises the intricate question of the influence of religion on morality. Is the connection necessary or accidental? It would not be difficult, for example, to show that the Pagan Cetewayo was throughout the Zulu troubles a pattern of justice as compared with our eminently Christian High Commissioner, Sir Bartle Frere, or that so public-spirited a citizen and infidel as Mr. Charles Bradlaugh would be a much more trustworthy custodian of other people's moneys than the pious directors of the City of Glasgow Bank.

But granted that a man's religion has little or no influence over his moral conduct—what then? Man *will* ponder the strange problem of his destiny, and those who believe that religion is a mere mental infirmity must be prepared boldly to sum it up in the terrible words of Richter, "Of the world will become a world-machine, of God a force, and of the second world a coffin."

Such teaching, it can hardly be doubted, would profoundly alter the hopes if not the moralities of the more energetic portion of the human family. Burns in his most despairing poem sang—

> "The poor oppressed honest man
> Had surely ne'er been born
> Had there not been some recompense
> To comfort those who mourn."

No comfort, alas! no recompense. In such sore plight humanity, I fear, would be disposed to say with Marcus Antonius, "It were well to die if there be gods, and sad to live if there be none."

With respect to the question of a Republic, Mr. Morley's attitude, as might be expected in so courageous a political thinker, is clearly defined. He recognises that until the Republican banner is boldly unfurled we who are Radicals are condemned to strike at phantoms. He is, of course, at the same time no partisan of any revolution other than a revolution of public opinion. In his powerful treatise on "Compromise," he says:—"Our conviction is not, on the present hypothesis, that Monarchy ought to be swept away in England, but that Monarchy produces certain mischievous consequences to the public spirit of the community. And so, what we are bound to do is to take care not to conceal this conviction; to abstain scrupulously from all kinds of action and observance, public or private, which tend ever so remotely to foster the ignoble and degrading elements that exist in a Court and spread from it outwards; and to use all the influence we have, however slight it may be, in leading public opinion to a right attitude of contempt and dislike for these ignoble and degrading elements, and the conduct engendered by them." This is not the language of saponaceous bishops or of turtle-fed aldermen, but it is "the voice of sense and truth," albeit it was never heard at the Guildhall.

With nearly all that Mr. Morley has written on Voltaire, Rousseau, Diderot, Turgot, and the French Revolution, I cordially concur. To Robespierre alone I think he has done scant justice, while to Burke he has been more than kind. With the impartiality of a judge, and the insight of a statesman rather than of a man of letters, he has succeeded in dispelling much of the obscurity in which Mr. Carlyle is chiefly responsible for having involved the greatest movement of the mind of modern Europe. Carlyle's "French Revolution" is undoubtedly a work of genius, but so has a lurid "nocturne" by Mr. Whistler being pronounced to be a work of genius. The trouble is that neither has the smallest resemblance to the original. The time is coming when, it is to be hoped, the English people will have forgotten all about the "sea-greenness" of Robespierre, and remember only his unquestioned and unquestionable "incorruptibility."

Mr. Morley's objection to Carlyle's bogey does not lie in a nickname, but I think he would, perhaps, have regarded Robespierre with a kindlier eye if he had not been the author of the dictum: "*Atheism is aristocratic. The idea of a Great Being who watches over oppressed innocence and punishes triumphant crime is essentially the idea of the people.*"

Mr. Morley's admiration for Burke I am wholly unable to comprehend. To bracket him with Milton is like comparing a penny whistle to an organ. Nay, those who thought only of dining when he thought of convincing were not so culpable as has been insinuated. It would have been greatly to the advantage of England and of Europe if Burke had never crossed St. George's Channel.

As a practical politician, Mr. Morley has strenuously exerted himself to secure two great objects—to level down the Church politically, and to level up the working class socially, with a view to unite the whole people in the pursuit of national as distinguished from sectional ideals. As president of the Midland Institute, in 1876, he delivered a remarkable address on "Popular Culture" in the Birmingham Town Hall, an address which will be found to embody opinions of the highest wisdom and sentiments of the noblest aspiration. It ends thus, and with it this notice must also end.

"When our names are blotted out and our place knows us no more, the energy of each social service will remain, and so, too, let us not forget, will each social disservice remain like the unending stream of one of Nature's forces. The thought that this is so may well lighten the poor perplexities of our daily life, and even soothe the pang of its calamities; it lifts us from our feet as on wings, opening a larger meaning to our private toil and a higher purpose to our public endeavour; it makes the morning as we awake to its welcome and the evening like a soft garment as it wraps us about; it nerves our arm with boldness against oppression and injustice, and strengthens our voice with deeper accents against falsehood, while we are yet in the full noon of our days, yes, and perhaps it will shed some ray of consolation when our eyes are growing dim to it all, and we go down into the Valley of Darkness."

II.

ROBERT WILLIAM DALE.

———◆———

> " Well done ! thy words are great and bold ;
> At times they seem to me,
> Like Luther's in the days of old,
> Half battles for the free."

RADICALISM is like a great world-haven which many ships reach by divers ocean tracks. It is a generous fruit which grows on trees of many species. The editor of the *Fortnightly*, about whom I had somewhat to say in the preceding article, and the lion-hearted pastor of Carr's Lane Chapel, Birmingham—what a contrast !

How far apart their motives—how closely allied their public aims !

The earnest "rationalist" and the earnest religionist are sworn bothers in political conflict; the one because, like Abou Ben Adhem, he is content to be written down simply "as one that loves his fellow-men," the other because he is penetrated by the apostolic conception that he is a "co-worker" with his Divine Master in the sacred cause of humanity.

Mr. Dale is a political Christian, a sort of spiritual utilitarian of a remarkable type—the best living embodiment of the traditions of the sect to which Oliver Cromwell belonged. Not orthodox certainly, as the Scribes and Pharisees hold orthodoxy, but still, for so powerful an intellect, strangely orthodox.

"I am very sensible," says Swift, in his "Argument to Prove that the Abolishing of Christianity might be attended by some Inconveniences," "how much the gentlemen of wit and pleasure are apt to murmur and be shocked at the sight of so many daggled-tail parsons who happen to fall in their way and offend their eyes; but, at the same time, these wise reformers do not consider what an advantage and felicity it is for great wits to be always provided with objects of scorn and contempt in order to exercise and improve their talents and divert their spleen from falling on each other or on themselves. . . . We are daily complaining of the great decline of wit among us, and would we take away the greatest, perhaps the only, topic we have left?"

Well, if there are any such great wits about who have a desire to exercise their talents in this particular way, I should strongly recommend them to go down to Birmingham and break a lance with the minister of Carr's Lane Chapel. He is a man of the people, and will give them a kindly welcome. If they do not find him at home in his formidably-equipped study, deep in the production of some systematic theological treatise on the Atonement or the Ten Commandments, they will be pretty sure to discover him either at a Liberal Ward Committee, at the Liberal Association Rooms in consultation with the taciturn strategist Schnadhorst, or haranguing an obstreperous multitude of electors in the Town Hall. When he is disengaged he will be at their service, and if they get much amusement at his expense I wonder.

A happier, heartier man than Mr. Dale—he disclaims the "Rev.," as a rag of priestcraft—I never met, combining as he does in no ordinary measure the laureate's desiderata of manhood—"heart, head, hand." His practice squares with his theory of life to a nicety. His soul is in his work. Like Cromwell, he prays to God, and keeps his powder dry. What good, he is never tired of asking, is the petition, "Thy will be done on earth as it is in heaven," if a man is not prepared at the call of duty to take off his coat and descend into the political arena to wrestle with the powers of Conservative darkness? In one of his "Nine Lectures on Preaching," delivered as Lyman Beecher Lecturer at the University of Yale, Connecticut—a series of papers not less distinguished by practical wisdom than literary merit—he told the students of the theological faculty:

"In your pastoral preaching you ought not to omit to illustrate the law of Christ in relation to public duty.

"Perhaps you have sometimes met good people who have informed you in a tone of spiritual self-complacency that they have never been in a polling-booth. They do not seem to understand that the franchise is a trust, and that it imposes duties.

"A Secretary of State might as well make it a religious boast that he habitually neglected some of the work belonging to his department. The duties of an individual voter may be less grave than the duties of an official politician, but neglect in either case is a crime against the nation.

"I think it possible that the time may come when men who refuse to vote will be subjected to Church discipline, like men who refuse to pay their debts. The plea that the discharge of political duty is inconsistent with spirituality ought to be denounced as a flagrant piece of hypocrisy. It is nothing else. The men who urge it are not too spiritual to make a *coup* in cotton or coffee. Although they profess to be alarmed at the spiritual terrors of the ballot-box and of an occasional hour in a political committee-room, they are not afraid that their spirituality will suffer if they spend eight hours every day in their store or their counting-house. Their spirituality is of such a curious temper that it receives no harm from pursuits—no matter how secular—by which they can make money for themselves, but they are afraid of the most disastrous consequences if they attempt to render any service to their country. The selfishness of these men is as contemptible as their hypocrisy. They consent to accept all the advantages which come from the political institutions of the nation, and from the zeal and fidelity of their fellow-citizens. . . . People who are so very spiritual that they feel compelled to abstain from political life ought also to renounce the benefits which the political exertions of their less spiritual fellow-citizens secure for them. They ought to decline the services of the police when they are assaulted, they ought to refuse to appeal to such an unspiritual authority as a law court when their debts are not paid, and when a legacy is left them they ought piously to abstain from accepting it, for it is only by the intervention of public law that they can inherit what their dead friends have left them.

"For men to claim the right to neglect their duties to the State on the ground of their piety, while they insist on the State protecting their persons, protecting their property, and protecting from disturbance even their religious meetings in which this exquisitely delicate and valitudinarian spirituality is developed, is gross unrighteousness. It is as morally disgraceful as for a clerk to claim his salary from his employer after leaving other men to do the work for which his employer pays him."

Plain speaking of this sort from the Carr's Lane and other Nonconformist pulpits of Birmingham has materially helped to preserve the borough from the arrow of Burnaby which flieth by day, and the pestilence of Jingo which stalketh by night.

Mr. Dale was born in London, in December 1829. His early education was received chiefly at a private school in Finsbury Square, kept by a Mr. Willey. After a brief period of probation as an assistant master, he removed to Birmingham to attend Springhill College, a training school of the Congregationalists, the religious denomination of his parents. Here he remained for the whole curriculum of six years, and in 1853 he graduated at London University, carrying off the gold medal in the department of Philosophy and Political Economy. Among his tutors at Springhill was Henry Rogers, author of the once popular work, "The Eclipse of Faith." Rogers had a fine literary taste, with which he did not fail to imbue his pupils. A strong friendship sprang up between the old man and Dale, and to this day the latter acknowledges his obligations to his master with almost juvenile warmth.

Another remarkable friend of Dale's youth was a man renowned in the world of Evangelical Nonconformity, John Angell James. He was for over half a century the pastor of Carr's Lane Chapel, and Dale had no sooner finished his studies than he was appointed his colleague and successor. James imagined that he himself was a staunch Calvinist. But Calvinism his successor could not swallow, and shortly after his appointment he one Sunday opened a vigorous fire on its cardinal dogma, and set the congregation by the ears. James appealed to by alarmed church-goers, magnanimously defended his colleague:

"He is a young man," he said; "but the root of the matter is in him. Wait; you will see."

They waited, but did not see, for the young man hardened his heart; and to this day he repudiates the doctrine which "sends ane to heaven and ten to hell, a' for Thy glory," as unscriptural and revolting.

James himself had a naïve excuse for practically banishing it from his preaching. "Ah, well," he would say, "you see the Scriptures don't say much about it."

In relation to eternal punishment, Mr. Dale's position is that of an exegetical Darwin. He believes that hereafter the spiritually fittest will alone ultimately survive. With him the spiritual and not the material is the real. There is a Light which lighteth every man that cometh into this world, be he Jew or Gentile, Christian or Pagan. It is a plastic theory, of which much may be made by a humane mind. Accordingly, Mr. Dale is a very cosmopolitan sort of Christian. He is a strong admirer of Mr. Moody, of Moody and Sankey fame, and he is a sworn friend at the same time of Mr. Crosskey, the leading Unitarian heresiarch of Birmingham—

> "Of old things all are over old,
> Of good things none are good enough;
> He'll show that he can help to frame
> A Church of better stuff."

The Carr's Lane congregation consists of over fifteen hundred "souls," though I fear their pastor counts them as frequently by "votes." They are largely composed of working men and small tradesmen—nearly all Liberals. A sprinkling are quasi-Conservatives; among the latter a wealthy alderman, about whom Mr. Dale tells with glee how he described one of his special expositions of Christian truth as "a brilliant farrago of democratic nonsense."

And this has struck me as a peculiar feature of Birmingham Radicalism. It is intense without being bitter or personally rancorous. It may be different in the actual throes of an election contest, which I have never witnessed; but ordinarily there is a gratifying exhibition of mutual respect among political opponents. There is, at all events in the Dale family, a kindly tendency to regard a Tory as an "undeveloped Liberal," who will do better by-and-by. The political evangel, like the religious, is not completely closed to any.

I shall never forget my first impression of the Dale household. A ward election was impending at the time, and Mrs. Dale, a lady not less remarkable than her husband for vigour of mind and public spirit, was in the thick of it canvassing the women electors, note-book in hand, as if the salvation of the borough depended on the issue. I had always regarded canvassing as more or less demoralising work, but it depends largely on the spirit in which it is conducted. Mrs. Dale was a model canvasser, using no argument even with the most ignorant which did not appeal to their better reason. The result was mutually beneficial. The accomplished lady had her sympathies with the poor braced, and her knowledge of their wants extended, while her less fortunate sisters had their political education, to some extent at least, improved by coming in contact with a superior mind.

The interest taken in politics by the youngest members of the family, hardly in their teens, would have been comical if it had not been so genuine and intelligent.

The political soundness of Birmingham Mr. Dale traces

back to the old Dr. Priestley leaven, which is still at work in the community. The good which that great man did has not been interred with his bones. The Tory mob of his day stoned him, but the present generation has built him a worthy sepulchre.

The solidarity of the Birmingham Liberal vote is less easy to account for. Mr. Dale thinks the large number of small employers of labour, who are only a few degrees removed from the condition of their *employés*, has much to do with it, and he is probably right. There is more of what the French call *egalité* in Birmingham than in any other town in England. No doubt there are snobs there, as elsewhere; but I have not had the misfortune to meet them. Rich men like Mr. Chamberlain are devoted to Radical principles, and that sets the fashion. Given, moreover, culture and religion on the same side, and the worst Conservative foe that remains to be overcome is ignorance.

This last-named obstacle to the triumph of Radicalism Mr. Dale has set himself vigorously to combat. He was one of the most strenuous champions of the famous National Education League, which had for its object the complete separation of religious from secular instruction in Board schools. To seek to disestablish religion in the Church, and to hasten to establish it in the school, did not seem to some Nonconformists too glaring an inconsistency. The minister of Carr's Lane thought otherwise, and was returned at the first School Board election in the purely "secular" interest, along with Chamberlain, Dawson, Wright, Dixon, and Vince. They were in a minority on account of the inexperience of the party managers in working the cumulative vote. At the ensuing election, however, they succeeded in securing a bare majority, and public education in Birmingham was "secularised" at a blow. Since then, alas, there has been a certain retrogression.

The Board, which consists of fifteen members, is subdivided into five committees—Finance, Education and School Management, Sites and Buildings, General Purposes, and Night

Schools—and it requires no small amount of skilful manipulation to supply each of these with a Liberal chairman. Mr. Dale has acted as chairman of the hardest-worked of all the committees—viz., Education and School Management. He is, moreover, under the new Government scheme for the better conduct of the Grammar School, with its large revenues, a Governor, having been appointed to that honourable office by the University of London. But though the School Board of Birmingham has discharged its duties with exemplary efficiency, Mr. Dale is opposed on principle to the multiplication of such authorities. He would strengthen the local Parliament, the Birmingham Town Council, and place every civic interest in its keeping. The Corporation already manages the gas and water supplies, and Mr. Dale would not shrink from charging it with the control of education and of the liquor traffic as well. I cannot but think he is right. Everything that tends to fritter away the authority and dignity of our municipalities is an injury to the public spirit of a community, and there is no surer mode of bringing about a result so undesirable than the senseless multiplication of local boards. It is the latest application of one of the most ancient maxims of tyranny—*Divide et impera.*

There is neither inside nor outside Parliament a more eloquent and uncomprising advocate of Church Disestablishment than Mr. Dale. He approaches the question primarily from the old Puritan standpoint—viz., that the State cannot rightfully legislate for the Church. The latter is to the former what the conscience is to the individual. The things of Cæsar and the things of God must be kept asunder—*Regnum meum non est de hoc mundo.* The union of Church and State is a foul *liaison* which use can never convert into just matrimony. Such is his theory.

Now for a statement of the practical disadvantages of the Anglican Establishment. " To a Nonconformist," he says in his "Impressions of America"—a series of admirable sketches, political, social, educational, and religious, contributed to the *Nineteenth Century*—travelling in America one of the freshest sensations arises from the absence of an ecclesiastical Establishment. In England I am reminded wherever I go that the State is hostile to my religious opinions and practices. Diocesan Episcopacy, in my judgment, deprives the commonalty of the Church of many of their rights and releases them from many of their duties; but in every parish I find an Episcopal clergyman who, according to Mr. Forster's accurate description, is a servant of the State. Though I am a minister of religion, the civil Government has placed me under the spiritual charge of the Vicar of Edgbaston; that excellent gentleman is my pastor and religious teacher. I am not obliged to hear him preach, but the State has thought it necessary to entrust him with the duty of instructing me in Christian truth, and celebrating for my advantage the Christian sacraments. The doctrine of baptismal regeneration seems to me a mischievous superstition, but I cannot say this to anybody without being in revolt against a great national institution.

"Now and then I am bound to liberate my conscience, and I tell my congregation what I think of the doctrine; but within a couple of hundred yards there are two national buildings, in which, under the authority of the State, the State clergy give thanks to Almighty God for the regeneration of every child they baptise, and in which grown men and women are taught that in baptism they were made members of Christ, children of God, and inheritors of the kingdom of heaven. The law is against me. It tolerates me, but condemns me. It barks, though it does not bite. It describes me as being among those people in divers parts of this realm who, 'following their own sensuality and living without knowledge and due fear of God, do wilfully and schismatically refuse to come to parish churches.' It has provided a book of Common Prayer, that 'every person within this realm may certainly know the rule to which he is to conform in public worship.' I am permitted to break the rule, but the rule stands. It is the policy of the State to induce the country to accept or retain religious doctrine which seem to me to be erroneous, and an ecclesiastical polity which seems to me to be unfriendly to the free and vigorous development of the religious life. The position of a Nonconformist in this country is, to say the least, not a pleasant one. His religious work is carried on in the presence of a Government which condemns his creed, condemns his modes of worship, condemns his religious organisation, and sustains the authority of a hostile Church. In the United States I breathed freely."

Towards the close of 1875, Mr. Dale and the Rev. Guinness Rogers delivered a series of vigorous Disestablishment addresses at Bradford, Liverpool, Leeds, Manchester, Norwich, and Derby. They have been reprinted by the Liberation Society, and should be in the hands of every advocate of Disestablishment.

Mr. Dale has travelled in the East and in the West. He has visited Egypt, the Sinaitic Desert, and Palestine. His American wanderings, however, have borne the most valuable fruit. His published "Impressions" of the States are the best complement to Sir Charles Dilke's "Greater Britain" with which I am acquainted. They supply exactly the sort of information one desires with regard to that mighty theatre of new social and political experiments. That so many competent observers are now turning their footsteps towards the Far West is a subject for unqualified congratulation :—

> "Was the Mayflower launched by cowards,
> Steered by men behind their time?
> Turn those paths towards Past or Future
> That make Plymouth Rocks sublime?"

It is a Western and not an Eastern policy of which England stands most in need. Overthrow the aristocracy of this country and there will be no insuperable barrier to a grand reunion of the two great branches of the English-speaking race.

When the pressure of Mr. Dale's pastoral and political duties is considered, the tale of his literary labours is immense. They include a "Life of John Angell James," a volume of "Week-Day Sermons." "The Atonement," which ran through seven editions in four years, "Lectures on Preaching," "Discourses on Special Occasions," "The Ten Commandments," "Lectures on the Epistle to the Hebrews," an "Essay on Lacordaire," another on "George Dawson," "A Reply to Mr. Matthew Arnold's Attack on Puritanism," "The Necessity for an Ethical Revival," etc. Besides contributing to the *British Quarterly*, the *Fortnightly*, the *Contemporary*, and the *Nineteenth Century*, he has acted as joint editor of the *Eclectic Review*, and for seven years as editor of the *Congregationalist*, the organ of his denomination. In regard to many of these multifarious matters I am far from being able to see eye to eye with him, but he is always earnest, honest, able, tolerant, the steady, stout-hearted friend of civil and religious liberty, as he understands civil and religious liberty. In one of the hymns compiled by Mr. Dale, still sung at Carr's Lane Chapel, I read—

> "Unlearn not the lore thy Wycliffe well learned,
> Forsake not the cause thy Milton approved,
> Forget not the fire where thy Latimer burned,
> Nor turn from the truth thy Cromwell so loved."

To younger Radicals among us, who draw inspiration from less venerable historic sources, such injunctions may appear superfluous. But they are still real to many of the best men and women in England with whom it should be our pride and pleasure to co-operate. Mr. Dale can pour new wine into old bottles without accident. He is likewise perfectly familiar with the uses of the newest bottles of Liberalism, as will be discovered by anyone who cares to read his presidental address delivered to the members of the Birmingham Junior Liberal Association in October 1878. He is one of the most effective platform speakers in Great Britain, and would make a heaven-born parliamentary candidate for a great popular constituency. Is it past praying for that such a man should be translated from Carr's Lane, Birmingham, to the wider sphere of usefulness at St Stephen's, Westminster?

III.

JOSEPH ARCH.

> "Men rough and rude pressed round
> To hear the praise of one
> Whose heart was made of manly, simple stuff
> As homespun as their own."

SINCE Wat Tyler perished by the hand of the assassin Mayor of London, Walworth, the agricultural labourers of England have had no more sincere and capable leader than Joseph Arch. To sketch his career is in a great measure to depict the condition and characteristics of his class, a numerous and important section of Englishmen, of whom, until quite recently, less perhaps was known for certain than of Afghans, Zulus, or the Ten Lost Tribes. For centuries they had been forgotten helots, mute bearers of other men's burdens, the starved, unlettered, hereditary bondsmen of "merry England." Their misery gave the lie direct to our boasted prosperity and freedom. The statue might be imposing, but the feet were obviously of clay. "And behold the tears of such as were oppressed, and they no comforter: and on the side of the oppressors there was power." Yea, very great power and very terrible oppression. On the agricultural labourer of England rests to this day the curse of the Norman Conquest, the economic damnation of the "three profits" of which our "miraculous Premier" is so enamoured that he has taken to demonstrating that the arrangement is a law of nature.

The English labourer is the true *servus servorum*, the slave of the farmer, who is in turn the slave of landlord and parson. On him presses with crushing weight the whole fabric of "society." He is the subject-matter, the *corpus vile* of the Great Unpaid. Where were the judicial dignity of Justice Shallow but for the peccant Hodge who pilfers a turnip, gathers a mushroom, or knocks over a hare? Where were the pride of " officers and gentlemen," were there no regiments of full privates recruited from rural England to command? On whom could the so-called National Church unctuously enjoin contentment with the condition of life wherein it has pleased God to place them were there no serfs of the soil among her presumed adherents?

Indeed, for many generations the combination of powers spiritual and temporal against the English agricultural labourer has been so irresistible that the marvel is he has the smallest manhood left. Reform after reform has passed him by unheeded, or rather has increased the distance between him and other classes of the community. The Protestant Reformation deprived him of the charities of the monasteries, and in their place put in force poor laws of unexampled barbarity. It found him sunk in ignorance, and it kept him so. In time Reform Bills came, but who should bestow franchises on a being so abject? Free trade gave a new impetus to British commerce, but, let the economists explain it as best they may, the Manchester cornucopia never poured any of its abundance into Hodge's lap. He was seemingly beyond the beneficent operation even of economic laws. For five-and-twenty years he had with more or less variation been going from bad to worse. So much indeed was this the case that the opening of 1872 found the actual tillers of English soil in a state of " depression" bordering on actual famine. Then it was that the Agricultural Labourers' Union took root, and Mr. Joseph Arch first became known to the public as the Moses who had been raised up to lead his down-trodden brethren out of the house of bondage. Like his prototype, he might have gone over to the oppressor, much to his own advantage, in the capacity of land steward to a local Pharaoh, but he had resisted the temptation, and when the hour struck the man was ready.

Joseph Arch, founder and president of the Agricultural Labourers' Union, was born in November 1826, at Barford, a beautiful village, of some eight hundred souls, about three miles from the historic town of Warwick. All about are stately mansions of the great, and Shakespeare's Avon winds close by through lovely meadows studded with majestic trees. Like himself, Arch's father and grandfather were industrious, ill-requited hewers of wood and drawers of water. Howbeit,

> "Let not Ambition mock their useful toil,
> Their homely joys and destiny obscure;
> Nor Grandeur hear with a disdainful smile
> The short and simple annals of the poor."

The life story of Mr. Arch's father is short enough and sad enough. Unlike his son he was a man of peace, disposed in all things to conform to the behests of the powers that be, but he "drew the line somewhere," and not to his advantage. He was sufficiently ill-advised to refuse to sign a petition in favour of the Corn Laws, and so became by one rash act a "marked man," on whom "quality" never after smiled. For more than fifty years he toiled, and when at last he was no longer able to drag his weary limbs to the fields, he took to bed, and sorrowfully turned his face to the wall. The savings of a lifetime of painful industry and frugality amounted to four shillings and sixpence! The *dénouement* I cannot better describe than in the words of the Rev. Mr. Attenborough, whose faithful sketch of Mr. Arch I cordially recommend to those who may wish further information regarding the origin of the National Agricultural Labourers' Union, and the early career of its founder:—

"The worn, crumbling Arch, just tumbling down, was to be propped up with 'good support,' and there was four shillings and sixpence towards providing it. 'Give him some beef tea, get him a drop of good wine if you can, and take this prescription to the chemist's.'

"The poor patient's friends sat wondering, and weighing his four and sixpence against the doctor's counsel; it was nowhere. The old man wept, knowing he was, after all his work, to become a burden to those he loved, and who, as he knew, had barely enough for themselves.

"'I be afeard, Joe, the parish will give thee nothin' for me, be'n as yer a Dissenter.' Joe was not anxious they should, but Joe's wife had been in the habit of earning a couple of shillings a week at charing, and now that the old man wanted nursing, she had to give this up and stop at home. To the guardians Arch made a reasonable offer.

"'Gentlemen, I don't want you to support my aged father; but if you will give my wife one shilling and sixpence towards nursing him, now that she is cut off her charing, I shall be much obliged to you; it isn't much; it's less than the loss of my wife's earnings, and nothing towards the expense.'

"'Certainly not, Arch, your father can go to "the house," and you must pay one and sixpence towards his support.'

"'Good morning, gentlemen. I'd sooner rot under a hedge than he should go there.'

"The old man lingered for ten months, and during the last few weeks of his life the parish, against Arch's will, but with the consent of his wife, allowed him one shilling and sixpence and a loaf! Then he died, and his son bought him a coffin, and hid him down in the earth on whose broad bountiful breast there seemed to be no room for him. Fifty years a worker, thirty years a ratepayer, a life's saving of four shillings and sixpence, a choice between the workhouse and his son's poor cottage, eighteenpence and a loaf for two months—this was the life story of Arch senior!"

Nor was this in ante-union days an isolated instance of hardship. On the contrary, so far from being the exception, it was the rule. Work as hard and live as sparingly as one might, the inevitable goal was the workhouse. Wages would admit of no other result, and this in Christian Jingo England, with its "miraculous Premier" and its capacity for undertaking unlimited campaigns! The thought burns like a hot iron, and the warning word "Beware!" rises to indignant lips—

> "Lest, when our latest hope is fled,
> Ye taste of our despair,
> And learn by proof in some wild hour
> How much the wretched dare."

It was not from his father, but from his mother that Mr. Arch inherited his moral stamina. She was a woman of well-defined views in religion and politics, leaning strongly towards Nonconformity and Radicalism. She could both read and write—rare accomplishments for one in her lowly station of life—and before her boy was six years of age he could, thanks to her tuition, do likewise.

Thereupon he was sent to the village school, where he remained for two years and three-quarters, and then his education was pronounced complete. Money was wanted above all things in the Arch household, and at the ripe age of eight years and three-quarters young Arch commenced to earn his livelihood as a bird-scarer or "crow-kepper," with wages at the rate of fourpence per diem. In South Warwickshire the living scarecrows are dressed as nearly as possible like the more common inanimate objects with which farmers are wont to adorn their potato fields. They are supposed to be more effective than the voiceless stationary "keppers," inasmuch as from dawn till eve they move from field to field, emitting all manner of strange and alarming sounds. Their garb is, however, so grotesque that the birds, it is hinted, draw near for the purpose of laughing at them, and so the provident husbandman's laudable aim is frustrated.

At ten years of age Joseph was considered ripe for the more responsible occupation of plough-driving. All day long the poor lad would trail his heavily-clogged boots by the side of the horse, to whose gearing he would occasionally have to cling from sheer exhaustion. Thereupon the furrow would bulge, and the incensed ploughman, dexterously hurling at him a great clod, would lay him prone, face downwards, on the just upturned soil.

Nor did material hardships constitute his sorest trials. As he grew older and entered on his "teens," he was promoted to drive a team in harvest-time, and felt himself every inch a man. His employer thoughtlessly taking advantage of his youthful elation of spirits, plied him with excessive quantities of liquor, and but for the peremptory steps taken by Mrs. Arch to keep her boy in the strait path of sobriety, the apostolate of the agricultural labourers might have been rendered for ever impossible in the person of Joseph Arch. In his sixteenth year this kind, judicious mother was no more, but her admonitions were indelibly impressed on her son's mind. To his mother Arch ascribes whatever good he has been able to achieve.

At twenty years of age, Arch's character was no longer to form. He was a local preacher, and earning the highest wages to be made as an agricultural labourer—viz., eleven shillings a week. Several eligible opportunities occurred for bettering his condition, but he resolved instead to "stand by the old man."

Shortly after he married the daughter of a local artisan, a woman of great natural endowments, both of head and heart. Though uneducated, technically speaking, she is, I think, superior to her husband as a speculative politician. At every step she has stimulated his zeal by steady devotion to great principles—greater, perhaps, than it would naturally occur to him to advocate.

In due course two children were born to them, and Arch's wages unhappily fell to nine shillings a week. Four persons to maintain at the rate of, say fourpence per head per diem! The thing Mrs. Arch declared could not be done, and so she took a bold step. She partially returned to her ante-nuptial employment, while her husband took up his tools and scoured the country in quest of more remunerative work than was to be had in the neighbourhood of Barford. For months he never crossed his own threshold. In his wanderings he encountered poverty beside which even the Barford standard was one of comparative plenty. In Herefordshire he found able-bodied men with wives and families toiling from morning till night for seven shillings a week. With one of these he once lodged. How the wife and children subsisted Arch could never ascertain, but the husband fared thus:—" Breakfast, a dry crust; dinner, ditto; supper—the great meal of the day—sometimes 'scald-chops,' a dainty dish, consisting of broken bread moistened by pouring hot water upon it, and sometimes a pint of cider warmed over the fire and a crust dipped into it. This from Monday till Saturday, and on Sunday *occasionally* a bit of bacon!"

He beheld the tears of the oppressed, and they had no comforter, and he vowed in the bitterness of his heart that if ever an opportunity should present itself he would try to be that comforter. The clock struck sooner than he expected.

Presently he was enabled to return to Barford to undertake "jobs" which required the assistance of other "hands." As an employer he was not merely considerate but generous. His own specialty as an agricultural labourer is hedge-cutting—he is the champion hedge-cutter of all England.

All his life Mr. Arch has been addicted to reading. His earlier studies were chiefly of a pietistic character. He devoured the Bible, the "Pilgrim's Progress," Pike's "Early Piety," "Pearson on Infidelity," *et hoc genus omne*. He still preaches to vast audiences, generally twice, and sometimes three times on Sundays. Originally a Primitive Methodist, he has latterly laid aside the shibboleths of sect altogether and taken his stand on the common ground of Christ's humanitarian precepts and the example of his spotless self-sacrificing life. His experience as a local preacher in addressing large audiences is to a great extent the secret of his success as a political agitator.

The National Agricultural Labourers' Union was started in this wise: "On the 5th of July 1872"—I quote Mr. Arch's own unvarnished narrative of "The Rise and Progress of the N.A.L.U."—"two farm labourers, named Henry Perks and John Davis, were sent by their fellow-labourers from Wellesbourne, in Warwickshire, to the village of Barford. The object of the deputation was to wait upon me to ask me to help them to form a union. . . . . Fortunately I was at home when they arrived. I went inside to see the men, who said, 'We are come over to see you about our having a union. We formed a bit of one under the hedge the other day; but we can't go on very well without some one to put us right. The men are all ready for it, and we appeal to you.'

"'But,' I said, 'do you mean to stick together?'

"'Yes,' was the reply.

"'Well, now,' said I, 'you go back and get some of the best men in Wellesbourne, and ask Mrs. Baker to let you have the clubroom, and I will be over on Wednesday night at seven o'clock. But, remember, you must be prepared for conflict, as the farmers will be sure to oppose you.'

"The reply was, 'You come, it can't be worse for us than it is.'"

Thus simply was the "Revolt of the Field," the most remarkable social upheaval of the day commenced. The news spread like wildfire, and on the Wednesday night Mr. Arch addressed over a thousand fellow-labourers under a great chestnut tree at Wellesbourne.

Meeting followed meeting in rapid succession. Arch was ubiquitous and untiring, and at last, at a memorable meeting at Leamington, the National Union was formed, with Joseph Arch as chairman, assisted by an executive committee of twelve labourers and an influential consultative council, comprising Professor Beesly, Mr. Jesse Collings, Mr. J. C. Cox, Mr. Ashton Dilke, the Hon. Auberon Herbert, Mr. E. Jenkins, and others.

The moderation of the demands of the union was no less

remarkable than the violence of the opposition offered by landlords, parsons, and farmers. Bishops menacingly alluded to "horseponds" as fitting receptacles for agitators. Then followed the memorable Chipping Norton prosecution and conviction of labourers' wives and the important trial at Faringdon to test the right of public meeting, where Sir James Fitzjames Stephen held a brief for the union with such signal success.

But it is not my business to write a history of the N.A.L.U. Suffice it to say that in most instances the immediate object of the union has been attained. Wherever the men have stood manfully by the union, wages have gone up, agricultural depression notwithstanding, from 15 to 20 per cent. In south Warwickshire, wages which in 1872 stood at from 10s. to 12s. now range from 13s. to 15s. a week.

Within the executive of the N.A.L.U., harmony, I regret to say, has not uniformly prevailed. The urban unionists, who have exerted themselves, I believe, with perfect disinterestedness for the emancipation of the agricultural labourer, have never regarded Mr. Arch's lead with much confidence, and the latter has not failed to reciprocate this sentiment of distrust. The reason, I think, is that Mr. Arch is a thorough agricultural labourer, with all the virtues and some of the failings of his class. He has seen so little real generosity exhibited towards the serfs of the soil that he is somewhat over-suspicious on their account. He fears the Greeks, even when they bring gifts to his clients, and this attitude, I am bound to say, has not always been without justification. It served him notably in Canada when he came to negotiate with the unscrupulous ring of emigration crimps who, in the fall of 1873, formed the Macdonald Cabinet. Canada is, in truth, a country where it is difficult to say whether the rigour of the climate or the corruption of the Government is the more unendurable. If he had listened to the warbling of the official sirens and deported large numbers of English labourers to the inclement shores of Canada, it would have been enough to wreck the union for ever.

Mr. Arch's sojourn in the United States was less satisfactory. The New York working men, intending a great compliment, had advertised him to speak at the Cooper Institute without his consent—*more Americano*. He declined, with quite unnecessary bluntness. He did not proceed far enough west, for there, if anywhere, is it possible to find the Promised Land of the English agricultural labourer. On a future tour of inspection it is to be hoped he will repair so great an oversight, inasmuch as it is pretty certain that emigration has all along been the sheet anchor of the union. Under the auspices of the N.A.L.U., and partly aided by its funds, some 700,000 souls have left our shores, or migrated from country to town, since 1872. At that time members could with difficulty pay 1½d. a week to the union; now the subscription is 2¼d., and there is still a solid phalanx of 25,000 subscribers.

But the good work is hardly begun. The labourer has to obtain the franchise, and the land has to be completely *defeudalised* before Mr. Arch's mission will have been fulfilled. I have never met a man who, from personal observation, has grasped so comprehensively the evils of our land monopoly. In his own neighbourhood Mr. Arch is an encyclopædia of information regarding the past and present produce of the various adjacent estates. Within the last twenty-five years cattle and sheep, he will tell you, have in most cases decreased by more than one-half without a single rood of pasture land being broken up. Instead of "three profits," there will hardly be enough for one if the present system is to obtain much longer. Feudalism is eating itself up, in South Warwickshire at least. These be truths which no one could inculcate with greater authority at St. Stephen's than the founder of the N.A.L.U., and there it is to be hoped Mr. Arch will, after next election, have an opportunity of explaining *his* view of the "three profits," and who ought to reap them.

IV.

EDWARD SPENCER BEESLY.

> "Thou, Humanity, art my Goddess: to thy law
> My services are bound; wherefore should I
> Stand in the plague of custom?"

LAST issue in writing of Mr. Joseph Arch I ran no inconsiderable risk of losing sight of the man in the magnitude of the cause with which his name is identified. This week I am in similar and greater peril; for if it be one thing to face National Agricultural Unionism as the subject-matter of Radical effort, it is quite another to tackle the whole duty of man—the Religion of Humanity—as revealed in the fulness of these later times by Auguste Comte.

To those who know anything of the writings of that extraordinary man I need scarcely say that, whatever may be thought of his ulterior conclusions, his was one of the most powerful, laborious, and all-embracing intellects of any time or clime. If one cannot accept his ideas it is still necessary to revise one's own in the light of them, for as Moses was fitted for his mission by being learned in all the learning of the Egyptians, so assuredly Auguste Comte was superlatively conversant with all modern sciences, with astronomy, physics, chemistry, biology; and being so conversant, he made, some sixty years ago now, a notable discovery. He found that each of these sciences had in the course of its development passed through three stages —a theological, a metaphysical, and a positive. Take, for example, life in man and brute—what is it? The answer of primitive man, the theological answer, is, God breathed into their nostrils the breath of life, and they became living creatures. Then came the metaphysical explanation: they live because their blood is pervaded by a mysterious sublimated essence called "vital spirits," or "physiological units." Then at last the question *why* they live is given up as hopeless, and it is only asked how they live, and by what means the conditions of life can be modified for their profit or loss. This is the last or positive stage which is ultimately reached in every science.

From 1822 to 1842 Comte was busily engaged in verifying the above profound generalisation in detail. Heureka! He had found a master-key to the whole history of mankind, religious, philosophical, moral, and political. The foundations of a true science of sociology might at last be confidently laid. The gods and the metaphysicians might now be safely, nay, advantageously, bowed out of the great Temple of Humanity, in appropriate niches of which should be placed such miscellaneous benefactors of the race as Moses, Christ, Mohammed, the Buddha, St. Thomas Aquinas; Plato, Socrates, Æschylus, Confucius, Shakespeare, Dante; Thales, Archimedes, Newton, Kepler; Ariosto, Cervantes, Molière; Julius Cæsar, Trajan, Danton, and a great company of other prophets who, in their day and generation, had worked hard in the sacred cause of Humanity, without, of course, apprehending very clearly what they were about.

Some of them, no doubt, had concerned themselves much about supernaturalities, immortalities, and such like childish things, according as they were in the theological or metaphysical stage; but they had all agreed in this, "to live not for themselves, but for others."

Here then is the "Open Sesame" of the Future. The pillars which support the great fane of Humanity are three—Affection, Order, Progress; the first representing the principle; the second, the basis; the third, the end of the new creed. And whosoever builds on any other foundation let him be Anathema Maranatha. Not quite so strong as that, perhaps, but still not far from it; for good Comtists attribute the sum of political strifes and social miseries to the conflict which necessarily arises from the fact that large masses of mankind are some of them still in the theological, some in the metaphysical, and only an elect few in the positive stage of belief. Until all have been brought into the positive fold wars and rumours of wars are inevitable. Like other millenniums, alas, that of the Positivists has been postponed *sine die*, and to a necessarily distant day too.

I should be sorry indeed if anyone were to suppose that the above is other than the faintest outline of the creed of which the learned Professor of History in University College, London, is so devoted and fearless an exponent. It cost him ten years' patient study to attain to settled convictions on the subject, and even yet he is not in the priesthood of Positivism. He is only a sort of lay deacon, or stalwart doorkeeper, at the Temple of Humanity. This being so, I feel that it is not a little presumptuous in me who have given but little attention to this new and most difficult of *cults*, to attempt in any way to pass judgment on it; and were it not that Mr. Beesly's political conduct and historical writings have been so directly inspired by Comtism, I should most willingly give it a wide berth.

There is so much that is admirable, and so many things at the same time that traverse one's most cherished opinions—prejudices, a Comtist would doubtless say—in the system of Comte, that it becomes a matter of no ordinary difficulty to review Mr. Beesly's career, simple as have been the incidents, with impartiality and discrimination.

Edward Spencer Beesly was born at Feckenham, Worcestershire, in January 1831. His father was vicar of the place, a sincere, sober-minded Evangelical of the old school, who kept up intimate relations with the leaders of his own party in the Church, and with few others.

His son Edward he found leisure to educate at home till the young man was of age to be entered as a student at nowise illustrious " Wadham," Oxford. This home-training may in some measure account for the fact that *the* Englishman who in public life has most frequently and audaciously made light of the tenderest susceptibilities of all manner of reputable people "with gigs," is in the bosom of his family a model of gentleness and every domestic virtue.

At Wadham College Mr. Beesly was lucky in his friendships, having for tutor Mr. Congreve—then the Rev. Richard—and for fellow-students Mr. Frederic Harrison and Mr. J. H. Bridges. Congreve was a man of admitted ability—one of the most accomplished Aristotelians of his day. Sincere but eccentric, no one was very much astonished when one fine morning it was rumoured in Oxford that he had been formally admitted into the Church of Auguste Comte. In time he was followed by Beesly, Harrison, and Bridges; Beesly, as I have said, taking ten years to acquaint himself with the evangel of the Parisian before relinquishing that of the Nazarene.

In 1854 Mr. Beesly graduated with honours, and was appointed an Assistant Master in Marlborough College. Subsequently he sought for and obtained the position of Principal of University Hall, Gordon Square, London, in succession to Dr. Carpenter, who had been preceded by Mr. Hutton, now of the *Spectator*, by the gifted Arthur Clough, and nominally by F. W. Newman, the first Principal designate who had never acted. The Hall is tenanted by students of all religious denominations, and no proselytising is permitted. There is a complete *pax ecclesiastica* maintained at University Hall almost unknown in similar institutions.

In 1860 Mr. Beesly was appointed Professor of History in University College, an office the duties of which he was peculiarly fitted both by predilection and training to discharge.

The Professor in his class-room is always interesting. He is unconventional without being familiar, and he has a happy knack of presenting the purely human aspect of his subject, however far it may appear to be removed from the domain of current interests, which seldom fails to leave the desired impression. The Comtian principle of the continuity of human life enables Mr. Beesly to irradiate the darkness of the past by the light of the present with no ordinary success.

The last time I was in his class-room—the class is a mixed one of young ladies and gentlemen, the propriety of whose behaviour is a standing disproof of the fears of timid moralists—he was comparing the cardinal features of the religion of ancient Rome with those more particularly of Christianity. The great goddess of the Romans was really Roma, the "abstract double" of the Eternal City. There was one Rome built by the hands of many generations of Romans, and another built up by the imaginations of many generations of Quirites. This process of creating a divinity after their own image did not shock the Roman people. They were in the theological stage of development. Well, it struck me very forcibly that this delusive object of Roman worship was hardly less an imposture than the object of Comtist veneration, the Being of Humanity. The Being of Humanity is the thinly disguised "abstract double" of an indefinite number of men and women, past, present, and to come, "mostly fools," with a considerable infusion of knaves. I for one absolutely refuse to worship at the shrine of such a Mumbo Jumbo. Having been once brought out of the theological wilderness by a process so painful, I positively decline to be again led back into it by a shabbier road than I entered it.

Of course I shall be told that I do not understand the Comtist religion, or perhaps that I am incapable of understanding it; for, like all possessors of absolute truths, Comtists have a short way with unbelievers. My only consolation is —and I admit it is a poor one—I am still in a majority in this country. I do not forget that Christianity was once in a minority of one, and if the avowed English co-religionists of Mr. Beesly number only some sixty or seventy souls at present, I am free to grant that they have among them proportionally by far the best brains in England. And they are diligent in season and out of season—zealous in every good work as they understand good works. Mr. Beesly's labours in connection, for example, with the translation of Comte's "Politique Positive" into English are enough to make any member of the Company of Biblical Revisers blush for very shame. He is likewise a frequent contributor to the columns of *La Revue Occidentale*, the organ of the Orthodox Positivists, conducted by the Primate of the body, Pierre Laffitte, a personal disciple of Comte.

It may be necessary to explain how it comes to pass that Mr. Beesly is an orthodox and not a heterodox Positivist. The seamless coat of Comte has, alas, already been rent. Dr. Congreve has disavowed the headship of Laffitte, and so has become schismatic, taking half of the Comtist Church in England and its dependencies with him. He has turned his back on Paris, as Henry VIII. turned his back on Rome. He has set up an independent island Church, and may be regarded as a sort of Comtist Protestant.

On the other hand, Mr. Beesly, Dr. Bridges, Mr. Harrison, Mr. Vernon Lushington, Mr. Cotter Morison, and others still remain Ultramontanes, repairing from time to time to Paris to engage in the solemnities which annually take place at Comte's old abode on the anniversary of his death. The house is kept exactly as when the founder of the new religion died, and is the sacred rendezvous—the kaaba—of the faithful. The meeting-place of the Orthodox is the Cavendish Rooms, Mortimer Street, Langham Place, where a course of lectures of an expositional character are delivered on Sunday evenings during the winter months by Mr. Beesly, Mr. Harrison, and other qualified laymen.

It remains to glance at some of Mr. Beesly's political opinions, acts, and historical writings, which are one and all penetrated through and through by the principles and spirit of his master, Comte. They have all for their central idea or governing principle the far-reaching Comtian dictum: "The working class is not, properly speaking, a class at all, but constitutes the body of society. From it proceed the various special classes, which we regard as organs necessary to that body." Woe to the aforesaid special classes if they cease to be necessary organs. Woe to Mr. Gladstone, woe to Earl Beaconsfield, woe to Parliament, woe to all men who are unduly friendly to special classes. Let them but show their baneful partiality, and the Professor will smite them with remorseless impartiality. To him the Trojan Whig and the Tyrian Tory have ever been much alike. Nay, he has even been known to speak disrespectfully of parliamentary institutions themselves, as Sidney Smith said Lord Jeffrey once spoke depreciatingly of the Equator. He has scoffed at the respectability of our middle class, and treated our greatest plutocrats as if they were nobodies. In all things he is pre-eminently un-English, affirming, as he does, the immense superiority of Frenchmen and French institutions over Englishmen and English institutions. England's function among the nations is merely to play the part of the " horrible example." She will do nothing at home that is not base and hypocritical; nothing abroad that is not tyrannical and suicidal. The cup of her iniquities is almost full to overflowing.

Mr. Beesly would give up India to-morrow, to say nothing, of course, of Afghanistan. He would make an ample apology to Cetewayo, and replace him on the throne of Zululand. He would surrender Gibraltar to Spain, and make a present of Ireland to Mr. Parnell, or to anybody else who might care to take it off our hands. He would concentrate all our military and naval strength in and around Great Britain, and having thus fortified the island by lopping off its rotten outlying members, the country would be in a position to enter on the discharge of international duties meet for civilisation, conformable to the Religion of Humanity.

England, along with France, would then be in a position to protect free Denmark, free Holland, free Belgium, from German or other autocratic aggression, and as opportunity occurred a blow for the resuscitation of Poland might perchance be struck. The Neo-Imperialists, at all events, can hardly be expected to regard this as the " voice of sense and truth," but it is unquestionably Positive Politics as understood by Auguste Comte, and his disciple is not the man to shrink from any of the consequences of his master's teaching.

With respect to only one point in this programme do I care meantime to pronounce an opinion. The Comtists have never ceased to protest against our conquests in Hindostan and our opium wars with China. Mr. Beesly in particular has lifted up his voice against these cold-blooded enterprises, which fill the mind of every sagacious observer with the gloomiest forebodings, with an energy that does him the greatest credit. It is one of the saving graces of the Comtist creed that it includes the most abject sons of men in the adorable Being of Humanity. They may be in the backward metaphysical state, like the Hindoos, or in the yet more unredeemed theological condition of the Zulus, but they are not, therefore, fit subjects for Christian oppression. They are where the most civilised peoples once were, struggling, weary and footsore, along the dusty highway of human progress which all must tread. If they fall among thieves, it is ours to play the part of the good Samaritan and lift them out of the ditch into which the footpads have cast them. But we, alas, are the footpads. I shall not speedily forget the righteous indignation with which Mr. Beesly recently spoke to me of the Zulu war. He felt the misdeeds of our representatives as a stain on his personal honour. The name of Frere, even more than that of Eyre, ought to go down with infamy to the latest posterity.

The mentioning of Eyre recalls to my mind an incident in Mr. Beesly's career which brought down on his head an extraordinary torrent of journalistic and other invective. At a public meeting held in connection with the Broadhead murders in 1867, he somewhat infelicitously observed that Eyre "had committed his crime in the interest of employers, just as Broadhead had committed his crime in the interest of workmen." The wealthy class, he argued, had approved, while the working class had condemned murder. This was enough; he was declared to have "apologised" for Broadhead's crimes, and even to have converted him "into a hero." So far was this from being the fact that it was subsequently proved that Mr. Beesly had on the first intimation of the atrocities gone out of his way to urge the unions to "ferret out any member guilty of a breach of the law and drag him to justice." This was, however, not enough. A victim was wanted, and for a time the vials of class calumny continued to be poured on the Professor's devoted head. Had he been a weak man he would have succumbed to the violence of the storm. As it was he stood erect and immovable as a pillar, and the tempest gradually died away.

But the Broadhead incident was by no means Professor Beesly's first offence against society. On the 28th day of September 1864 he had actually presided at the first meeting of "the International," in a room of St. Martin's Hall, Long Acre. There Tolain submitted his memorable project, and Marx, Eccarius, Odger, Lucraft, Llama, and Wolff were named as a provisional committee. Here at least was one highly educated English gentleman with the courage of his opinions whom no political Mrs. Grundy could intimidate.

In 1875 occurred the iniquitous conviction of the five cabinet-makers, Read, Weiler, Ham, Hibbert, and Matthews, for the offence of picketing. Again, Mr. Beesly came boldly to the front. During the term of their imprisonment he lectured at the Eleusis Club on their behalf; when they were released he was among the first to welcome them at the prison-door; and he presided at the complimentary dinner at which they were subsequently entertained, supported by the Hon. L. Stanley, Mr. John Morley, Dr. Congreve, Mr. Ashton Dilke, Professor Hunter, and others.

In March 1877 died George Odger, the Epaminondas of English politicians. He was interred in the Brompton Cemetery, and from a broken column near his grave Professor Beesly pronounced a befitting eulogium on his career in presence rather than in the hearing of a countless multitude.

"George Odger," he said, "was not only a good but a great

citizen, one who put his public in the first rank of duties, and was prepared to sacrifice all private interests to that consideration"—a meed of praise not less deserved by the eulogised dead than by the living eulogist. There is not, I am sure, a more inflexibly honest politician or cultivated gentleman in England than Professor Beesly.

But I am bound to say that I think many of his political conceptions are mistaken. Like all Comtists, his admiration for France is excessive, and he dangerously undervalues the importance of parliamentary government. I acknowledge with gratitude the immense sacrifices which the French People have made in the cause of human emancipation. France is pre-eminently

> "The Poet of the Nations.
> That dreams on and wails on
> While the household goes to wreck."

All the same I cannot conceive with Mr. Beesly that English workmen, as such, have any very vital stake in the evolution of the social and political life of France. If they cannot, with the aid of the less selfish and more intelligent section of the middle class, combine in their own way to establish on the ruins of Monarchy and Aristocracy in England a stable Republic, not based on birth and privilege, but on merit and equal rights, then let them throw up the sponge, once and for all, and, betaking themselves, not in their thousands, but their millions, to the free, open-armed United States of America, leave behind them a solitude wherein their oppressors may meditate at their leisure on the consequences of their own selfishness and folly.

A word or two on Mr. Beesly's vigorous vindication of Catiline, Clodius, and Tiberius, and I am done. To him these besmirched historic personages are standard-bearers of the Roman Revolution, the lineal descendants of the illustrious Gracchi and of Drusus. According to this view Cato and Cicero, Brutus and Cassius, were the Beaconsfields and Salisburys, while the Catilines and the Clodii were the Dilkes and Chamberlains of the time. The cause of the latter triumphed eventually when Julius Cæsar crushed the Senate and became the Saviour of Society—the great world prototype of personal rulers.

In a sense the advent of Roman Imperialism was a popular gain. It replaced many tyrants by one. But it gave the death-blow to whatever little public spirit remained in Rome, and that calamity was irreparable. I grant the Republican Oligarchy was largely corrupt and oppressive. Unhappily, it never occurred to anyone to renovate the Roman Legislative Assemblies by the admisson of representatives from the provincial Communes. Representative government as now understood was the discovery of a later age. As it was, Cato and Cicero, Brutus and Cassius, saw the image of constitutional freedom receding day by day, and they clung desperately to her skirts. In such evil times Radicals became Conservatives, and Conservatives ostensible Radicals.

Mr. Beesly seems to me to forget that even a hateful middle class may be crushed at too great a cost. Like all Comtists, he is too partial to able men placed in authority by brute masses. For my part, had I lived in the days of Brutus and Cassius, I am certain that I should have been on the losing side at Philippi, just as I should have been at the *coup d'etat*, or as I should be if ever M. Gambetta, for example, were to show symptoms of following in the footprints of Napoleon.

V.

CHARLES HADDON SPURGEON.

> "God forgive me! If ever I
> Take aught from the Book of that Prophecy,
> Lest my part, too, should be taken away
> From the Book of Life on the Judgment Day."

FROM Professor Beesly's Comtism to the Rev. Charles Haddon Spurgeon's Christianity—what a distance to travel! Mr. Beesly once somewhat uncharitably accused Mr. Gladstone of being more concerned about his "contemptible superstitions than about politics." What would he not say of the views of the Pastor of the Metropolitan Tabernacle? You might search the whole world and find no one whose mind was more thoroughly under the domination of theological ideas than Spurgeon's. To a Positivist the reverend gentleman must appear like a survival not of the fittest, but of the unfittest—a painful anachronism to remind good Positivists and advanced thinkers generally of the lowly estate from which they have emerged. Not even reached the metaphysical stage; and yet Mr. Spurgeon has thousands and thousands of excellent men and women who hang on his every word, spoken and written, as if it were the very bread of life.

With hardly an attempt at direct political propagandism, Mr. Spurgeon contrives to be the greatest single influence in South London in favour of Liberalism. At elections, School Board and Parliamentary, his followers display an energy and discipline which leave nothing to be desired. They are men of faith, who do not lose heart in times of adversity and reaction. Their human sympathies as well as their spiritual have been warmed by the flame which burns in the bosom of the devout and fearless Great Heart of the Metropolitan Tabernacle.

If the common characteristic of men of progress, of genuine Radicals, be that they "live not for themselves but for others," then it would be hard to find a better Radical than Mr. Spurgeon. As his Divine Master went about doing good, so has His disciple ever struggled hard to follow in his footsteps. So much I readily grant. My heart is entirely with this pure-minded, unsophisticated believer, but my unsanctified head will not, alas, follow it. I go to the Tabernacle and I admire the vastness of the audience, the simple, unconventional eloquence of the preacher, the pith and mother-wit of many of his sayings; but on the whole the phraseology, if not strange, is almost meaningless to me, and I return to my place about as little edified as if the good man had been talking in some dead language to which I had no key. Instead of attracting me, his familiarity with the Almighty and His ways repels me. He is more intimate with *Him* than I am with my dearest friend. Is this the unredeemed condition of the theologically-minded spoken of by the Prophet Comte? I ask myself; or what is it?—

> "It is growing dark ! . . . .
> I come again to the name of the Lord !
> Ere I that awful name record,
> That is spoken so lightly among men,
> Let me pause awhile and wash my pen ;
> Pure from blemish and blot must it be
> When it writes that word of mystery."

To Mr. Spurgeon there is no mystery at all. He *knows* the decrees of God, and he has escaped the wrath to come. Hallelujah ! Mr. Spurgeon is a converted man ; and that makes all the difference.

Now, how was he converted? This becomes an important question, for on his early conversion hangs the whole of Mr. Spurgeon's future career. He is one of the elect, and in regard to so important a matter I much prefer that he should speak for himself. The event took place on December 15th, 1850, in the Primitive Methodist Chapel, Colchester, in Mr. Spurgeon's sixteenth year.

"It pleased God in my childhood to convince me of sin. At last the worst came to the worst. I was miserable; I could do scarcely anything. My heart was broken in pieces. Six months did I pray—prayed agonisingly with all my heart, and never had an answer. I resolved that in the town where I lived I would visit every place of worship in order to find out the way of salvation. I felt I was willing to do anything and be anything if God would only forgive me. I set off, determined to go round to all the chapels, and I went to all the places of worship, and though I dearly venerate the men that occupy those pulpits now, and did so then, I am bound to say that I never heard them once fully preach the gospel. I mean by that, they preached truth, great truths, many good truths that were fitting to many of their congregation, spiritually-minded people; but what I wanted to know was, How can I get my sins forgiven? And they never once told me that. I wanted to hear how a poor sinner under a sense of sin might find peace with God, and when I went I heard a sermon on 'Be not deceived; God is not mocked,' which cut me up worse, but did not say how I might escape. I went another day, and the text was something about the glories of the righteous; nothing for poor me. I was something like a dog under the table—not allowed to eat of the children's food. I went time after time, and I can honestly say that I don't know that I ever went without prayer to God, and I am sure there was not a more attentive hearer in all the place than myself, for I panted and longed to understand how I might be saved. At last one snowy day—it snowed so much I could not go to the place I had determined to go to, and I was obliged to stop on the road, and it was a blessed stop to me—I found rather an obscure street, and turned down a court, and there was a little chapel. I wanted to go somewhere, but I did not know this place. It was the Primitive Methodists' Chapel. I had heard of these people from many, and how they sang so loudly that they made people's heads ache; but that did not matter. I wanted to know how I might be saved, and if they made my head ache ever so much I did not care. So sitting down, the service went on, but no minister came. At last a very thin-looking man came into the pulpit, and opened his Bible and read these words: 'Look unto me and be saved, all the ends of the earth.' Just setting his eyes upon me as if he knew me all by heart, he said, 'Young man, you are in trouble.' Well, I was, sure enough. Says he, 'You will never get out of it unless you look to Christ.' And then, lifting up his hands, he cried out as only, I think, a Primitive Methodist could do, 'Look, look, look! It is only "look,"' said he. I saw at once the way of salvation. Oh, how I did leap for joy at that moment! I knew not what else he said. I did not take much notice of it, I was so possessed with that one thought. Like as when the brazen serpent was lifted up, they only looked and were healed. I had been waiting to do fifty things, but when I heard this word 'Look!' what a charming word it seemed to me. Oh, I looked until I could almost have looked my eyes away, and in heaven I will look on still in my joy unutterable."

Here, then is an authentic narrative of the election of Charles Haddon Spurgeon; and what could be more ingenuous? He was converted by the word "look," as the sinful old Scotchwoman was brought from nature to grace by the solemn emphasis with which Dr. Chalmers pronounced the word Mesopotamia. In a similarly unhappy frame of mind George Fox sought advice from a clergyman and was admonished to "drink beer and dance with the girls." There is in truth a great variety of cures for such spiritual maladies. Edward Spencer Beesly finds great joy in believing in Comtism, John Henry Newman in embracing Romanism, and Charles Haddon Spurgeon in flying to the iron rock of Calvinism. They are all converted from uncertainty to certainty. *O ter quaterque beati!* I would to Heaven I were as sure of anything as these men are of everything. Similar phenomena are common among Mohammedans and Buddhists.

The great mistake that is made by such religionists as Mr. Spurgeon is to suppose that there is no law of conversions as of other mental moods. A true grammar of spiritual assent has yet to be written, and when that has been fairly executed by some competent investigator of psychological phenomena like Professor Bain, for example, there will be nothing startling or abnormally significant in the experience of the pastor of the Metropolitan Tabernacle. The element of mystery will inevitably be eliminated, and evangelical conversions will come perchance to be classified as a sort of measles or small-pox of the intellect.

Charles Haddon Spurgeon was born at the village of Kelvedon, in Essex, in June 1834. Like so many other families who have left their mark on the religious life of England, the Spurgeons are the descendants of pious Continental refugees. Driven from the Netherlands by the persecutions of Alva, they settled in Essex and produced a line of pastors—each of them remarkable in his own way—which has remained almost without a break until now. Preaching has become quite a hereditary occupation or passion with the Spurgeons. In the phraseology of the sects, "They have never wanted a man to stand before the Lord in the service of the sanctuary."

Mr. Spurgeon's grandfather, James Spurgeon, was for over half a century pastor of the Independent Church at Stambourne, in Essex. "Like Luther," says his grandson, in an article in the *Sword and the Trowel*, "he had a vivid impression of the reality and personality of the great enemy, and was accustomed to make short work with his suggestions."

An extraordinary narrative follows, which I fear must be ranked with "contemptible superstitions." He had been converted under a particular tree in a wood, and the devil, appearing to him in a dream, threatened to tear him to pieces should he venture to repair to the hallowed spot by a particular path. Greatly daring, he went, and discovering, of course, no fiend at the tree, he exclaimed, "Ah, cowardly devil, you threatened to tear me in pieces, and now you do not dare to show your face." Instead, however, of finding Satan at the rendezvous, his eye lighted on what was much to be preferred—viz., a massive gold ring, for which, mysteriously enough, there was no claimant.

But the sequel to the story is the best. The old man continued annually to visit the spot for devotional exercises, till at last a wheat field occupied the site of the wood. He then knelt down among the wheat to pray, but had hardly commenced when he was sternly reminded that his sacred grove had not been cut down for nothing, and that he must seek the Lord elsewhere. "Maister," cried a harsh voice on the other side of an adjoining hedge, "thayre be a creazy man a-saying his prayers down in the wheat over thayre!"

John Spurgeon, the son of this venerable grove-worshipper, and father of the subject of this sketch, was the second of a family of ten. For many years he was engaged in business in Colchester, but, like so many of his family, he eventually drifted into the ministry, doing duty successively at Tollesbury; Cranbrook, Kent; Fetter Lane, Holborn; and at Islington.

When a mere child, his son, Charles Haddon Spurgeon, became an inmate of his grandfather's house at Stambourne, and at once came under the most pietistic influences. When ten years of age (see *Sword and Trowel*) a man of God, the Rev. Richard Knill, made him the subject of a prophecy, which, of course, came to pass.

"Calling the family together, he took me on his knee, and I distinctly remember his saying, 'I do not know how it is, but I feel a solemn presentiment that this child will preach the gospel to thousands, and God will bless him to many souls. So sure am I of this that when my little man preaches in Rowland Hill's Chapel, as he will do one day, I should like him to promise me that he will give out the hymn commencing—

> 'God moves in a mysterious way
> His wonders to perform.'"

This sort of half-insinuated miracle is of not infrequent occurrence in Mr. Spurgeon's writings, and it is by no means the most satisfactory feature. Whenever I stumble on such things I recall the story of the unsanctified Yankee politician, who said he did not so much object to twaddle as to the people who ignominiously believed in it. Twaddle, he admitted, might have its uses.

There were two taverns in this shrewd man's town of unequal repute; one of them was the head quarters of the anti-Masonic leaders—anti-Masonry was the "cry" of the hour—the other was the resort of the body of their followers. At the beginning of the legislative session our politician had taken up his quarters at the tavern frequented by the anti-Masonic rank and file. After a little while, however, he astonished the anti-Masonic leaders at the other tavern by presenting himself at their table. "What brings you here?" they asked; "we thought you had cut us to go to the other place." "So I did," he replied, "but I can't stand the nonsense of your d— anti-Masons down there!" "Well," they laughingly responded, "how have you bettered yourself here, for we are all anti-Masons too?" "True enough," said the clear-headed legislator; "but there is a great difference; those d— fools down yonder believe in it!"

It is this unfaltering "believing in it," nevertheless, that is at once the source of Mr. Spurgeon's weakness and of his strength. When Robespierre made his first appearance in the Assembly he was derided by all but Mirabeau, who, more discerning, observed, "That man will go far; he believes every word he says." So it is with Mr. Spurgeon. He has gone a long way, and will continue to go a long way, for he believes every word he says. So has it been with Newman, who firmly mooring his bark to the rock of Papal Infallibility, has become a Prince of the Roman Church. One only requires to shut one's eyes and walk by faith in order to achieve great things, yet there are disadvantages connected with this contemning of one's sight. I have, for example, been at pains to glance at most of the productions of Mr. Spurgeon's prolific pen, and I can find nothing that does not bear an utterly ephemeral impress. His mind, it is true, is thoroughly saturated with the ideas and the literature of the Hebrew race, the least scientific of all the great nations of antiquity, but I cannot discover that he is abreast of any other kind of knowledge. The sacred writings of other peoples are seemingly sealed books to him. Neither by the development hypothesis nor by the comparative historical method—the two great clarifiers of modern thinking—has Mr. Spurgeon apparently benefited in the least.

In a lecture on "The Study of Theology," delivered before the Young Men's Christian Association at Newington, he explained the manner in which he dealt with refractory texts. When books failed him he offered, he said, this prayer, "O Lord, teach me what this means," and he added, "it is marvellous how a hard, flinty text struck out sparks with the steel of prayer."

I admit the sparks, but I desiderate the light of a genuine scholarship; and though it would be most unjust to speak slightingly of Mr. Spurgeon's acquirements, I cannot but think that his influence for good would have been immensely more lasting had he acted on his father's sensible advice, and subjected himself to a sound collegiate training before becoming a teacher of other men.

The motive which determined him to reverse the sound maxim, *disce ut doceas*, was characteristic. "Still holding on to the idea of entering the collegiate institution, I thought of writing and making an immediate application; but this was not to be. That afternoon, having to preach at a village station, I walked slowly in a meditative frame of mind over Midsummer Common to the little wooden bridge which leads to Chesterton, and in the midst of the common I was startled by what seemed to me to be a loud voice, but which may have been a singular illusion. Whichever it was the impression it made on my mind was most vivid. I seemed very distinctly to hear the words, 'Seekest thou great things for thyself, seek them not!' This led me to look at my position from a different point of view, and to challenge my motives and intentions. . . . Had it not been for these words, I had not been where I am now," etc.

Either a loud voice or a singular illusion, but in any case good enough to prevent a lad of eighteen, already acting as a pastor at Waterbeach, from seeking to complete his legitimate studies! "Backed like a weasel, or very like a whale" —it is all the same. Well, one might think such things, but if I were Mr. Spurgeon I should not say them. However they may affect the unthinking mass, they cannot but make the judicious grieve. They are a direct incentive to ignorant spiritual self-sufficiency.

What is the consequence to Mr. Spurgeon himself? He began to preach when he was sixteen, and between his earliest and his latest discourses there is but little to choose, whether as regards matter or manner. From the first he was popular—a great preacher, but a very indifferent thinker—the prophet of incipient reflection, the high priest of emotional religion.

He had scarcely passed his nineteenth year when he was appointed pastor of his present metropolitan charge. His first London sermon, in December 1853, was addressed to 200 hearers; in three months' time he counted auditors by the thousand. Since then he has touched nothing which has not prospered, and his industry has been enormous. In 1859 was laid the first stone of the vast Metropolitan Tabernacle, which, completed in 1861 at a cost of £31,332, accommodates with ease an audience of 6000 persons.

In connection with the Metropolitan Tabernacle, and owing its origin to Mr. Spurgeon's persistency, is the Pastors' College, an institution maintained at great cost for the education of Baptist preachers; the Stockwell Orphanage, the Colportage Association, and a great variety of other benevolent institutions, large and small, which bear eloquent testimony to the enduring zeal of Mr. Spurgeon in promoting what he regards as the truest interests of humanity.

In addition to all these achievements, Mr. Spurgeon's publications of one kind or other have been innumerable. Of his sermons some twenty-two volumes have already been published, and single copies have been known to attain a circulation of 200,000.

Who shall say that the theological age of the world has yet been outlived? And it is not because Mr. Spurgeon preaches soothing doctrines to his flock that they are attracted by him. He is the mainstay of Calvinism in England. The elect few alone are to be saved; the rest go to eternal perdition. He will not hear of the smallest limitation to their torments. This diabolic dogma, worthy of the man who betrayed the noble Servetus to the stake—a man head and shoulders above Calvin, both as a theologian and as a man of science—is not worthy either of the head or heart of the pastor of the Metropolitan Tabernacle. Were it true the creature would then indeed be more just than the Creator, and all but the vilest reprobates would refuse to become "breeders of sinners." Virtuous men would everywhere conspire to bring the race to speedy extinction, so as to baulk the malevolent Demiurgus of his prey. The doctrine is rendered for ever incredible by its very enormity. I took some exception to the Religion of Humanity in the preceding article, but this may be called the Religion of Inhumanity, and it I totally repudiate. "A plague on both your houses!" more especially the latter. Burns was more humane, and peradventure not less Christian, when he wrote of the "arch enemy"—

> "But fare ye weel, Auld Nickie Ben,
>   Oh, wad ye tak' a thought and men',
> Ye aiblins might, I dinna ken,
>   Still ha'e a stake:
> I'm wae to think upon yon den,
>   E'en for your sake."

At the London School Board election of 1870, Mr. Spurgeon materially aided in cementing the compromise by which Scripture teaching has been retained in rate-supported schools. He forgot the admonition of Christ, "Render unto Cæsar the things that are Cæsar's, and to God the things that are God's." He called in the arm of the flesh to levy rates from Atheists and all manner of unbelievers for the support of what was delusively termed non-sectarian education. In but too many instances those who have most urgently demanded the disendowment of religion in the Church have rushed with the greatest haste to endow it in the schools. They have abolished Church formularies and made every teacher a formulary unto himself or herself. Instead of one creed being taught, we have at present twenty or more in full swing, for I defy Mr. Spurgeon or any other to impart non-sectarian Biblical instruction. The thing is impossible.

Mr. Spurgeon's recent discourse on the Present Crisis was what may be described as a model political sermon. "'But,' saith one, 'we hope we shall have national prayer.' I hope so too; but will there be a national confession of sin? If not, how can mere prayer avail? Will there be a general desire to do that which is just and right between man and man? Will there be a declaration of England's policy never to trample on the weak, or pick a quarrel for our own aggrandisement? Will there be a loathing of the principle that British interests are to be our guiding star instead of justice and right? Personal interests are no excuse for doing wrong; if they were so we should have to exonerate the worst of thieves, for they will not invade a house until their personal interests invite them. Perhaps the midnight robber may yet learn to plead that he only committed a burglary for fear another thief should take the spoil and make worse use of it than he. When our interests are our policy, nobility is dead and true honour is departed.

"Will the nation repent of any one of its sins? If stern

reformation went with supplication, I am persuaded that prayer would prevail; but while sin is gloried in my hopes find little ground to rest upon. It may be that my text will be the sole answer of the Lord: 'I will go and return to my place till they acknowledge their offence and seek my face; in their affliction they will seek me early.'"

VI.
JAMES BEAL.

> "We cannot bring Utopia by force,
> But better, almost, be at work in sin
> Than in a brute inaction browse and sleep."

THERE is not in England's vast Metropolis, or peradventure in all England, a Radical who during the last thirty years has more consistently acted on this principle than Mr. James Beal, of 20 Regent Street, auctioneer and land agent. His name may be comparatively unfamiliar to some of my readers, but it ought not so to be.

He is the typical Radical citizen of London—a *bourgeois* untainted by any of the political failings of the English middle class. These consist of indifference to the claims of intellectual superiority on the one hand, and to the demands of suffering humanity on the other. The British shopkeeper is not without his virtues, but he is neither the friend of thinkers nor of the proletariate. In both these respects Mr. Beal has risen conspicuously above the class to which he belongs, while assiduously and intelligently striving to promote its legitimate interests. For more than a quarter of a century this busy, bustling auctioneer has contrived to devote some portion of his day—often the best portion of it—to the furtherance of this scheme or that of municipal or national reform. Without fee or reward, in evil and in good report, he has gone steadily forward, studying, writing, lecturing, organising on behalf of some good cause or other—

> "One of much outside bluster; for all that,
> Most honest, brave, and skilful."

Mr. Beal has made the public interest his interest to an extent that has not been excelled by any private citizen of the day. His achievements bear eloquent testimony to the good which it is possible for individual Radicals to effect who may never even aspire to a seat in the House.

The self-forgetfulness which enables such public-spirited citizens as Beal to feel greater pleasure in returning to Parliament political thinkers of the eminence of Mill and Morley than in being themselves returned is one of the most hopeful signs of English public life. It points to the ultimate conquest of Philistia by the forces of humanity and right reason, and in that sacred warfare Mr. Beal has earned for himself imperishable distinction. In Phlisitia he is not of it. On the contrary, he has assailed the Philistines in their chief strongholds of vestry, guild, and corporation with a vigour which has caused them to tremble behind their entrenchments. But I must not anticipate.

Mr. Beal's public work, like his private business, has been of a strictly practical character, and will be best treated in brief chronological sequence. Whatsoever his hand has found to do he has done it with his might. There are many good men willing to discharge public duties at the solicitation of others. But Mr. Beal is not one of these. It has been his function to invent duties for himself and others, as the sequel will show:—

> "No man is born into the world whose work
> Is not born with him; there is always work,
> And tools to work withal for those who will;
> And he who waits to have his task marked out
> Shall die and leave his errand unfulfilled."

James Beal was born in Chelsea (Sloane Square), in February 1829. His father was a respectable old Tory tradesman, who had originally come from Yorkshire. He died before Beal had completed his seventeenth year, living long enough, however, to satisfy the subject of this memoir that he and his male parent possessed few or no sympathies in common. It was different with Beal's mother. She was a woman as remarkable for vigour of mind as of body, and from her her son inherited most of his mental and physical characteristics. Without brothers, and without access to his father's sympathies, Beal naturally enough "took after" his strong-minded mother, whose memory he still reverently cherishes.

There was no London School Board in those times, and young Beal's education was accordingly of a somewhat meagre kind. He attended several local schools, kept by private teachers, but never got beyond the "beggarly elements" of the three R's. He was eventually put to business in his fourteenth year, the consequence being that Mr. Beal is substantially a self-taught man. No one who has gone through the regular scholastic mill could doubt this for one moment. The matter of his writings is always excellent, but the manner is generally very rugged. His arrows have terrible barbs, but no feathers. They do not kill at long range, but they are very formidable in a hand-to-hand encounter. As a journalist, the directness, not to say the fury, of his method of attack, so different from that of the professional scribe, arrests and is bound to arrest attention by its very novelty, if for no better reason.

Mr. Beal's business training was in every way more fortunate than his educational. He commenced as clerk in a solicitor's office, and before he had completed his sixteenth year he had mastered Blackstone and acquired a general knowledge of legal forms and principles, which could not fail to be of the greatest use to him as a man of business in after life.

About this time he had fortunately few companions except his books, and these he read with avidity, storing up much valuable information, which he shortly found most serviceable. One of his few friends happily possessed a large and well-selected library, and Beal having the run of it, did not neglect the opportunity to make up for the shortcomings of his school training.

Subsequently Mr. Beal entered the office of an upholsterer,

but before he was twenty-one he found himself a partner in the extensive auctioneer and land-agency business of which he has now for many years been the principal. This Radical of the Radicals has bought and sold more real estate, let and hired more aristocratic mansions, than perhaps any land agent in England. Such a fact, so antecedently improbable, speaks volumes for the integrity and capacity of the man.

In 1848 Mr. Beal began to apply his mind to politics " in earnest "—that is to say, he became a confirmed and immovable Radical. He had previously induced his father, much to the old man's subsequent astonishment, to record his vote for Cochrane, then Radical candidate for Middlesex—a thoroughly characteristic act; for Beal, with all his fiery zeal, has a wonderful knack of converting foes into friends, if only an opportunity of exerting his personal influence is afforded him. His own mind is so thoroughly made up that he will speedily make up yours if you are not on your guard. He became a member of the "Discussion Classes" which then met at the National Hall, Holborn, and there he made the acquaintance of such well-known apostles of Radicalism as Hetherington, Lovett, Watson, and Place.

The first reform with which his name is associated was the abolition of the penny stamp on newspapers. Brougham had succeeded, in 1834, in effecting a reduction of the obnoxious impost from fourpence to a penny, and Hetherington, Place, Beal, and others, in 1848, formed a committee for its total removal. In furtherance of the movement, Beal, in 1849, published an excellent pamphlet, entitled "A Few Words in Favour of the Liberty of the Press and the Abolition of the Penny Stamp on Newspapers." The committee was ultimately merged in an association for the repeal of both the advertisement duty and the paper duty, objects which were eventually attained.

In 1850, Mr. Beal contributed to the *Freeholder* a valuable series of letters on the land question. They were reprinted in 1855, and a second edition, entitled "Free Trade in Land," appeared in 1876. Both as regards theory and practice the author shows himself a thorough master of his subject. He has read and he has observed, and both reading and observation have convinced him that our whole system of land tenure is simply barbarous.

From 1851 to 1855 he was actively engaged in establishing freehold land societies throughout England and Scotland. Many suburban estates were bought and subdivided among the shareholders as sites for cottages, one out of many advantages of the arrangement being that thousands of artisans, then without the franchise, were thus enabled by a flank movement to obtain it.

About the same time Mr. Beal came prominently forward in the character of an ecclesiastical reformer, addressing a series of trenchant letters to the Bishop of London on certain Popish practices observed in the Church of St. Paul, Wilton Place, and of St. Barnabas, Pimlico. A memorable action, "*Westerton and Beal* v. *Liddel*," ensued. The legality of Ritualism had never been legally challenged since the Reformation. Mr. Beal appeared in person before the Privy Council, and obtained a favourable judgment, but without costs, which were cheerfully defrayed by public subscription. The agitation resulted in the Public Worship Act, and the end is not yet.

In 1857, Mr. Beal entered on a long and arduous struggle with the gas companies of the Metropolis. These companies had "districted" London among themselves, and ruled the consumers with a rod of iron. Mr. Beal contrived to effect a combination of vestries against the companies—on the principle, I suppose, of setting a thief to catch a thief—and after a contest which lasted all through '57, '58, '59, and '60, the Metropolitan Gas Act was passed, which improved the quality of the gas supply, limited its price, curtailed dividends, and effected a net saving to the consumers of £625,000 per annum,—a sum equivalent to the entire School Board rate.

Not satisfied, however, Mr. Beal in 1868 had another bill for the further amendment of the Metropolitan gas supply introduced into Parliament. Its history was peculiar. The Metropolitan Board of Works opposed it, and the Corporation of the City of London appropriated it, the Metropolitan Board, subsequently reporting, with the consistency which distinguishes it, that the Act had immensely benefited the City!

In 1873 yet another gas bill was introduced, with the approval of the Board of Trade. Its object was to amalgamate the various companies, with a view to facilitate the eventual purchase of their united undertakings by the yet unborn municipality of the Metropolis. The result was so far satisfactory. All the companies north of the Thames were unified, while those south of it were reduced to four in number.

In 1870, Mr. Beal induced the Government to give notice of its intention to improve the water supply of London. Unfortunately the good intention, like so many others, went to pave the unmentionable region spoken of by Dr. Johnson; but the subject has not been allowed to drop. It has been demonstrated at influential public meetings recently held that the present Metropolitan water supply is unsatisfactory as regards purity, cost, and the poundage principle of assessment. Put the water supply under representative instead of company control, and it is calculated that £150,000 per annum can readily be saved to the ratepayers. Next session Mr. Cross stands pledged to deal with the question, and it can hardly be that he should deviate far from the lines drawn by Mr. Beal, who first set the stone rolling.

In 1876, Mr. Beal broke new and most important ground. Fearing least an increased education rate should render the cause of scholastic enlightenment unpopular, he set himself to investigate other possible sources of revenue, and an altogether remarkable series of papers on "The Corporation Guilds and Charities of the City of London," contributed to the *Dispatch*, and signed "Nemesis," was the result. The revelations were simply astounding. The Corporation, with a revenue of £600,000 per annum derived from the "common good," the Liveries with more than £1,000,000 issuing out of trust funds, and the City Charities with a good £100,000 annual income, were shown to be one vast network of corruption and malversation. *Ab uno disce omnia.*

In 1513, the Mercers held 160 acres of trust land, located chiefly in Marylebone and Westminster (Bradbury's trust). They now retain eight and a half acres, and no man can or will tell what they have done with the rest of the estate. The eight and a half acres yield a rental of £27.575, and the trustees make a return to the Charity Commissioners of a fixed "annual payment of £1, 10s. per annum to St. Stephen, Coleman Street." Having done this, they feel they have discharged their duty towards the "pious founder" and the public, and pocket the little balance for the trouble they have taken. In New York, certain malefactors connected with Tammany Hall, who in a similar manner sought to convert public trusts to private uses, speedily found their way to the Tombs amid a hurricane of popular execration. If they had been in "famous London town" they would have been central figures at the Lord Mayor's Show, clothed, not in sackcloth and ashes, but in purple and fine linen, the observed of all observers.

Mr. Beal holds, and I heartily agree with him, that these nefarious city jobbers must be compelled to disgorge at least half their revenues for Metropolitan education, or justice will remain a laughing-stock. Mr. Beal, almost single-handed, has carried dismay into their camp. The Grocers' Company has given £25,000 to the London Hospital, and the guilds are organising a technical college to cost £20,000 per annum. But these are not tokens of genuine repentance. They are mere dissembling peace-offerings to be set aside by the public with contempt.

The existence of so many anomalies and gigantic abuses convinced Mr. Beal, as early as 1861, that what is really wanted is a single municipality for the whole of London. In that year a Committee of the House, before which Mr. Beal was examined, considered the whole subject, and ever since his views have been rapidly winning public approval. Mill, Buxton, Elcho, and Shuttleworth have each unsuccessfully brought in bills embodying Beal's ideas. Latterly Mr. Gladstone has promised his powerful support, and placed the reform of the municipality of London at the head of his long list of " unredeemed pledges." Eventual triumph is accordingly as good as certain. When it comes it will be the cleansing out of the biggest Augean stable in Christendom.

Mr. Beal, as is well known, was the moving spirit in the generous electioneering effort which in 1865 resulted in the return of the late John Stuart Mill for Westminster free of expense, and it was owing to his enlightened action that the first London School Board had among its members such distinguished men as Lawrence, Huxley, and Morley. And, unwearied in well-doing, he is again at his post. What he did for Mill he is resolute to do for the greatest of his disciples, John Morley, and for Sir Arthur Hobhouse. Voluntary subscriptions have poured in so generously for the impending contest that there has already been banked a sum almost sufficient to fight the battle of intellect and worth against vulgar wealth and bastard Imperialism. May the fickle divinity that controls elections second his praiseworthy efforts!

Mr. Cross's vaunted Artisans' Dwellings Act Mr. Beal would have rendered workable, if the right hon. gentleman had only had the good sense to profit by his advice. His plan was not to enforce sales to the local authority, but to compel the owners of dilapidated tenements themselves to incur all risks in connection with the pulling down and re-erection of condemned buildings owned by them. As it is, the Metropolitan Board is at a standstill, having lost £800,000 of the ratepayers' money in the vain attempt to sell the sites of "rookeries" for as much as they cost. Verily, wisdom is justified of her children.

In conclusion, it may be said that in no progressive movement, national or municipal, since 1848 has Beal failed to play a manly and singularly disinterested part. In 1851, when Joseph Hume and Sir Joshua Walmsley endeavoured to revive public interest in parliamentary reform, Beal "stumped" London for them, and materially helped to convince Earl Russell of the inexpediency of adhering to his "finality" policy. He had his reward in the legislation of 1867.

In 1857 appeared "Beal's History of the London Joint-Stock Banks," contributed originally to the *Bankers' Circular* —an interesting and useful production. In 1859 he published a trenchant exposure of the confessional in the Church of England.

In 1866 was founded by him the Metropolitan Municipal Association, and subsequently the Guilds Reform Association, both of which bodies have rendered excellent service in preparing London opinion for necessary changes in local government.

Nor have Mr. Beal's sympathies been confined to London or England exclusively. He was a determined partisan of the North during the American civil war, and at a public meeting held in London in the interest of the Confederates he tore down the "Palmetto flag" from the wall, and trampled it under foot at the risk of serious personal violence.

When Garibaldi was wounded at Aspromonte he raised a fund of £1000 to send out Professor Partridge to give the noble general the benefit of first-rate surgical skill.

Indeed, as I have said, it is impossible to mention almost any good pie for thirty years past in which this indefatigable friend of humanity has not had a finger. One stands simply amazed at the multitude of his good deeds, which have no smack of self-consciousness. It would be impossible to imagine a reformer with less cant or nonsense about him than Beal. He has no "unction" of any kind—a hearty, sharp, decisive man, ordained to be a Radical and pioneer of progress from the foundations of the world. "Wha does his best," said Burns, "will whiles do mair." James Beal, methinks, has oft done mair.

VII.

MONCURE DANIEL CONWAY.

> "His hearers can't tell you on Sunday beforehand
> If in that day's discourse they'll be Bibled or Koraned,
> For he's seized the idea (by his martyrdom fired)
> That all men (not orthodox) *may be* inspired."

MR. CONWAY'S inspiration may be questioned, but none will gainsay his total heterodoxy. If he is not a prophet it is not his fault—he is the least orthodox preacher in London. "His faith has centre everywhere, nor cares to fix itself to form."

The congregation of South Place Chapel, Finsbury, are Nonconformists who non-conform very much. Their Bible is called "The Sacred Anthology"—a book of ethnical Scriptures, collected and edited by Mr. Conway. The purpose of the work is simply moral. "He has aimed," he says in the preface, "to separate the more universal and enduring treasures contained in ancient Scriptures from the rust of superstition and the ore of ritual," and he has succeeded in his aim. To good Rationalists "The Sacred Anthology" ought to be what "The Garden of the Soul" is to good Romanists. "The utterance does not wholly perish which many peoples utter; nay, this is the voice of God."

At South Place, the condemnation of the Pharisees who for a pretence make long prayers is not incurred. No prayers are offered up. There has been substituted what is called "meditations" or moral soliloquies, and the finest music. The whole atmosphere of the chapel is "advanced" to such a degree that Unitarians of the older school when they occasionally enter it are almost as puzzled as orthodox Trinitarians what to make of it. The average intellectual level of the congregation is, I should imagine, the highest in London. Men and women who could not be induced to listen to any other preacher go readily to hear Mr. Conway. Nowhere will you find a finer collection of human heads. And yet Mr. Conway is not an orator in any sense of the word.

His predecessor, the celebrated W. J. Fox, " Publicola " of the *Dispatch*, and M.P. for Oldham, was a different man. He combined all the qualities of a popular, if heretic, preacher. It is what Mr. Conway says, and not how he says it, that attracts. He is hardly even a scholar in the strictly technical sense of the term, and in matters of detail he is occasionally inaccurate. But he is an original and fearless thinker, a born instructor of other men in whatever is true, beautiful, and good, with an ear delicately attuned to catch the faintest accents of the " still small voice " of conscience. What he hears in the closet he has the courage to proclaim from the housetop. His discourses consequently bear an oracular impress. They have, moreover, an aroma of mysticism, faint but sweet—a breath of New England transcendentalism, peculiarly grateful to unaccustomed Cockney nostrils.

It were curious to speculate what would happen if, say, Spurgeon and Conway were to exchange pulpits for a month or so. Both churches, I imagine, would be completely emptied. To the Eclectics of South Place Mr. Spurgeon's doctrines would be mere foolishness, while to the Calvinists of the Tabernacle Mr. Conway would be worse than a stumbling-block; he would be Antichrist. Yet there is a golden bridge over this terrible chasm of conflicting beliefs. Mr. Conway and Mr. Spurgeon have a common object for which they toil—viz., the moral elevation of mankind. Where this essence of all true religions is present, the form is of secondary consequence. Creed or no creed, for the good the path of duty is the same.

> "The soul is still oracular; amid the market's din
> List the ominous stern whisper from the Delphic cave within—
> 'They enslave their children's children who make compromise
>   with sin.'"

Moncure Daniel Conway, it need scarcely be recorded, is by birth an American. He was born in 1832, near Fredericksburg, Stafford County, Virginia, where his father, Walker Peyton Conway, a gentleman of independent fortune, enjoyed universal esteem. The elder Conway was both a county magistrate and a member of the State Legislature. The stock had come originally from Wales, and in the course of a century or more had multiplied rapidly in Stafford County. Intermarriage with other "leading families" of Moncures and Daniels had been very frequent. The Moncures were of Scottish Jacobite extraction, while the Daniels were English. The father of young Conway's mother was John Moncure Daniel, a graduate in medicine of Edinburgh University, and Surgeon-General of the United States army. Among her ancestors was likewise Stone, the first colonial governor of Maryland, while her grandfather, Thomas Stone, enjoyed the proud distinction of being one of the signatories of the famous Declaration of Independence. These were matters of some moment in a State where slavery was an institution and "mean whites" were treated with contempt.

Supported by troops of affluent friends and kinsmen, Conway's path in life seemed at its commencement nowise steep or arduous. As a politician he might hope to climb the ladder of power and dignity in the Republic easily and rapidly.

But the lion of slavery crouched in the way. His father was, unfortunately, a large slave-owner—a humane man, it is true, but still, like his neighbours, an owner of scores of human chattels. "Few," says Mr. Conway in his "Testimonies concerning Slavery," "are the really peaceful days that I remember having smiled on in my old Virginian home; the outbreaks of the negroes among themselves, the disobediences which the necessary discipline can never suffer to be overlooked, the terrors of devoted parents at the opportunities for the display of evil tempers and the inception of nameless vices among their sons, I remember as the demons haunting those days. I have often heard my parents say that the care of slaves had made them prematurely old."

Conway's early education was the best that the neighbourhood afforded. As a child he attended several private schools, and subsequently he became a pupil of the Classical and Mathematical Academy in Fredericksburg. Here he made rapid progress, and in due course was entered as an undergraduate of Dickinson College, Pennsylvania, where he graduated in 1849.

The students were mostly from Maryland and Virginia, with strong pro-slavery sympathies, and young Conway returned to his Virginian home in his eighteenth year as full of anti-Northern prejudices as the rest. He commenced the study of law at Warrenton, and while thus engaged fell under the influence of a remarkable man, his cousin John M. Daniel, the formidable duellist editor of the notorious *Richmond Examiner*. Daniel was the best educated man in Richmond, a profound student of Spinoza, Hegel, Kant, Fichte, Feuerbach, Fourier, Cousin, Voltaire. His range of vision far exceeded that of any man Conway had known, and it is scarcely to be wondered at that Daniel made a strong impression on his youthful kinsman's mind. He professed to rest slavery on a quasi-scientific basis of racial inferiority. " We hold," he declared in his journal, to which Conway became a contributor, "that negroes are not *men* in the sense in which that term is used by the Declaration of Independence. Were the slaves men, we should be unable to disagree with Wendell Phillips."

Thus fortified in his pro-slavery ideas, Conway's next step was to become the secretary of a Southern Rights, otherwise a Secessionist Club, whose sole *raison d'être* was to break up the Union in the interest of the " peculiar institution " of the South on the first available opportunity. So much for the pernicious teaching of his misanthropic cousin. But happily other considerations began to weigh with Conway. If circumstances had leagued him with the oppressor, kind Nature had made him at heart an irrepressible Radical.

In 1850, before the completion of his eighteenth year, appeared his first pamphlet, entitled "Free Schools in Virginia," which was distributed among the people and laid on the desk of every member of the State Convention, which met that year for the revision of the Virginian Code. I have read this plea for *free schools* to educate the "mean whites," and can only wonder that a lad of eighteen should have had the ability or patience to produce so masterly an appeal.

The effect was, nevertheless, most disappointing. He was virulently attacked by the journals as one who, by advocating a "mob road to learning," was jeopardising the very existence of Southern society. The mean whites, like the servile blacks, must be kept in ignorance. It is not, however, so long since representatives of our own "agricultural interest" were in the habit of giving expression to views equally enlightened.

But Mr. Conway was not thus to be put down. Reason, conscience, compassion told him that the cause he had espoused was just and beneficent. He had not taken it up as he had taken slavery, on trust. He had thought out the problem for himself, and he remained unshaken in his convictions. Whether he knew it or not, he had taken a distinct step away from the slave-holding oligarchy in the direction of freedom. In order to promote his laudable object he threw up the law and took to the gospel. He became a Methodist preacher, as the likeliest means of reaching the hearts and heads of the poor whites whom he desired to benefit. The Baltimore Methodist Conference speedily appointed him to the charge of some twelve congregations. One of these happily lay in a section of country settled by Quakers, and consequently unpolluted by any taint of slavery. He saw prosperous agriculturists and happy, free, educated negro labourers, and the scales began to fall from his eyes. He had never dreamed of such a state of society. At first he was bewildered, but an aged Quaker, whose acquaintance he had made, eventually enabled him to turn a steady, admiring gaze on the rising sun of Negro Emancipation :—

> "Up, up! and the dusky race,
> That sat in darkness long,
> Be swift his feet as antelope's,
> And as behemoth strong."

"Again," says Mr. Conway, "I visited the old Quaker patriarch, and told him with what delight I had found that the interior of Sandy Spring was even more attractive than its exterior.

"'Now, friend, can thee account for this evident superiority of the Friends' neighbourhood over the rest of this county, or of thy own State?'

"'Well,' I ventured, 'doubtless you have certain habits of thrift and industry which others have not.'

"'Perhaps it is so,' said the old man gravely; after which followed a long silence, which I felt belonged to him and was for him to break. Then he turned his eyes—at once luminous and keen—full upon me, and said,—

"'But there is *one* habit of our people to which thee will find, should thee search into it, is to be traced all the improved condition of our lands and our homes, that *is the habit of taking care that our labourers get just wages for their work. No slave has touched any sod in any field of Sandy Spring.*'"

These simple words converted the reluctant secretary of the Southern Rights Club into an uncompromising Abolitionist. Henceforth his duty with respect to the great social problem of his time and country was clear to him.

The change in his religious conceptions was no less striking. About the time of the Moody and Sankey revivals Mr. Conway gave an account of his own conversion almost unparalleled in its candour.

"It was my destiny to be born in a region where this kind of excitement is almost chronic. . . . When the summer came the leading Methodist families—of which my father's was one—went to dwell in the woods in tents.

About two weeks were there spent in praying and preaching all the day long—pausing only for meals—and during all that time the enclosure in front of the pulpit was covered over with screaming men and women and frightened children. . . . While I was there women came and wept over me; preachers quoted Scripture to me. No one whispered to me that I should resolve to be better, more upright, true, and kind. Hundreds were converted by my side, and broke out into wild shouts of joy. But I had no new experience whatever. I was not in the least a sceptic. I believed every word told me. Yet nothing took place at all. On a certain evening I swooned. When I came to myself I was stretched out on the floor with friends singing around me, and the preachers informed me that I had been the subject of the most admirable work of divine grace they had ever witnessed. I took their word for it. All I knew was that I was thoroughly exhausted and was ill for a week."

But he did not take their word for it for an unreasonable time. In 1852 his religious as well as his social ideas underwent modifications so important that he determined to betake himself to Harvard University, where the dominant theology is Unitarian. Here he graduated B.D. in 1854, having in the interval contracted lasting friendships with Emerson, Parker, Sumner, Phillips, and others, the best hearts and heads in the Republic.

After completing his studies he returned with fond hopes to his home in Virginia. But it was only to find that as an Abolitionist his own flesh and blood regarded him as a leper.

At last a company of young men confronted him in the street and warned him that he must henceforth regard himself as a perpetual exile from Virginia, kindly adding that he had been spared tar and feathers solely on his parents' account. Thereupon he again turned his steps towards the free North, and in 1854 he was appointed minister of the Unitarian church in Washington, but did not long find rest for the sole of his foot. An anti-slavery sermon which he preached in denunciation of the dastardly outrage on Senator Sumner by Preston Brooks led to his dismissal by the most liberal and anti-slavery congregation in Washington.

In 1856 he was invited by the Unitarians of Cincinnati to become their pastor, and there some of his most useful and brilliant discourses were delivered. But his mind was absorbed in the impending conflict with the slave power, and he ultimately became an Abolitionist lecturerer in Ohio and the Middle States. And his pen was as busy in the work of emancipation as his tongue.

In 1858 were published "Tracts for To-day;" in 1861 came "The Rejected Stone;" in 1862 "The Golden Hour." All these were powerful weapons put into the hands of the Abolitionists, "The Rejected Stone" in particular making a deep impression on the mind of the Martyr-President Abraham Lincoln.

Subsequently he became the first editor of the *Boston Commonwealth*, a high-class weekly, primarily started as an Abolition organ.

Meanwhile, his father and his two brothers threw in their lot with the Secessionists, the young men both receiving wounds in the fratricidal struggle.

At last, when the tramp of the Federal soldiers was heard in the streets of the little town whence Conway had been driven in 1854, he hastened to the spot to assist the slaves of his father's household to escape to the free North-west. By dint of great exertions he found the fugitives. The old woman who had nursed him sprang forward and folded him in her arms as if he were still a child. "Far into the night we sat together, and they listened with glistening eyes as I told them of the region to which I meant to take them, where never should they

'Feel oppression,
Never hear of war again.'

At Baltimore Railway Station all was nearly lost. A threatening mob beset the station, and the ticket agent peremptorily intimated, 'I cannot let these negroes go on this road at any price.' I simply presented my military order to this very disagreeable and handsome agent, and he began to read it. He had read but two or three words of it when he looked up with astonishment and said,—

"'The papers says these are your father's slaves.'

"'They are,' I replied.

"'Why, sir, you could sell them in Baltimore for fifty thousand dollars!'

"'Possibly,' I replied, whereupon (moved probably by supposing that I was making a greater sacrifice than was the case) the young man's face was unsheathed!

"'By God! you shall have every car on this road if you want it, and take the negroes where you please!'

"Then, having sold me the tickets, he gave his ticket-selling to a subordinate and went out to secure us a car to ourselves, and from that moment, though the imprecations around us went on, our way was made smooth."

In 1863, Mr. Conway was commissioned by the friends of Abolition to come to England to try to influence English as he had American opinion in favour of the Federal cause, and in this good work he was engaged when the Confederacy collapsed.

At that juncture South Place Chapel was in need of a pastor, and who so able to discharge the duties as this trans-atlantic Iconoclast and Idealist, who brought with him to the Old World the best manhood of the New?

In 1875 he revisited the West on a lecturing tour, and was received by his long-estranged family and by his countrymen generally with open arms. He was offered the pastorate of Theodore Parker's old church in Boston, but preferred to return to England, where the battle with theological obscurantism and political oligarchy is more arduous. England has sent so many of her good and brave men to America, that it is but right that the latter should begin to return the compliment.

Mr. Conway, needless to say, remains a staunch Republican. Like all intelligent American citizens whom I have known, the more he has studied our political institutions, the less he has been captivated by them. His little work, "Republican Superstitions," is the best commentary on the working of "our glorious constitution" that I know. Therein he shows, with incontrovertible logic, and complete mastery of details, that it is precisely the monarchical elements thoughtlessly or superstitiously imported into the constitution of the United States by its framers that have worked all the mischief in the Republic.

He would have but one Chamber, returned by equal constituencies, with a Chief Magistrate and Executive directly eligible by and responsible to the Legislature. A second Chamber, if it is opposed to the popular House, is noxious; if it is in harmony with it, it is superfluous.

Mr. Conway has learned by the sad experience of his own beloved Republic how disastrous a thing is the doctrine of State Rights or Home Rule. Let this Radical of Radicals speak a word in season to those undiscerning ones in England who in this matter seem in haste to confound purblind reaction with action, retrogression with progression.

"Could there be a more cruel concession made by England to Ireland than that very Home Rule for which so earnest a demand is now made? Whether England should concede complete independence to Ireland may be a question; but to raise up in Ireland ambitions that at some point must be checked, to give embodiment to aspirations and interests which no sooner reach their development than they will be certainly crushed, were the gift of weak indulgence, and by no means that of true generosity. For every concession the Northern people made to 'State Sovereignty' in the South, several thousand Southerners had to be slain in the end."

VIII.

CHARLES BRADLAUGH.

———◆———

" There is heresy here, you perceive, for the right
Of privately judging means simply that light
Has been granted to *me* for deciding on *you;*
And in happier times, before Atheism grew,
The deed contained clauses for cooking you too."

I HAVE been warned by kind friends who have been pleased to commend several of the foregoing sketches much beyond their deserts—friends whose good opinion I highly value—that whatever I do I must on no account allow " Bradlaugh " to appear in this series. To very many " Iconoclast " is still *monstrum horrendum cui lumen ademptum.* But my reply has invariably been, How are you to keep him out? The man is altogether too big to be passed over if one is not to lose sight of everything savouring of reasonable proportion. Besides, though due regard must be had to the " single life," it is of yet greater importance to consider the " type," and a more marked type of Radicalism than that which is incarnated in Mr. Charles Bradlaugh does not exist. He is the grim captain of that section of English Radicals, far more powerful than is generally supposed, who boldly inscribe on their banner the watchwords, Atheism, Malthusianism, Republicanism. These formidable isms, which philosophers have excogitated in the closet or whispered in the salon, Mr. Bradlaugh has with stentorian voice proclaimed from the housetop. It is not that his opinions differ so much from those entertained by many most re-

spectable and intelligent members of "society." His offence
consists in having conveyed the news to the "man in the
street." He has insisted on popularising doctrines which
"vested interests" desire to see imparted only to a select
body of initiated.

In all such matters, however, there are really but two
questions to be asked. Has the propagandist acted in good
faith? Has he been true to his own convictions? Now,
Mr. Bradlaugh is a very big man, as well in mind as in body,
and large objects ought never to be inspected with a micro-
scope. He has been the hero of a hundred fights, and it may
well be that he has not on all occasions conducted himself
with the perfect chivalry of a knight of romance. Still,
taking him all in all, and having due consideration for the
many hardships and temptations of a career such as his, I
cannot doubt that he has been valiant, singularly valiant,
for the truth as he has known it, and that he will be justly
regarded by posterity as one of the most remarkable figures
of his time and country.

His anti-religious ideas are in the main repugnant to me,
as I dare say they are to many of my readers; but let us
not judge Mr. Bradlaugh or any other public-spirited citizen
by our particular standard of spiritual rectitude. "Those
who have not the law are a law unto themselves, their conscience accusing or excusing one another." To his own
Master, to the light which lighteth every man who cometh
into this world, Mr. Bradlaugh must stand or fall. Judge
not that ye be not judged. Rather let us say, as did Oliver
Cromwell in a somewhat similar case, "Sir, the State, in
choosing men to serve it, takes no notice of their opinions;
if they be willing faithfully to serve it, that satisfies. I
advised you formerly to bear with men of different minds
from yourself. . . . . Take heed of being too sharp or
too easily sharpened by others against those to whom you
can object little, but that they square not with you in every
opinion concerning matters of religion."

It is a work of some difficulty to summarise the chequered

career of Mr. Bradlaugh. He himself has attempted it with indifferent success in a brief "Autobiography," clear enough so far as the narrative of events is concerned, but lacking somewhat in human interest.

He was born at Hoxton, in 1833. His father was a struggling, indefatigable solicitor's clerk, who could but ill afford to give his son Charles the scanty education which he actually received. At seven years of age he attended a National School in Abbey Street, Bethnal Green. Subsequently he was sent to a small private school in the same quarter, and in his eleventh year he completed his meagre educational curriculum at a boys' school in Hackney Road, having acquired little beyond a knowledge of the three R's. He is, consequently, for the most part a self-taught man, but he has taught himself to some purpose. His mind is in a splendid state of discipline. You can account for the fact when you see his library, which is as extensive as it is curious, the well-worn accumulations of a life devoted to stormy controversy abroad and intense study at home. I never remember to have seen such a serviceable collection of argumentative shot and shell as on Mr. Bradlaugh's shelves.

Mr. Bradlaugh was first employed as errand boy to the firm which his father served. In his fourteenth year he was equal to the more important duty of acting as wharf clerk and cashier to a firm of coal merchants in Britannia Fields, City Road. While so engaged the serious troubles of his life began.

In his sixteenth year he was a model young Christian, an enthusiastic Sunday-school teacher; altogether a promising neophyte of the Church as by law established. But he had not, like Mr. Spurgeon, attained to that chronic state of conversion, that sublime superiority to reason, which should enable him to dote with unutterable joy on such empty words as "Look, look, look!"

The Bishop of London was announced to hold a confirmation in Bethnal Green, and the incumbent of St. Peter's,

Hackney Road, in an evil hour, requested his youthful Sunday-school teacher to be prepared with suitable answers to any questions that might be put by the Right Reverend Father in God affecting the Thirty-Nine Articles and cognate matters. Like an obedient son of the Church, young Bradlaugh complied, and began to compare the Articles with the Gospels, but finding, as well he might, that they differed, he wrote a respectful note to his clergyman, asking to be piloted through one or two of his difficulties.

The ill-advised incumbent replied by informing the lad's parents that their son had turned Atheist, and that he had been suspended from his functions as a Sunday-school teacher for a period of three months. It is not given to the clerical profession, as a rule, to know much about human nature, but this was an exceptional blunder. I do not know that Mr. Bradlaugh is constitutionally a doubter—indeed, I think not—but he is a born fighter, a dialectical athlete revelling in the *gaudium certaminis* as a strong man rejoices to run a race.

The young tiger had tasted blood. He refused to attend church during the interval of his suspension as a teacher, and soon began to spend his Sundays elsewhere and otherwise. The time—1849—was one of great religious and political ferment, and Bonner's Fields, near where the Consumption Hospital now stands, was the habitual resort of disputants of all kinds. Thither Bradlaugh repaired to mingle with youthful ardour in the fray—at first on the orthodox Christian side, then as a Deist, and ultimately as a full-fledged Atheist or *ne plus ultra* Infidel.

How great a spark the rash, intolerant incumbent of St. Peter's had kindled! Mr. Bradlaugh's next step on the downward path was to become a teetotaller, and this brought matters to a crisis. At the instance of the reverend gentleman, Mr. Bradlaugh's employers gave him "three days to change his opinions or lose his situation." He might have swallowed one at a time, but "Beer *and* the Bible" made his gorge rise.

Rather than succumb the poor boy elected to go out from his father's house a social outcast, and throw himself on the stony-hearted world. Whether pride or principle had most to do with this Hegira it might be hard to say, but in any case the die was irrevocably cast. He soon became known as a boy preacher of the most audacious infidelity. But it did not pay. Unlike Spurgeon's godliness, Bradlaugh's ungodliness was by no means "great gain." In his seventeenth year he found himself reduced to such straits that he was compelled to enlist in the 7th Dragoon Guards, and with this regiment he served for three years in Ireland, and there he did not neglect his opportunities. He studied the grievances of the Irish people on the spot, and hence his never-failing sympathy with that much-enduring race. By his hand was drawn up the famous manifesto of the Irish Republic which ushered in the Fenian agitation.

In 1853, through the death of an aunt, he inherited a small sum of money, out of which he purchased his discharge, and returned to London, quitting the regiment with a "very good character" from his colonel, who all along treated him with marked consideration. He was soon lucky enough to find employment in the chambers of a solicitor named Rogers, a liberal-minded man, who was proof against all the shafts of anonymous bigotry which were showered on him as the harbourer of Iconoclast. In this office Mr. Bradlaugh acquired a knowledge of legal principles and procedure of which the most eminent counsel at the English Bar might well be proud. He again began to lecture in various Metropolitan Freethought institutions, more particularly the Hall of Science, City Road, of which my friend, Mr. Evelyn Jerrold, has recently given an account so just and graphic.

In 1855, Mr. Bradlaugh had his first encounter with the police authorities in regard to the right of public meeting in Hyde Park. He carried his point, and was publicly thanked by the Royal Commission of Inquiry for the value of the evidence given by him on the occasion.

In 1858, Mr. Edward Truelove, the well-known and personally estimable Freethought publisher, was arrested for issuing the pamphlet, "Is Tyrannicide Justifiable?" while Simon Bernard was at the same time incarcerated at the instance of the French Government for alleged complicity in the Orsini conspiracy. In the defence of both Mr. Bradlaugh rendered material assistance.

"In October 1860," said Mr. Bradlaugh in his "Autobiography," "I paid my first visit to Wigan, and certainly lectured there under considerable difficulty, the resident clergy actually inciting the populace to physical violence and part destruction of the building I lectured in. I, however, supported by a courageous woman and her husband, persevered, and, despite bricks and kicks, visited Wigan again and again, until I had *bon gré mal gré* improved the manners and customs of the people, so that I am now a welcome speaker there. I could not," he naively adds, "improve the morals of the clergy, as the public journals have recently shown, but that was their misfortune, not my fault."

In 1861, Mr. Bradlaugh was arrested at the instance of the Young Men's Christian Association of Plymouth, but he succeeded, thanks to his forensic skill, in wringing from an unwilling bench of magistrates a prompt certificate of dismissal. Mr. Bradlaugh then, in turn, raised proceedings against the Plymouth Superintendent of Police for illegal arrest. The verdict, one farthing damages, though unsatisfactory in the main, had yet two important results— it made the Plymouth authorities pay sweetly for their intolerance in the shape of costs, and it secured the right of free speech in Plymouth and adjoining towns.

In 1862 a Church of England clergyman was guilty of a foul libel affecting the late Mrs. Bradlaugh and her two amiable and highly accomplished daughters, whom to know is to respect. "This fellow," says Mr. Bradlaugh, "I compelled to retract every word he had uttered, and to pay £100, which, after deducting costs, was divided amongst various charitable institutions. The reverend libeller wrote me an abject letter begging me not to ruin his prospects in the Church by publishing his name. I consented, and he has since repaid my mercy by losing no opportunity of being offensive. He is a prominent contributor to the *Rock* and a fierce ultra-Protestant."

Mr. Bradlaugh's relations with the Anglican priesthood, it must be admitted, have at all times been most unfortunate.

To the Reform League, in 1867, Mr. Bradlaugh, at his own charge, rendered most valuable services — services which, when his connection with the association ceased, were handsomely acknowledged in writing by the president, Mr. Beales, and the secretary, Mr. George Howell.

To his marvellous courage and perseverance is it likewise owing that the last fetter has been struck off the Press of England. Up to 1869 every newspaper was required by law to give securities to the extent of £800 against the appearance of blasphemous or seditious libels. Mr. Bradlaugh, refusing compliance, printed his journal "in defiance of her Majesty's Government," and so repeatedly baffled the law officers of the Crown in their prosecutions that the statute had finally to be repealed, the late Mr. J. S. Mill writing thus to the defendant in connection with the event: "You have gained a very honourable success in obtaining a repeal of the mischievous Act by your persevering resistance."

Mr. Bradlaugh was likewise instrumental, after much costly litigation, in establishing the competency of Freethinkers to give evidence in courts of law. He carried a case in which his testimony as plaintiff was objected to from court to court till the Evidence Acts of 1869 and 1870 eventually relieved Freethinkers from a disability so grievous and unjust.

During the Franco-Prussian war, Mr. Bradlaugh took no active part in favour of either side till the installation of the provisional Republican Government. Then, as might have been expected, he used his utmost influence on behalf of France. Great meetings were held in London and in the leading provincial towns to express sympathy with the struggling Republic, which it was hoped might ultimately be able to drive the invader from French soil. Twice was Mr. Bradlaugh put under arrest—once by the Provisional Government, and once by M. Thiers—for his presumed support of dangerous sections of the Republican party, but his loyalty to the cause of free government in France did not go unacknowledged. The Tours Government thanked him for his fraternal efforts in a long and flattering letter signed by Gambetta, Crémieux, Glais Bizoin, and Fourichon, while M. Tissot, the French *chargé d'affaires* in England, and Emmanuel Arago, a member of the Provisional Government, addressed him individually, the last-named eminent man concluding his note with the words:—"Mr. Bradlaugh est et sera toujours dans la Republique notre concitoyen."

In 1873 Mr. Bradlaugh conveyed to the short-lived Republican Government of Spain the congratulations of a great Radical meeting held in the Town Hall of Birmingham, and was received by the Republicans of nearly every shade with open arms, notwithstanding an intimation, lodged by Mr. Layard in his ambassadorial capacity, that the Queen of England would regard any manifestations of confidence in Mr. Bradlaugh as a personal affront. The speech which the English iconoclast delivered at the great banquet given in his honour at Madrid was marked by singular moderation of tone. He was perhaps the first Englishman who foresaw the accession of the Alphonsists to power.

Towards the end of 1873, Mr. Bradlaugh visited the United States of America, and commenced an extensive lecturing tour, dealing with such subjects as English Republicanism, the Irish Land Question, etc. He lectured in all the chief towns of New England and the middle States, and met generally with a most cordial reception. At Boston, "the hub of the universe," the late Senator Sumner presided at Mr. Bradlaugh's lecture, with Wendell Phillips and Lloyd Garrison on the platform beside him. Mr. Sumner introduced the great bugbear of English public life as "the Samuel Adams of 1873," the Samuel Adams of 1766 being "that austere patriot always faithful and true" who spoke the first words of defiant protest against the tyranny of English monarchical rule in New England. The lecturer realised on an average the handsome sum of one hundred and sixty dollars per lecture.

On the occasion of the Prince of Wales' mischievous and insidiously planned jaunt to India, Mr. Bradlaugh was not wanting to the popular cause. He called the people together in Hyde Park, in which he may be said to have preserved the right of public meeting, and entered a spirited though unavailing protest against the subsidy, and petitions bearing 135,000 signatures were in consequence laid on the table of the House of Commons. The shameless Tichborne imposture he smote with the hammer of Thor, and throughout the late disgraceful Jingo episode in the history of the nation he was faithful even to the shedding of blood. At the second of the two memorable Jingo demonstrations in Hyde Park he would in all probability have been killed but for his enormous bodily strength and personal intrepidity. As it was his left arm, with which he protected his head from the savage blows of his assailants, fell powerless by his side before he could cleave his way with a heavy truncheon to a place of safety. Erysipelas supervened, and for three weeks his life was in peril. It is but fair to add that five of his foemen found their way to St. George's Hospital.

I have mentioned these matters with perhaps tedious minuteness, because in public life Mr. Bradlaugh, like politicians in better repute, has a right to be judged by his "fruits." It is but too common in respectable circles to regard him as a vulgar, self-seeking demagogue. Now, demagogue he may be, but certainly not in the objectionable accepted sense of the word. He has never concealed his anxiety to get into Parliament, but of all the roads by which St. Stephen's may be approached he has certainly chosen the least likely and the most arduous. He has been at a world of pains to spoil his own chances. All the great "interests" —royalty, aristocracy, plutocracy, church, chapel, public-house—have arrayed themselves against him. Yet excepting Mr. Gladstone, this man has perhaps the most attached personal following of any politician in England. This unique position he has won by his daring, by his intellect, by his Titanic energy, and by his general thoroughness of character. If he is not a real hero, he is a surprisingly clever counterfeit. In his own way, and by his own example, he has inspired many thousands of the most abject of his countrymen with reinvigorated feelings of self-reliance and renewed hope on earth. He has taught them the inestimable lesson of self-help, of righteous indignation against oppression.

On the other hand, like nearly all Atheists whom I have known, he is a consummate egotist. He who recognises in nature no power greater than himself almost necessarily rises rapidly in self-esteem. There is very little room left for the Christian virtues of patience, humility, charity. Indeed, these are pretty much what Mr. Bradlaugh attributes to Christ as faults of character. There is no God, and Charles Bradlaugh is his prophet. This is the secret of his power. Not that I mean to affirm in the least that Bradlaugh's egotism is incompatible with the common weal. In a different way from Beesly or Spurgeon he has arrived at certainty. That is all. He might say, like Faust—

> "No scruples or doubts in my bosom dwell
> Nor idle fears of devils in hell."

Hurrah for the "Everlasting No!" On this sure foundation let the edifice of human happiness be erected. Absolute selfishness more or less enlightened—call it individualism, or by whatever name you will—is the way, the truth, and the life. Whenever any great world-synthesis of religious or moral ideas has broken down, this has been the inevitable result of analysis. But the human race can never permanently live on negations. In the heat of conflict, while the old system is dying and the new is unborn, they may appear almost like Gospel truths, but when the ground has once been fairly cleared their significance is at an end. Men once more begin to recognise in nature a more profound purpose, a more all-pervading intelligence, a more sacred continuity than before. Comte attempted to piece together the broken links of our faith, but failed. Mr. Bradlaugh merely dances an Indian war-dance in paint and feathers among the *débris*. It is, in my opinion, a poor and questionable occupation for so able a man. The Deliverer is yet to come, and there are many signs that he cannot now be far off. Meantime wise men will possess their souls in patience, awaiting with confidence the dawn of the better day.

But all this has little to do with Mr. Bradlaugh's politics, which are of this world, and not of the next. He is peculiarly wanted at this moment at St. Stephen's, where a disease worse than paralysis has seized on the legislative body. If the corpse can be revivified, he is the man to do it; and if I were a Northampton elector, Christian or Infidel, I should spare no effort to secure his return, if on no higher ground than on this, that desperate diseases require desperate remedies.

I am, moreover, bound to say this in favour of Mr. Bradlaugh as a politician, that in all my experience I have never known him take the wrong side on any public question. And what he has been in the past he will be in the future. He could not now betray the people though he were to try. He has peculiar claims on Northampton. Thrice has he contested it, and on each occasion has he come nearer winning. It is a disgrace to any system of government pretending to be representative that the acknowledged chief of militant English Republicanism, and what is of less consequence, of organised Secularism, should have no voice in the Legislature of a country which he has done so much by ceaseless toil to preserve from sinking into political apathy. A better plea than the exclusion of Mr. Bradlaugh from the House of Commons could not be adduced in favour of Mr. Hare's scheme of proportional representation.

It remains to glance, however briefly, at Mr. Bradlaugh's published writings. These consist chiefly of theological and political essays. Of the former, the philosophical or expositional portion is, for a very different reason, about as worthless as those of Mr. Spurgeon; while the historical, as for example the lives of David, of Jacob, and Jonah, are, to say the least, very amusing, though I should scarcely have thought the game worth the candle. Of his political works, on the other hand, all are accurate and of immediate interest. "Hints to Emigrants to the United States," in particular, no intending emigrant should be without. It is a plain, unvarnished tale told by the most competent and impartial observer who has ever yet applied his mind to this important subject. His sketches of Cromwell and Washington, though biography is by no means his forte, display statesmanlike insight. I conclude with the words of final "Contrast":—

"A fitting emblem for Oliver Cromwell is presented by the grandly glorious Western sunset. Still mighty in the fierceness of its rays, few eyes can look steadily into the golden radiance of that evening sun; the strongest must lower their glances, dazzled by its brilliance. Every cloud is rich with ruddy gilding, as if the mere presence of that sun made glorious the very path it trod. And yet, while one looks, the tints deepen into scarlet, crimson, purple, as though that sun had been some mailed warrior, who had gained his grand pre-eminence by force of steel, and had left a bloody track to mark his steps to power. And even while you pause to look, the thick dark veil of night falls over all, with a blackness so cold, complete, and impenetrable as to make you almost doubt the reality of the mighty magnificence which yet has scarcely ceased. In the eventide of his life's day such a sun was Cromwell. Few men might look him fairly in the face as peers in strength. His presence gives a glory to the history page which gilds the smaller men whom he led. And yet Tredah and Worcester, Preston and Dunbar, and a host of other encrimsoned clouds compel us to remember how much the sword was used to carve his steps to rule. And then comes the night of death—so thickly black that even the grave cannot protect Cromwell's bones from the gibbet's desecration. And not unfittingly might the sunrise, almost without twilight, in the same land, do service as emblem for George Washington. He must be a bold man who, in the mists and chills of the dying night, not certain of its coming, would dare to watch for the rising sun. And yet, while he watches, the silver rays, climbing over the horizon's hill, shed light and clearness round; and soon a golden warmth breathes life and health and beauty into blade and bud, giving hope of the meridian splendour soon to come. George Washington was the morning sun of a day whose noontide has not yet been marked—a day of liberty rendered more possible now that slavery's cloud no longer hides the sun; a day the enduring light of which depends alone on the honest Republicanism of those who now dwell in that land where Washington was doorkeeper in Liberty's temple."

IX.

JAMES ALLANSON PICTON.

> " Come wander with me," she said,
> " Into regions yet untrod ;
> And read what is yet unread
> In the manuscripts of God."

JAMES ALLANSON PICTON, the author of "The Mystery of Matter," is one of those rare persons who, to use his own quaint phrase, have "gone through Materialism and come out at the other side." Such an explorer, it will readily be admitted, well deserves a place in this or any other series of pioneers of progress. But I would rather not be the chronicler of his toilsome journey. No wonder if the St. Thomas' Square congregation, Hackney, found difficulty in following their spiritual guide on his dim and perilous way. But though the path which Mr. Picton has cleft through the Materialistic jungle be arduous for ordinary mortals to tread, it is in my opinion the best that has yet been cleared. "Narrow is the way that leadeth unto life, and few there be that find it." Mr. Picton makes a clean sweep of the supernatural, but imparts to the natural a lofty significance which more than compensates for the loss. "All forms of finite existence may, for aught I care, be reduced to modes of motion; but motion itself has become to me only the phenomenal manifestation of the energy of an infinite life in which it is a joy to be lost. To me the doctrine of an eternal continuity of development has no terrors, for believing matter to be in its ultimate essence spiritual, I see in every cosmic revolution a 'change from glory to glory, as by the Spirit of the Lord.' I can look down the uncreated, unbeginning past without the sickness of bewildered faith. *My Father worketh hitherto.* My sense of eternal order is no longer jarred by the sudden appearance in the universe of a dead, inane substance foreign to God and spiritual being."

> "Thus at the roaring loom of time, I ply,
> And weave for God the mantle thou seest him by."

All religions properly so-called conceive of phenomena as the outcome of an eternal, incomprehensible Power, " which makes for righteousness" throughout the universe. Every irreligious system, on the other hand, regards the phenomenal altogether apart from its source. The question then arises, which way of looking at the mighty enigma is the more philosophic? The Positivists reply, and Mr. Bradlaugh replies, "We know nothing of the source, nor can know." But their parade of ignorance almost presupposes the reality of that of which they profess to be ignorant.

"The same intellectual constitution which makes science possible, the impulse to seek after the reason of things and their completeness, implies in its very germ an already existing, though inarticulate, belief in ultimate substance and in an infinite unity. Further, the very fact that our mental faculties cannot work without suggesting this dim majesty which is beyond their ken, compels a constant reference thereto, which, as it is involved in the laws of thought, cannot be without practical import."

Our Positivist brethren will, of course, seek to impugn the validity of such reasoning, but they are, as a rule, persons so superstitiously anti-superstitious that their objections may be discounted almost by anticipation. In any case, Mr. Picton believes that he has passed clean through the prevalent Materialism and emerged into a spiritual effulgence which irradiates in some degree the darkest crannies of human destiny. He has unbounded faith, that is to say loyalty, to the Divine Will, as he apprehends it.

But if his own faith in the Eternal overflows, his charity towards those who have stopped midway in the ascent of the Materialistic Hill of Difficulty is equally without limit.

"Take the philosopher," he says, "who thought out, or thinks he has thought out, his system of the universe. Finding no place therein for a God such as he was taught to speak about and dream about in his childish years, he calmly says, "there is no God at all. . . . He is confident in his system of the universe, and is assured that it always works together under the same conditions to the same ends. He would stake his life upon the certainty that impurity and duplicity and dishonesty must bring misery and confusion into the Commonwealth. Now, such a man has far more trust in the Lord than ever he supposes. Through despair of presenting that inconceivable Being in any form whatever to his consciousness, he fancies that he dispenses with the thought entirely. But the more nearly he comes to a realisation of oneness in that system of the universe which he thinks he has wrought out, the more nearly does he come to the thought of God. The more confidently he rests in the certain working of moral as well as of physical laws, the more does he manifest that which, in our minds, is equivalent to trust in the Lord. Under any form of religion, and under no form of professed religion, then, the exhortation of the text, 'Trust in the Lord and do good,' may be carried out and its creed asserted."

In a word, Mr. Picton's charity induces him to ascribe religion to the professedly irreligious. He compels them to come in.

Discussing the problem of the immortality of the soul, he says:—

"We should not repine if the larger life beyond death remains a hope too grand for any earthly form. I live; this I know. And all around me is a Power, immeasurable, inscrutable, of which I can only think that it lives more grandly and mightily than I, folding me in its embrace and making a reverent feeling of my own nothingness the supreme bliss. Whence I came I know not; whither I go I cannot tell. But every moment of true communion with the Infinite opens out eternity. Whatever tenfold complicated change has happened or may come, however strangely the bounds which now limit my personal life may be broken through, however unimaginably my consciousness of God may be enlarged, it is impossible that the more real can be merged in the less real, and while material phenomena are but phantoms, God Himself only is more real than I."

The above quotations give but a faint impression of this remarkable work, "The Mystery of Matter," which, along with an earlier volume, "New Theories and the Old Faith," goes further towards revivifying true religion by rendering it credible, than all the heavy tomes of orthodox theology which have appeared within the last decade.

Mr. Picton has combined science, logic, disciplined imagination, and fervent piety in the execution of a task of immense difficulty, and the result is a cogent testimony to the indestructibility of essential religion in the soul of man:—

> "Still Thou talkest with Thy children,
> Freely as in old sublime;
> Humbleness and truth and patience
> Still give empire over time."

James Allanson Picton was born in Liverpool, in the historic year of reform 1832. His father, whose name was recently so honourably before the public as the originator and chairman of the Liverpool Free Library and Museum, was then a well-to-do architect, a staunch Liberal in a community abounding in political reactionaries, a cultivator of letters in a hive of commercial industry. He is the author of the "Memorials of Liverpool," a model work of the kind, and would now have been occupying the mayoralty chair in the Town Council but for the domination of a Tory majority, which the last municipal election has happily reduced to unwonted insignificance.

At an early age young Picton was sent to what was then known as the High School, the upper branch of the Mechanics' Institution, where up to his sixteenth year he continued to make steady progress in all the ordinary and some of the extraordinary branches of study.

On leaving school, Picton entered his father's office, and for the next three years of his life diligently set himself to master the requirements of the paternal profession, which, if he had continued to follow it, would pretty certainly have been to him a lucrative calling. But eventually he abandoned it for, as he believed, a higher, if less remunerative, occupation.

Inspired from his youth up with philanthropic sentiments, Picton had become an enthusiastic Sunday-school teacher, and this experience led him to think of the ministry as a suitable sphere of action.

He was never very orthodox in his religious beliefs—how could a mind capable of such profound speculation so be?—but he had an eye to his main object, the moral elevation of the poor and ignorant, and he decided that the pastoral fulcrum of Independent Nonconformity was the best for his purpose—which may be doubted.

Accordingly, at nineteen years of age he resumed his studies, and was entered simultaneously as a student of the Lancashire Independent College and of Owens College, Manchester. At the latter institution he stood first in classics at his final examination. In 1855 he took the Master's degree in classics at London University, and his academic studies were at an end.

In 1856 Mr. Picton's career as an Independent minister began. The start was not promising. Suspected of heterodoxy, he was black-balled by the zealous shepherds of the Manchester Ministers' Meeting, who appear to have applied to him pretty much the now somewhat obsolete argument, "He is an Atheist. *Ecce signum,* he doesn't believe in the Devil."

> "Careless seems the great Avenger ; history's pages but record
> One death-grapple in the darkness 'twixt old systems and the Word.
> Truth for ever on the scaffold, Wrong for ever on the throne—
> Yet that scaffold sways the future, and behind the dim unknown
> Standeth God within the shadow, keeping watch above his own."

The orthodox pastors, however, had gone a step too far. Public opinion strongly manifested itself against such an act of barefaced intolerance, and by a suspension of rules Mr. Picton was admitted to the pastorate of a congregation at Cheetham Hill, Manchester.

His work lay chiefly among the poor and destitute, for whom no man seemed to care. For the children he composed a model little "Catechism of the Gospels," and for the instruction of adults he and Mr. Arthur Mursell delivered weekly lectures on suitable subjects in the large room of a "ragged school."

In 1862, however, while thus beneficently engaged, the bull's-eye of orthodoxy was again turned on him. In connection with the centenary of "Black Bartholomew," he published a discourse entitled "The Christian Law of Progress," which was pronounced to be "of dangerous tendency." Thereupon the heretic removed to Leicester, where he succeeded to Dr. Legge's charge, but his "tendencies," it is deplorable to relate, became worse instead of better. He fell into bad company, particularly that of Mr. Coe, the Unitarian minister, and a powerful contingent of Radical working men, whom he was in the habit of addressing in his chapel on Sunday afternoons on such unhallowed topics as "True Radicalism," "The Rights of Man," the death of Earnest Jones, the Jamaica outrages under Governor Erye, etc.

As in Galilee, so in Leicester, the common people heard their teacher gladly, but the uncommon folks took a different view of the matter. What amounted to a vote of want of confidence in Mr. Picton's ministry was passed, and though very active steps were taken to prevent his departure from Leicester, the heresiarch felt constrained to turn his face towards our metropolitan Babylon, which, with all her drawbacks, is generally large-hearted enough to welcome able and earnest exponents of the most diverse opinions, whether religious or political.

In 1869 Mr. Picton succeeded to the pastorate of St. Thomas' Square, Hackney. Here his "tendencies" were as bad as ever. He resumed his evil habit of Sunday lecturing, and the intelligent artisans of the neighbourhood flocked to hear him. For two successive seasons the critical period of English history from the reign of Elizabeth to the Revolution of 1688 was subjected to systematic criticism, and Mr. Picton was never more gratified than by the appreciation of solid instruction exhibited by his auditors.

A working men's club was next started, an institution which survives in the Borough of Hackney Working Men's Club, one of the most useful and prosperous undertakings of the kind in London.

In 1870 preparations for the first London School Board election began, and Mr. Picton was among those who were solicited by the electors to offer themselves as candidates. He complied, and though then necessarily but little known to the general London public, secured a seat through the devotion of his friends, more particularly those of the working class. And the confidence then reposed in him was twice renewed with even greater emphasis by the constituency. For three years he filled a most responsible post on the Committee of School Management, before which are laid all the details of school affairs.

Throughout an advocate of "education, secular, compulsory, and free," he was not unnaturally believed by many besides myself to have deserted the Radical standard in favour of the present immoral "compromise" of the religious difficulty—the offspring of a foul *liaison* between Church and Chapel. But this, I am assured, is a misapprehension of Mr. Picton's position. Finding that the compromisers, while pretending to exclude from the schoolrooms one catechism, had practically introduced as many creeds as the total number of sects to which Board teachers belong, he exerted himself with very limited success to mitigate the evil by increasing the moral at the expense of the theological instruction.

As it is, Mr. Picton, after nine years' hard work on the Board, has been compelled, chiefly by the unsatisfactory state of his health, to seek a temporary respite from public duties, and the minds of our children are meantime at the mercy of a motley crew of Romanist, Anglican, Ritualist, Baptist, Presbyterian, Unitarian, and Atheist instructors to make or mar at their good pleasure. The result is easy to predict—a general sapping of the foundations both of religion and morals. Birmingham in this matter has fallen low enough, but she has not yet reached the metropolitan depth of degradation.

Some months ago Mr. Picton resigned his pastorate of the St. Thomas' Square congregation, and he is at present enjoying a well-merited rest from his labours. He does not intend to resume ministerial functions, I believe, but possibly to throw his entire energies into literary and political pursuits.

The gifted authoress of "The True History of Joshua Davidson" hazards the prediction that if Christ, who "went about doing good," were to reappear on the earth in our day, it would be in the character of a Radical politician; and if it is meant simply that the platform and the press are now more powerful agencies for good or evil than the pulpit, it were hard to differ from her.

Able, single-minded men like Picton are sadly wanted in Parliament, and the Churches will, as a rule, be glad to be rid of persons of such "dangerous tendencies." His political contributions to the *Fortnightly*, *Macmillan*, and the *Weekly Dispatch* have, apart from his platform utterances, marked him out as a vigorous political thinker, on whom Radical constituencies should keep an eye. He is a tried soldier in the ranks of Democracy, who well deserves promotion at the people's hands, all the more so because he would be the last to seek it.

X.

FREDERICK AUGUSTUS MAXSE.

> "To side with truth is noble
> When we share her wretched crust,
> Ere her cause bring fame and profit
> And 'tis prosperous to be just."

IT is now several years since I first chanced to meet Rear-Admiral Maxse at a Reform Conference, but until quite recently I have had no opportunity of verifying my early impressions. These, with certain reservations, were of a most favourable kind, and they have been abundantly confirmed on closer acquaintance.

Maxse is what so very few Englishmen are, an idealist in politics, a singularly poor hand at a compromise. Instead of accommodating his theory to the facts, he strives to bend the facts to his theory. With sailor-like single-mindedness, he has an awkward trick — awkward in a politician—of making use of language in order to express his meaning instead of concealing it, as a good wire-puller should. His more candid political friends, consequently, complain that he cannot be got, even at critical electoral seasons, to recognise the advantage of calling a spade an elongated agricultural implement. Hence the damning suspicion which obtains in certain quarters that the Admiral is, with all his ability, "impracticable." An Englishman and not "practical!" How could such a one hope to enter in at the strait gate which leadeth to St. Stephen's? Impracticability were a grievous fault, and grievously did the gallant Admiral answer it at Southampton in 1868, and in the Tower Hamlets in 1874. But the fault, and I frankly admit its existence, lay at least as much with the Admiral's critics as with himself. If he were too much devoted to the ideal, they were too little. I agree, for once, with the prophet of "sweetness and light," that "Philistia has come to be thought by us as the true Land of Promise; the born lover of ideas, the born hater of commonplaces, must feel in this country that the sky over his head is of brass and iron."

Now, Admiral Maxse is a born lover of ideas, a born hater of commonplaces, and he has never been adequately able to apprehend how inaccessible are the vast majority of his countrymen to such sentiments. In this sense has he shown himself really impracticable. Among a quicker-witted and more logical people, like the French, the chances are that he would have found himself quite at home. He ought to have known Englishmen better. A London constituency, unlike a Parisian, will always prefer a gluttonous alderman with a marked aversion to the letter *h*, to the profoundest philosopher or to the truest philanthropist. Blessed is the cultivated Radical who expects little of the average English elector, for he shall not be disappointed. Admiral Maxse, I have heard it said, has been seriously disappointed by his political experiences. Not disappointed, though disenchanted he has certainly been. But like other true soldiers of Democracy, he has "learned to labour and to wait."

The disillusioning process is always a painful one for a lofty, ardent nature like Maxse's, but it is salutary all the same. It does not alter by a hair's-breadth one's sense of duty, while it teaches invaluable lessons of method and adaptation in relation to the social environment. Progress, though inevitable, is seldom to be obtained by a *coup*:—

> "We see dimly in the present what is small and what is great,
> Slow of faith, how weak an arm may turn the iron helm of fate."

Frederick Augustus Maxse was born in London in the year 1833. He is now consequently in the full vigour of manhood, lithe of limb, and intrepid of carriage, every inch an "officer and a gentleman." He is on the Retired List, but in an emergency he might well become the Blake of a Second Commonwealth. Speculative, perhaps somewhat chimerical, in religion and politics, he is yet obviously a man of action, a born commander of men. His father, James Maxse, was a Tory squire of the old school, who had inherited immense wealth honourably acquired by the Maxse family as merchants in Bristol. He was one of the best heavy-weight riders across country of his generation, and as for his feats, have they not been duly recorded by Nimrod in connection with the famous Melton Meets? On the mother's side the Admiral is a Berkeley, his mother being Lady Caroline Maxse, daughter of the fifth Earl of Berkeley. The Berkeleys have for generations been noted for great physical toughness and consistent political Whiggery, the late "Ballot" Berkeley, M.P. for Bristol, being Maxse's uncle. Family politics, however, never influenced the Admiral's opinions in the least. He left home too early for that. He was afloat in his thirteenth year, having previously attended successively good private schools at Brighton, Hampton, and Paris. In Paris he acquired a mastery of the French language, which he has since found of the greatest benefit. His interest in French politics is at least as keen as in those of his own country. He is on terms of intimacy with nearly all the great men of the Third Republic, with whom he has so much more in common than with the ruck of English Liberals.

Excellent busts of Hugo and Gambetta—the best I have, seen—adorn his mantelpiece at The Chestnuts, Wimbledon, where all things bespeak the apple-pie order of the Captain's Cabin. One room is entirely hung with marine drawings, consisting chiefly of ships in which the owner has sailed. His first ship, which he joined on passing the examination then set to cadets, was the *Raleigh*, Captain Sir Thomas Herbert. The *Raleigh* sailed for the South American station, where she remained for three years. There was a naval brigade on shore to protect the town of Monte Video, and the *Raleigh* lay lazily off the coast to succour the marines if need were. These three years Maxse as good as completely lost. He was supposed to learn navigation, but the chaplain who was his instructor knew little or nothing about the subject which he was supposed to teach.

In his sixteenth year he returned to England, but was speedily again afloat as midshipman in H.M.S. *Frolic*, Captain Vansittart. The *Frolic* went to the Mediterranean. In 1852 he served as lieutenant on board H.M. sloop *Espiègle*, in the West Indies, whence he was invalided home just in time to take part in the Crimean war. He was appointed acting flag-lieutenant to Sir Edmund Lyons, and sailed for the scene of conflict. No sooner had the allied troops disembarked than his commanding officer recognised his special fitness to act as naval aide-de-camp to Lord Raglan. He was attached to the headquarter staff in naval uniform, but with a cavalry sword. Prompt, daring, intelligent, an opportunity for earning distinction was not long in occurring. He carried an important message to the fleet from headquarters, riding across the head of the Bay of Sebastopol, a distance of fifteen miles, through a territory alive with Cossacks and fugitive Russian regulars. Happily the gallant youth accomplished his task in safety, but it might well have been otherwise. So much was Lord Raglan impressed with this act of courage that he made it the subject of special commendation in an early despatch, and young Maxse was at once promoted to the rank of Commander. The Admiral, who is as modest as he is brave, makes light of the matter, but the example was much needed, and it had its effect on older officers, who, it may be remembered, were at the time much hampered in the discharge of their military duties by "urgent private affairs." Maxse was subsequently engaged in the battle of Inkermann, and witnessed "the Six Hundred" ride "into the jaws of death, into the mouth of hell," at Balaklava, his brother, Colonel Fitzhardinge Maxse, acting on the occasion as aide-de-camp to Lord Cardigan. On the death of Lord Raglan, whose memory he fondly cherishes, he returned with his remains to England on board H.M.S.

Caradoc, and was shortly afterwards appointed to the command of the steam corvette *Ariel*, in the Mediterranean. Thereafter his promotion in the service was, and would have continued, rapid, but circumstances arose which tended materially to divert his thoughts from purely professional objects.

Maxse's education had been purely naval. It ought, I think, to have been literary or philosophic. Ideas take possession of him with overpowering force. He is their servant rather than their master. He has read extensively and closely, but with passion, I do not say prejudice. The consequence is that he is at times apt to see objects in considerable disproportion, a defect which a more systematic scholastic training in youth would have done much to cure. While yet a "middy," he had read star-eyed Shelley, and the humanitarian impression made on his mind has never been effaced. The seeds of Radicalism were thus early laid, though they took some little time to germinate:—

> "There is no wind but soweth seeds,
> Of a more true and open life,
> Which burst, unlooked for, into high-souled deeds,
> With wayside beauty rife."

Let us hear the Admiral's own account of his conversion to the gospel of aggressive Radicalism:—"My profession has been that of a naval officer. I was brought up to the tune of 'Rule Britannia' and 'Britons never shall be slaves.' Ignorant of politics, when at sea I was indifferent to politics. If I had been polled for my vote as a young lieutenant, I dare say I should have voted Conservative—indifferentism forming a main element of Conservatism. What made me an active politician was, when I came to live on shore, observing the condition of the English agricultural labourers. I found that a large number of Britons *were* slaves, slaves to artificial oppressive circumstances, for the maintenance of which the governing classes stood, in my eyes, responsible; and upon the discovery of this I determined that if during the whole of my life I could carry but a single handful of earth towards the foundation of a better state of society, that handful I would carry." Accordingly the Admiral, acting on his well-worn maxim, "People who do not care for politics do not care for their fellow-creatures," has twice, as has been said, sought the suffrages of popular constituencies.

At Southampton, in 1868, he addressed himself more particularly to questions affecting the land and education. He is a fluent, forcible speaker, too earnest to be amusing, but always attractive because instructive. You feel that his mind is made up, and that what he says he will infallibly perform. But he does not see the by-play of electioneering, and from sheer honesty of purpose and detestation of chicane, he falls into the most obvious traps laid for him by the enemies of his cause. "Leading questions" are put to him which he answers with ruinous candour. He knows nothing of the Scotsman's art of answering one inconvenient question by asking another. He seems never even to have profited by the illustrious example of Mr. Gladstone's "three courses," which intimates to the caviller—" You pays your money and you gets your choice." It is seemingly impossible to get into the Admiral's head what is almost an axiom in electioneering, viz., that the shortest line that can be drawn between two political points is often a mighty circumbendibus. Neither at Southampton nor in the Tower Hamlets did the gallant Admiral evince the smallest appreciation of these elementary campaigning truths.

In the Tower Hamlets, though personally an abstainer, he took strong ground against the Permissive Bill, and he would have nothing to do with the publicans. Both parties, of course, voted against him. Again, Liberal Churchmen would have none of him because of his strong advocacy of disestablishment, while the Nonconformists, to their everlasting discredit, threw him completely overboard because of his advanced views regarding the opening of museums on Sundays. The committee of the Tower Hamlets Nonconformist Liberal Association had actually the indecency to issue a manifesto during the contest, wherein, after promising that they had carefully considered the claims of the various candidates, they went on to say,—" Captain Maxse, by his advocacy of the opening of museums on Sunday, and his sympathies in favour of 'Home Rule,' precluded a consideration of his name."

This being the enlightened verdict of Little Bethel, the defeat of the Radical candidate is not, perhaps, much to be wondered at, especially when it is added that only 17,000 electors took the trouble to go to poll for five candidates out of a constituency of 32,000. Some of these "fixes" the gallant Admiral could never be put in again, the advocates of the Permissive Bill, for example, having themselves abandoned their measure, and in its stead substituted "local option," a change of front which will enable Admiral Maxse and many other genuine Radicals in future to render them willing aid. By way of equivalent it will be their duty to help to keep off the land-sharks that prey on candidates of such exceptional honesty of purpose as the Admiral. His high courage, resolute purpose, and lofty enthusiasm would be a very clear addition of strength to the flaccid Radicalism of St. Stephen's. His failings outside Parliament would very closely resemble virtues inside.

Admiral Maxse's name is closely identified with several questions of vital interest to the nation, more particularly with Electoral Reform, Land Tenure Reform, Religious Equality, National Education, the Enfranchisement of the Agricultural Labourers, and Woman Suffrage. He has probed the inequalities of our representative system to the core, and if there be anyone who still believes in the delusion that this is a self-governed land, and has any desire to know the naked truth, I cannot do better than recommend him to peruse Maxse's pamphlet, "Whether the Minority of Electors should be Represented by a Majority in the House of Commons?" Thirty thousand electors, he shows, in small constituencies elect forty-four members of Parliament, while 546,000 in large boroughs return only thirty-five. Thirty thousand electors thus outvote 546,000. At the last general election 18,000 electors of Manchester, who recorded their votes in favour of a candidate, failed to return him, while 18,000 electors, living in petty boroughs or rural constituencies, seated no fewer than thirty honourable members! Fourteen thousand electors in Buckinghamshire return eight members; 50,000 in Lambeth have but two allotted to them.

Commenting on such stupendous anomalies, the Admiral indignantly observes,—" The splendid outcome of our parliamentary system is that a minority of electors appoint a majority of members of Parliament, and the majority of electors appoint their minority to be steadily outvoted and beaten, and all the while statesmen and journalists vie with one another in national brag, and tell the deluded people that they are blessed above all other peoples in their institutions and in their laws. And the story is circulated so persistently that at last, as people are ultimately convinced by a perpetual advertisement, they think that it is even so."

During the autumn of 1874, chiefly through the exertions of the Admiral, was formed the Electoral Reform Association. It had for its chief object the equalisation of constituencies, and started with the promise of a most useful career. It made shipwreck, however, unfortunately over the question of Woman Suffrage, against which Admiral Maxse set his face with, I think, most injudicious vigour. It is a problem which may be safely left for such goody-goody sentimental people to solve in their own fashion as we see voting for incompetent women in preference to competent men in School Board elections.

I have read with some curiosity the Admiral's " Woman Suffrage, the Counterfeit and the True—Reasons for Opposing Both," and can only feel astonishment that he should have been at so much pains to argue so stoutly either on the one side or the other. Female suffrage would have done very well if only the Admiral had had the good sense to let it alone. It is a topic which females and feminine men should be permitted wholly to monopolise. It will please them, and do no one much injury.

As a member of the executive council of the Land Tenure Reform Association, Maxse did yeoman's service. He lectured on the subject in various towns, and always with effect. At the great public meeting held in Exeter Hall in March 1873, presided over by the late John Stuart Mill, Admiral Maxse moved the first resolution, and anticipated in his speech much that is now being forced on public attention by the agricultural distress which has set in with such severity. The Association was perhaps before its time somewhat; but its attitude was prophetic.

Maxse's best known pamphlet, which has had a deservedly large circulation, is entitled "The Causes of Social Revolt," being the substance of a lecture delivered in London, Portsmouth, Bradford, Nottingham, and other towns. It will repay careful perusal.

It is not often that Admiral Maxse has concerned himself about foreign affairs, but his letters to the *Morning Post* on "the German Yoke" in Alsace-Lorraine were most valuable contributions towards the proper understanding of a nefarious "imperial" proceeding which it is safe to prophesy will yet cause much blood and many tears to be shed. The bravest of the brave and a Crimean hero, he has been throughout our "spirited foreign policy" a steady anti-Jingo and a foe to militarism. Indeed, wherever the Admiral has erred it has been on the side of a frankness rare in English public life. With his aristocratic and professional connections he might years ago have entered Parliament, either as a nominee of the Whigs or the Tories. Instead of that, "he humbly joined him to the weaker side" with the usual result. His choice of sides is an eloquent and spontaneous testimony to the grievances endured by the English people at the hands of an oppressive oligarchy. Such men as Frederick Augustus Maxse are an honour to any class, but belong to none. Their capacity for self-sacrifice is their true patent of nobility, and that no sovereign can either confer or take away.

XI.

THE HON. AUBERON HERBERT.

———◆———

"They are slaves who dare not be
In the right with two or three."

WHEN a patrician like the Hon. Auberon Edward William Molyneux Herbert comes to figure as a strenuous people's tribune, it is not unnatural that his motives should be subjected to searching analysis. Of thorns men do not ordinarily gather figs, nor of aristocratic bramble-bushes gather they democratic grapes. Nevertheless, when it does happen that grapes are produced in such circumstances, they are sometimes of the choicest quality. They are like the strawberry that has ripened under the nettle. In the society of a man like Herbert you feel that *Noblesse oblige* is not quite an empty phrase. There is a certain chivalry in his Radicalism, a knight-errantry if you will—a combination of courage and courtesy, gentleness and independence, which it would be hard indeed to match in these unromantic days:—

"For manners are not idle, but the fruit
Of loyal nature and of noble mind."

By one or two critics I have been accused of fanatical abhorrence of aristocracy; but it is not so. On the contrary, I should say of such men as Herbert, "I have not found so great faith, no not in Israel." I could name several members of his order who, for purity of motive, sense of justice, and genuine love of their fellow-men, have no superiors, or perhaps equals, in the ranks of those whose political principles may be said by comparison to bear interest. The aristocracy of England has never been absolutely without some redeeming representatives. If it had been wholly noxious it could not have survived so long. But it was founded in conquest and rapine, and it has all along clung to birth and not merit, as the chief justification of its existence. The House of Lords is the most extraordinary anachronism in the political world. The idea of a hereditary legislator is even more absurd than that of a hereditary butcher or baker, and if Englishmen had had any sense of the ludicrous the peerage would have been laughed, if not kicked, out of existence long ago. Notwithstanding some appearances to the contrary, the baronage of England, Mr. Herbert maintains, and I agree with him, is now as effete as the Sublime Porte. There is but one thing they can now do with advantage—efface themselves as speedily as possible, and fall into line in the great army of democracy, which, often retarded in its advance, never really turns back; which, "like death, never gives up a victim."

When an aristocrat by birth becomes a democrat by reflection, when a Royalist by association becomes a Republican by sympathy, the process of conversion can never be without interest. Those of us who, like myself, were at no time anything if not Radical, are apt to set but too little store by principles which one in Mr. Herbert's position prizes like so much treasure-trove. Converse with Mr. Herbert on such matters and you are made to feel as if you had been entertaining angels unawares. The ethical superiority of the Radical creed which you may have assumed he will demonstrate to you with a freshness of logic and a fervour of conviction that I have never heard surpassed. Not that I agree with all or nearly all of the practical conclusions at which he has arrived. Of some of these I shall have a few words to say by-and-by. It is the frank, generous spirit, void of the faintest suspicion of *arrière pensée*, in which he approaches every political problem that is the great matter.

Auberon Herbert was born in London, in 1838, his father being Henry, third Earl of Carnarvon, and his mother Hen-

rietta Anna Howard, niece of the twelfth Duke of Norfolk.
The father of the first Earl of Carnarvon, the Hon. Major-
General William Herbert, was a son of the eighth Earl of
Pembroke. Henry, the first earl, was raised to the baronage
as Lord Porchester of High Clere, Southampton, in 1780, and
in 1793 he was made Earl of Carnarvon. He was a gentleman of intrepid bearing, and is said to have earned his claim
to a peerage by drawing his sword and threatening to run
Lord George Gordon, of riotous memory, through the body
unless he undertook on the spot to withdraw the mob from
the precincts of St. Stephen's. The second earl affected
Whiggery; the third, the author of "Portugal and Gallicia,"
an authoritative book of travel of no inconsiderable literary
merit, was a Tory; while the fourth, the late Colonial Secretary (Mr. Herbert's brother)—whose resignation was the first
clear intimation to the country that Beaconsfield and the
Jingoes in the Cabinet meant serious mischief—it is hoped
will eventually sever his connection entirely with the uncon-
stitutional party, and join the Liberal party, with which he
is so much more in sympathy.

Mr. Herbert is married to Lady Florence Amabel, a
daughter of the sixth Earl of Cowper. She is a woman as
remarkable for simplicity of manners as for the vigour
of her intellect and the kindness of her heart. If Mr. Herbert is speculative, she is the incarnation of common sense.
Tennyson's daughter of a hundred earls was not one to be
desired. It is different with Lady Florence. She has fewer
airs than the opulent green-grocer's wife round the corner,
who might learn much from her in domesticity. With her
as with her husband, *noblesse oblige*.

Mr. Herbert's early education was superintended by tutors,
to the personal rather than to the scholastic influence of
some of whom he was much indebted. In 1857 he proceeded to Oxford, where he became a student of St. John's
College, but studied steeple-chasing and kindred pursuits
more than the ancient classics or any other kind of literature. The spirit of adventure was strong within him, and

after two years of desultory reading he determined to enter the army so as to see service abroad. Accordingly in 1859 he joined the 7th Hussars at Canterbury, and subsequently served in India for a period of sixteen months, attaining the rank of lieutenant. Here, perversely enough, he was as studious as at Oxford he had been idle. He edited a little magazine called the *Crusader*, and began to qualify himself for staff duties. With this object in view he returned to Oxford to complete his University curriculum, and graduated B.C.L. in 1862. On taking his degree, not caring to resume his military career, he devoted himself to University tuition, and subsequently obtained a "Founders' Kin" Fellowship.

In 1864 the man of "blood and iron" had matured his first great crime by procuring the invasion of Schelswig-Holstein by an irresistible Austro-Prussian army. Mr. Herbert, deeply sympathising with the gallant Danes, abandoned his academical pursuits and hastened to the Dybböl lines in order to encourage the defenders by succouring their wounded. He rendered valuable aid; was oftener than once under fire, and became a great favourite both with officers and men. The Government subsequently signalised its gratitude by conferring on him for his labour of love the Order of the Danneborg. The distinction was otherwise well merited, for Mr. Herbert pleaded the Danish cause with the English people in a series of "Letters from Sönderborg" in a way that would have stirred their hearts to active intervention if anything could have aroused them from their apathy. When England is prepared to fight innumerable campaigns, it is, alas! not done on behalf of Danes, but of Turks—not for freedom but for despotism.

The Sönderborg letters are replete with manly feeling and shrewd military observation. They have been republished in a little volume, entitled "The Danes in Camp," which every student of Bismarckian rascality ought to peruse. I make but two brief extracts illustrative of its tone : "As you will easily conceive, the conduct of England has placed neither our nation nor our policy in a favourable light. The

Danes are sorely hurt at our desertion of their fortunes. They feel it the more acutely because between them and England there has existed a silent brotherhood. English is the language which is taught in their schools and colleges, and which forms a regular part of their education. Their customs, their feelings, their ways of thought, their character, and sometimes their very look, are English. To English literature they have turned in the attempt to oppose it to that of Germany. English is the language which they seem to have chosen even in preference to French or German, which would have afforded a better link of communication between themselves and the nations of that great continent on whose outer edge their fortunes are cast, and to which they cling desperately, with nothing but the bravery and the stern virtues of the old Norse race to maintain them on their narrow foothold."

"Dark as are the clouds, and cruel as is the game which is being played out, I am determined to remain constant to my belief that I have both visited Arcadia and seen a 'patriot army.' Do you blame me in this nineteenth century for cherishing two such illusions, if illusions they are?"

While I am about it, I may as well finish the record of Mr. Herbert's warlike experiences. No sooner had he left the Dybböl lines than he sought those before Richmond, where the silent, inflexible Grant had at last got Secession firmly by the throat. The taciturn General gave him a kindly reception, but was not to be "drawn." Not a man on the staff could move him to the faintest demonstrativeness. At last a dispute arose as to the distance between two places. One officer said five miles, another four, another six. "Three and a half," interjected Grant, with a tone of decision. He alone was right. The General had been drawn, and everybody was satisfied. President Lincoln, to whom Mr. Herbert was introduced at Washington, impressed him very differently. Sagacity and honesty were his obvious characteristics. His implicit trust in Grant made Grant be trusted. The General had many enemies, some of whom accused him of intemperance. "*Does* Grant get drunk?" asked the President of one of these maligners. "They say so." "Are you *quite* sure he gets drunk?" "Quite." The President paused, and then gravely ejaculated, "I wonder where he buys his whisky?" "And why do you want to know?" was the astonished rejoinder. "Because, if I did," replied Lincoln, "I'd send a barrel or two of it round to some other generals I know of."

When Mr. Herbert went to America he was still a Conservative. What he saw and heard, however, on the great Republic was not without its influence on his future conduct. "The easy, powerful current of life, the mixture of classes, the respect shown to all, made a deep impression on me. Ready to see all the faults of democratic government, I saw them, and yet felt the power and depth of the tide, as if I had passed from some narrow lake out on the sea."

In the Franco-German war Mr. Herbert was once more a ministering angel to the wounded. "When in the Luxembourg train I heard the sound of firing, jumped out, took my place in a coach going to a nearer point, saw the battle of Sedan going on from a rising ground, collected some lint, and with a large pitcher of water started for the field. It was a long distance, and I found myself for the greater part of my road absolutely alone. The villages through which I passed were almost entirely deserted. In the afternoon the firing ceased. It was nightfall before I reached the field. Some German officers asked for a drink of my water, but considerately accepted my excuse that it was for the wounded. . . . In the morning I found a country house full of wounded French who had not yet been taken to hospital. I spent the whole morning in applying the few simple lessons I had received in washing wounds and bandaging, and I think the belief that they had a doctor amongst them, which I took care not to disturb, did more good to them than my bandages. It was a pretty little country house, and as I tore up sheets and curtains for what I wanted I could not help thinking of the return of the luckless owners, who, however, perhaps came back with an exceedingly grateful feeling that any house at all remained to them." This simple narrative admirably illustrates the leading features of the writer's character—his self-reliance and his humanity.

To come now to Mr. Herbert's political acts and principles, which should have been reached sooner. He started life, to be sure, as a Tory, but I cannot discover that he had ever the root of the matter really in him. He called himself a Conservative long after he had become more Liberal than most Liberals. At Oxford, however, he must have had the reputation of being a sound Conservative, for he was elected President of the Union Debating Society over a Liberal opponent, and in 1865 he stood unsuccessfully for Newport, Isle of Wight, in the "Liberal-Conservative" interest. In 1866 a safe Conservative seat was offered to him, but he had resolved to throw overboard the Irish Church, and with the Irish Church necessarily went the safe seat. More decided steps followed. He went down to Newport and frankly told his old friends that he could no longer conscientiously act with them; and, what testified still more strongly to the sincerity of his motives, he resigned his private secretaryship under Sir Stafford Northcote, and engaged in the less lucrative occupation of furthering various working-class movements in which Mr. Hodgson Pratt took an interest. The conversion was complete, but not sudden. It had been produced by several considerations, the cumulative effects of which were simply irresistible. On his way to serve in India he had stopped long enough in Venice to take sides against the Austrian tyrant, and on his return to Oxford the writings of Mill, more particularly his famous treatise on "Liberty," Buckle's "History of Civilisation," and the personal influence of Goldwin Smith, had the effect, so to speak, of regenerating his entire political nature. When he made the final plunge into Radicalism he felt like an escaped prisoner on the first day of freedom.

In 1868 he made a gallant but unsuccessful effort to wrest

a seat from the Tories in Berkshire. It was not long, however, before a much more suitable constituency sought and secured his services. In 1870 he was returned for Nottingham by a large Radical majority, and remained in Parliament till the dissolution of 1874, when, to the disappointment of many enthusiastic friends and supporters, he retired from the representation of the borough. His health had suffered, and his notions of the true functions of a Legislature had in the interval undergone a change of which he could not at the time foresee the consequences. He required leisure to think them out. But of this more anon.

In Parliament Mr. Herbert was not, generally speaking, a *grata persona*. He was too conscientious to be a good party man, too Radical all round both for Conservatives and Liberals. The cut and colour of his coats, moreover, scandalised honourable members. They were light green when they ought to have been of a more sombre hue, and it was oftener than once debated by certain of the weaker brethren whether the Speaker's attention might not with advantage be drawn to the irreverent attire of the member for Nottingham. This, however, was not Herbert's greatest enormity. In seconding Sir Charles Dilke's famous motion respecting the Civil List, and commenting on the justly-suspected frauds connected therewith, Mr. Herbert, while alluding to the actual occupant of the throne with all the superstitious reverence which a degraded public opinion could possibly exact, had yet the manhood to affirm his conviction that a Republic is preferable to a Monarchy in a community such as ours. Thereupon one honourable member "spied strangers in the gallery," and had the Press ejected, while a noble lord manifested his loyalty to the Crown by "cock-crowing!" So great was the uproar, raised chiefly by the "party of order," that for the space of an hour the member for Nottingham could scarcely ejaculate more than a word or two at a time. The Speaker pronounced the scene the most "painful" he had ever witnessed; yet I have never heard anyone allege that Herbert uttered one untrue or offensive syllable in his speech. The fault was entirely with the fault-finders. It was the old story—Great is Diana of the Ephesians; the silversmiths were all in arms. Howbeit,

"They have rights who dare maintain them ;
   We are traitors to our sires,
Smothering in their holy ashes
   Freedom's new-lit altar fires.
Shall we make their creed our jailor ?
   Shall we, in our haste to slay,
From the tombs of the old prophets
   Steal the funeral lamps away
To light up the martyr fagots
   Round the prophets of to-day ? "

The religious provisions of the Scotch Education Bill of 1872 Mr. Herbert criticised with commendable candour and a rare appreciation of the evil effects of ecclesiastical uniformity on the character of the Scottish people. The justice of his strictures, to which no member from Scotland dared give expression, was gratefully acknowledged by enlightened Scottish opinion.

In 1873, in criticising the Army Estimates, Mr. Herbert took occasion to impugn the organisation and question the efficiency of our standing army. He proved by irrefutable statistics that the British army is consumed by loathsome disease, and thinned by incessant desertion to an extent that is almost incredible. " Officers and gentlemen," needless to say, were horrified, more especially when they were told by a member, who might be regarded as one of themselves, that a territorial citizen force, a simple extension of the Volunteer system, would be more effective in the field than a standing army, and incomparably less costly to the British taxpayer.

Mr. Herbert's kindly nature was never seen to greater advantage than in the untiring efforts he made " to provide for the protection of wild birds during the breeding season." He set forth the virtues of thrushes, blackbirds, jays, and sparrows with something like paternal pride, and begged the House, with a genuine ardour which aroused its sympathy, "to have compassion on creatures which were so entirely within their power." So true it is that—

> "He prayeth well who loveth well
> Both man and bird and beast."

Since Herbert has been out of Parliament he has devoted himself to agricultural pursuits, but no serious call to public duty has found him wanting. The Bulgarian atrocities filled his mind with horror. He came to London and "lobbied" for weeks in order to put courage into the breasts of timid Liberal members. The St. James's Hall conferences owed him much for the success which attended them, and he gave a striking proof of his personal intrepidity by presiding at the second anti-Jingo meeting in Hyde Park, where the Herculean strength of Mr. Bradlaugh with difficulty availed to save himself from a violent end.

As a politician, Mr. Herbert has latterly adopted the ultra-individualist theories of Mr. Herbert Spencer, and started a "Personal Rights and Self-Help Association" as the outward manifestation of his new faith. The Personal Rights Association abhors Socialism in every form. What is Socialism? It exists whenever the State does for individuals what they might voluntarily achieve for themselves. They are the best laws which repeal laws. The Church as by law established is a Socialist institution—down with it. National education is Socialist—down with it. The Poor Law is Socialist—repeal it. The Liquor Laws are Socialist—away with them. Factory legislation is Socialist—undo it. What is wanted is absolute free trade in everything—religion, ignorance, whisky, destitution, and overwork. The hotter war, the sooner peace. The individual must save himself. By throwing away the State crutch is it alone possible to learn to walk. The true sphere of government is merely to preserve the internal and external police of the realm. When more is attempted it is an illegitimate and baneful exercise of authority, an arrest of progress, a stunting of the national growth. Either the State must do everything for the individual, or the individual must do everything for himself. Neck or nothing! It is the ideal social democracy of Germany against the ideal individualist democracy of England. Unfortunately the problem is complicated, and will remain insoluble until monarchy and aristocracy have disappeared from both countries. A privileged aristocracy at the top of the social pyramid necessarily implies protected poverty at the base. Deal with the cause before you meddle with the effect. When some simple form of Republican government, based on universal suffrage, such as Mr. Herbert desires, has been attained, it will be time enough seriously to concern ourselves about the intrinsic consequences of Socialism and Individualism. With a completed democracy, socialist and individualist conundrums will solve themselves. Let Mr. Herbert seek first the Republic, and all else will be added to him.

XII.

EDWARD AUGUSTUS FREEMAN.

> " The Politics are base:
> The Letters do not cheer;
> And 'tis far in the deeps of History
> The voice that speaketh clear."

AMONG eminent English Radicals, Freeman, the historian, occupies a unique place. He goes forward by going backward. He is a Radical because he is a Conservative. He is a Democrat because he is a student of antiquity. Addressing the Liverpool Institute in November last, he described himself as "belonging to that old-fashioned sect that dreads nothing so much as the change of novelty." It is his boast to be one of the trusty few who "cleave to the old faith that there is something in the wisdom of our forefathers, and that the right thing is to stand fast in the old paths." The Tories are dangerous innovators. Our political progress has consisted in setting aside "the leading subtleties which grew up from the thirteenth century to the seventeenth" and reverting "to the plain common sense or the eleventh or tenth, and of times far earlier." The most primitive institutions of the English race were based on universal suffrage. The Swiss Republic is the oldest polity in Europe, and the best. In all history there is hardly a more picturesque chapter than that with which Freeman's "Growth of the English Constitution" opens: "Year by year, on certain spots among the dales and mountain-sides of Switzerland, the traveller who is daring enough to wander out of beaten tracks and to make his journey at unusual seasons, may look on a sight such as no other corner of the earth can any longer set before him. He may there gaze and feel what none can feel but those who have seen with their own eyes, what none can feel in its fulness but once in a lifetime, the thrill of looking for the first time face to face on freedom in its purest and most ancient form. He is there in a land where the oldest institutions of our race—institutions which may be traced up to the earliest times of which history or legend gives us any glimmering—still live on in their primeval freshness. He is in a land where an immemorial freedom, a freedom only less eternal than the rocks that guard it, puts to shame the boasted antiquity of kingly dynasties, which by its side seem but as innovations of yesterday. There year by year, on some bright morning of the spring-tide, the Sovereign People, not entrusting its rights to a few of its own numbers, but discharging them itself in the majesty of its own corporate person, meets in the open market-place or in the green meadow at the mountain's foot to frame the laws to which it yields obedience as its own work, to choose the rulers whom it can afford to greet with reverence as drawing their commission from itself. Such a sight there are but few Englishmen who have seen. To be among those few I reckon among the highest privileges of my life.

"Let me ask you to follow me in spirit to the very home and birthplace of freedom, to the land where we need not myth and fable to add aught to the fresh and gladdening feeling with which we for the first time tread the soil and drink in the air of the immemorial Democracy of Uri. It is one of the opening days of May; it is the morning of Sunday, for men there deem that the better day the better deed—they deem that the Creator cannot be more truly honoured than in using in His fear and in His presence the highest of the gifts which He has bestowed on man. But deem not that because the day of Christian worship is chosen for the great yearly assembly of a Christian commonwealth the more direct sacred duties of the day are forgotten. Before we in our luxurious island have lifted ourselves from our beds the men of the mountains, Catholic and Protestant alike, have already paid the morning worship in God's temple. They have heard the Mass of the priest or they have listened to the sermon of the pastor before some of us have awakened to the fact that the morn of the holy day has come. And when I saw men thronging the crowded church, or kneeling for want of space within on the bare ground beside the open door, and when I saw them marching thence to do the highest duties of men and citizens, I could hardly forbear thinking of the saying of Holy Writ, that 'where the Spirit of the Lord is there is liberty.'

"From the market-place of Altdorf, the little capital of the canton, the procession makes its way to the place of meeting at Bozlingen. First marches the little army of the canton, an army whose weapons never can be used save to drive back an invader from their land. Over their heads floats the banner, the bull's head of Uri, the ensign which led the men to victory on the fields of Sempach and Morgarten, and before them all, on the shoulders of men clad in a garb of ages past, are borne the famous horns, the spoils of the wild bull of ancient days, the very horns whose blast struck such dread into the fearless heart of Charles of Burgundy. Then, with their lictors before them, come the magistrates of the commonwealth on horseback, the chief magistrate, the Landamman, with his sword by his side. The people follow the chiefs whom they have chosen to the place of meeting, a circle in a green meadow, with a pine forest rising above their heads and a mighty spur of the mountain range facing them on the other side of the valley. The multitude of freemen take their seats around the chief ruler of the commonwealth, whose term of office comes that day to an end. The Assembly opens; a short space is first given to prayer, silent prayer, offered up by each man in the temple of God's own rearing. Then comes the business of the day. If changes in the law are demanded, they are then laid before the vote of the Assembly, in which each citizen of full age has an equal vote and an equal right of speech. The yearly magistrates have now discharged all their duties; their term of office is at an end, the trust which has been placed in their hands falls back into the hands of those by whom it was given, into the hands of the sovereign people. The chief of the commonwealth, now such no longer, leaves his seat of office and takes his place as a simple citizen in the ranks of his fellows. It rests with the free will of the Assembly to call him back to his chair of office, or to set another there in his stead.

"Men who have neither looked into the history of the past, nor yet troubled themselves to learn what happens year by year in their own age, are fond of declaiming against the caprice and ingratitude of the people, and of telling us that under a Democratic Government neither men nor measures can remain for an hour unchanged. The witness alike of the present and of the past is an answer to baseless theories like these. The spirit which made Democratic Athens year by year bestow her highest offices on the patrician Pericles and the reactionary Phokion still lives in the Democracies of Switzerland, and alike in the Landesgemeinde of Uri and in the Federal Assembly at Berne. The ministers of kings, whether despotic or constitutional, may vainly envy the same tenure of office which falls to those who are chosen to rule by the voice of the people. Alike in the whole Confederation and in the single canton, re-election is the rule; the rejection of the outgoing magistrate is the rare exception. The Landamman of Uri, whom his countrymen have raised to the seat of honour, and who has done nothing to lose their confidence, need not fear that when he has gone to the place of meeting in the pomp of office his place in the march homeward will be transfered to another against his will."

In the foregoing extract the reader has Freeman at his best—Freeman the Liberal politician and Freeman the devout Christian. His politics and his religion, like Gladstone's, inspire all his writings. His life has been one strenuous endeavour to vindicate by precept and example the noblest traditions of the one and of the other. As a man of Teutonic stock, he has at all times taken strong ground against unhappy Celts, and, as a follower of Christ, he has assuredly never shown undue compassion for the disciples of Mahomet. Yet it were hard to tax Mr. Freeman with prejudice. The strength and honesty of his intellect no man can question. Of historians he is the most industrious and accurate, and he is by no means deficient in imagination. In this last quality he is of course immeasurably inferior to a prose poet like Carlyle, but there is compensation. He has never sunk a *Vengeur*, and I could scarcely conceive of him having the philological credulity to connect "king" with "cunning man." History is but past politics, just as politics are present history. This cardinal truth Mr. Freeman, as a narrator of events, fully apprehends, and this it is that gives such lucidity and value to all his writings. He has, moreover, moral courage of the highest order, and admirable tenacity of purpose. To his own mind his objects are invariably clear, and he takes the most direct, if sometimes not the most pleasant, means of clarifying the minds of others. For such constitutionally inaccurate persons as Beaconsfield and Froude he has, like experience, proved himself a hard taskmaster, but the public has reaped the benefit of his occasionally "brutal frankness."

Yet with all these varied qualifications, moral and intellectual, Mr. Freeman is not without his limitations. His mind is a peculiarly English mind, strong in facts and shrewd at inferences, but weak and timid in the application of first principles. Original speculators like Spencer or Bain might logically overthrow the very foundations of his political and religious beliefs, and he would never know or care. He is an accomplished specialist in letters, and he is content so to be. Living all his days the life of a squire of his county, his habits of thought are as realistic as those of the class of which he is so great and unwonted an ornament. All the difference is that his historical recollection is better than theirs. Things that they regard as sacred by reason of their antiquity he knows to be of comparatively modern origin. In a note to "The Growth of the English Constitution" he makes the following manly declaration with regard to the monarchical superstition which is so sedulously fostered in this country: "There really seems no reason why the form of the Executive Government should not be held as lawful a subject for discussion as the House of Lords, the Established Church, the standing army, or anything else. It shows simple ignorance, if it does not show something worse, when the word 'Republican' is used as synonymous with cut-throat or pickpocket. I do not find that in Republican countries this kind of language is applied to the admirers of Monarchy; but the people who talk in this way are just those who have no knowledge of Republics, either in past history or in present times. They may very likely have climbed a Swiss mountain, but they have taken care not to ask what was the constitution of the country at its foot."

Edward Augustus Freeman was born at Harborne, in the neighbourhood of Birmingham, in 1823. He unfortunately lost both parents before he was one year old, his father, John Freeman, Esq., of Pedmore Hall, Worcestershire, dying at the comparatively early age of forty. His paternal grandmother, who resided at Northampton, became his guardian, and with her he had his home till his removal to Oxford in 1841. Before proceeding to the university, he had attended for several years a school at Cheam, Surrey, a private tutor, the Rev. Mr. Gutch, subsequently preparing him for matriculation at Trinity College. There his great talent and industry were not without their reward. He was elected a Scholar, and in 1845 he became a Fellow of his college. Twelve years later, after the publication of several of his historical works, he was made Examiner in Law and Modern History, and in 1873 Examiner in the School of Modern History. Both universities have vied with each other in recognising his vast attainments, Oxford conferring on him the honorary degree of D.C.L., and Cambridge that of LL.D.

Like many other Oxford men who have subsequently arrived at a knowledge of the truth as it is in Radicalism, Mr. Freeman was brought up in the strictest bonds of political and ecclesiastical Toryism. His grandmother had sown seed at Northampton which the Tractarians, then in the ascendant, watered at Oxford. Among his college friends was Patterson, now Monsignor, and other incipient Romanists of distinction. About this period, likewise, he wrote verses, and very good verses, too, as regard form, of an ultra-Royalist or Jacobite character, Carlos, a maternal ascendant who, tradition says, was the last man to strike a blow for the King at Worcester, being a favourite subject of his muse.

But so sound an intelligence as Freeman's could not long draw sustenance from such unrealities. In 1847 he married an estimable lady, the daughter of his former tutor, Mr. Gutch, and gradually put away the more childish things of political and ecclesiastical reaction. Slight, and it might be said almost whimsical, considerations at first weighed with him. Always an interested and critical student of history, Church history at first more particularly, he was struck with the unsatisfactory bearings of two ecclesiastical facts or fictions. Edward the Confessor had a wife, and the kingdom sorely wanted an heir to the Crown, but the saintly character of the monarch could only be sustained by practical celibacy. Was this asceticism rational sanctity? Again the salvation of some millions of unfortunate Swedes was made to turn on the sufficiency of the consecration of a particular bishop of the sixteenth century. Was this reasonable theology? Clearly the chaff of Ritualism must be separated from the older and more solid grain of Anglicanism.

The Tractarian movement was not, however, all loss to Mr. Freeman. It made him a profound student of architecture, and a clever sketcher of ecclesiastical buildings. In such matters he has often been consulted by the greatest authorities, among others by Sir Gilbert Scott. His " History of Architecture" (1849), "an Essay on Window Tracery" (1850), and "The Architecture of Llandaff Cathedral" (1851), his earliest publications, are still works of acknowledged merit.

While I am dealing with Church matters, I may as well note the progress which this enlightened Churchman has made in respect of the question of disestablishment and disendowment. He heartily supported the abolition of the Irish Establishment, and in 1874 he published a curiously tentative volume, in which he discussed the position of the English Church, arriving at the somewhat novel conclusion that the property of the National Church is not national property. Its revenues, he argues, are in precisely the same position as those of Nonconformist communions. The Sovereign Power, however, being absolute, may appropriate whatever it has a mind. A neater little juggle with Austin's definition of sovereignty I do not remember to have seen. True, the State may never have by any formal act, as Mr. Freeman alleges, endowed the Church as by law established; but surely Mr. Freeman will not deny that there was a time when the Church and the people were co-extensive, and in theory they are still one and indivisible. In practice the so-called State Church is merely a monopolising sect which has fraudulently appropriated the shares of all the other sects. These latter, when they are strong enough to bring sovereign authority to bear, will eject the dispossessor, and compel him to disgorge his ill-gotten gains. He would be a bold Churchman, indeed, who should propose to deal similarly with the revenues of Nonconformist communions. More recently, however, the attitude of the State Church towards the struggling Christian populations of Turkey has satisfied Mr. Freeman that, having ceased to act as the conscience of the nation, its moral justification is at an end. It is to be hoped Mr. Gladstone and other zealous Churchmen will likewise discern how faithfully the Nonconformists of England have done what the Established sect has so conspicuously left undone.

In the autumn of 1869 Mr. Freeman pricked the national conscience in a memorable manner regarding the "morality of field sports." He held up the barbarities of the battue to the shame and scorn of mankind. The withers of "quality" were mercilessly wrung, from those of the Prince of Wales downwards. There were numberless attempted defences, but not one that Mr. Freeman was not able to break down with the greatest ease. The contemptible hypocrisy of persons like his Royal Highness who act as patrons of societies for the prevention of cruelty to costermongers' donkeys, while themselves delighting in the cruel and unmanly massacre of tame pigeons and semi-domesticated pheasants, was thoroughly exposed in the course of the controversy, and a well-aimed blow struck at the heart of the abomination of the Game Laws, which have so long disgraced the statute-book of the country.

> "Strange that of all the living chain
> That binds creation's plan
> There is but one delights in pain—
> The savage monarch man!"

It is hardly necessary to say that, with perhaps the single exception of Mr. Gladstone, Mr. Freeman is the greatest living master of the Eastern question in all its details. He was four years of age when the battle of Navarino was fought, and he remembers the receipt of the intelligence. He may be said to have been interested in the emancipation of the Eastern Christians ever since. At the time of the Crimean war his pen was incessantly employed in combating the national madness. The number of persons in this country who then understood the real issues in the East was insignificant, and Freeman was one of the few. He may be said to have advocated the "bag and baggage" policy from the beginning. And he never lost sight of his object. When the City fell down and worshipped the Sultan on the occasion of his visit to London, Mr. Freeman almost alone entered a spirited protest against the base idolatry, and described the Oriental tyrant in befitting terms. When the Herzegovinian insurrection broke out he was one of the first who strove to range his countrymen on the side of the oppressed. By innumerable letters to the newspapers and speeches in various towns he did an immense deal to enlighten public opinion, and he succeeded personally in raising no less a sum than £10,000 in furtherance of the good cause. In 1877 he visited Greece, and was received by the people of such places as Zante, Corfu, Ithaca, and Athens with unbounded enthusiasm and gratitude. He addressed them in their own tongue, and, as he himself has related, was not merely cheered, but kissed by certain of his audience. Among the Christian population of the Balkan Peninsula the names of Gladstone and Freeman are deservedly regarded as household words.

The greatest impeachment in my opinion of the soundness of Mr. Freeman's political judgment was his justification of the annexation of Alsace-Lorraine—I beg a thousand pardons, Elsass-Lothringen—by the Germans at the conclusion of the Franco-German war. He boldly argued that Germany was entitled to rend from France a portion of territory which had once been Teutonic, whatever the inhabitants, who were notoriously French in sympathy, might say to the contrary. The consent of the governed, the necessary condition of free government, was nowise needed when the precious Teuton had his fish to fry. Now, I admit that France had many offences at her back for which it was right that she should atone, but had the "man of blood and iron" and the Majesty of Prussia none? What of bleeding Poland? What of Silesia? What of Hanover? What of Schleswig-Holstein? All this Pan-Teutonism conveniently overlooked. And what has been the result? A war of revenge has been rendered a dead certainty:—

> "Out of evil, evil flourishes;
> Out of tyranny, tyranny buds."

An imperial despotism has been established in Germany at least as detestable as that which Louis Napoleon Bonaparte set up in France. The iron of that tyranny has entered into the very soul of the German people, and so long as it can be pretended that a Gallic *revanche* is possible, there will it remain. How Mr. Freeman could have justified such a palpable sowing of dragon's teeth I have never been able to fathom.

In 1868, Mr. Freeman contested Mid-Somerset in the Liberal interest, but without success. His failure, I consider, was a public loss of no small magnitude. He is a good speaker, and his special knowledge would on many occasions in recent sessions have been of the highest utility in Parliament. For five-and-twenty years he was a Saturday Reviewer, and he wrote much in the *Pall Mall Gazette* in its more Liberal days. The House of Commons contains no member who, as a student of constitutional history, could compare for a moment with the author of the "Norman Conquest," the "History of Federal Government," and "Comparative Politics." Any legislature might well be honoured by the presence of such a scholar, and any constituency in the kingdom might be proud of such a representative.

O'CONNOR'S LIFE OF BEACONSFIELD.

PEOPLE'S EDITION.

LORD BEACONSFIELD:
A BIOGRAPHY.

BY T. P. O'CONNOR, M.A.

PRICE TWO SHILLINGS.

London:
W. STEWART & CO.,
THE HOLBORN VIADUCT STEPS, E.C.

OPINIONS OF THE PRESS.

A terrific exposure of the public career of Lord Beaconsfield.—*Spectator*.

A storehouse for all future writers of modern history.—*Athenæum*.

We know not where the history of the period it embraces can be found so succinctly narrated.—*World*.

The narrative throughout is most animated and eloquent.—*Nonconformist*.

It is a work of high literary excellence.—*Scotsman*.

Mr. O'Connor has told the story in the most graphic manner.—*Echo*.

Written in a critical spirit, and its permanent value is consequently greater.—*Time*.

An important political work, and one which cannot be too widely read. By far the completest work which has yet appeared.—*Manchester Examiner*.

One of the most important contributions to our literature that has lately appeared. The Book has a capital index.—*Sheffield Independent*.

Considered merely as a mine of facts, supersedes all others.—*Western Morning News*.

A very able and complete work.—*Western Daily Mercury*.

Mr. O'Connor has taken pains to collect a vast amount of information relating to the early incidents of Mr. Disraeli's public career.—*Daily Chronicle*.

Mr. O'Connor has availed himself of many sources of information within his reach.—*Bookseller*.

A most interesting and popular life of Lord Beaconsfield.—*North British Daily Mail*.

Just Published. Price 1s.

PARLIAMENT AND THE CONSTITUTION.

A Popular Explanation of the Forms and Usages of the British Parliament.

BY

A PARLIAMENTARY REPORTER.

London:
W. STEWART & CO.,
THE HOLBORN VIADUCT STEPS, E.C.

SYNOPSIS OF CONTENTS.

Election of Members—Assembling of Parliament—The Speaker—House of Peers—House of Commons—Petitions—Returns—Introduction of Bills—Queen's Speech—Questions—Motions — Estimates — Public Bills — Second Readings—Committee—Private Bills—Select Committees—Publication of Evidence—Sittings of Parliament—Rules of Debate—Prorogation—Privilege—THE CONSTITUTION—Ancient Rule—Conquest—Military Service—The Church—Constitutions of Clarendon—Courts of Justice—Progress of the People—Magna Charta—The House of Commons—Customs Duties—Constitutional Progress—The Rising of the Peasants—The Reformation — The Bill of Rights — Parliamentary Reforms.

*** *To those who would properly understand Parliamentary Debates, and to newspaper readers generally, this accurate and clearly written little manual should prove of very considerable value.*

JUST PUBLISHED, Crown 8vo, 2s., Superior Edition, 3s. 6d.

WILLIAM EWART GLADSTONE,

AND

WHAT HE HAS DONE:

A POPULAR BIOGRAPHY.

BY

SAMUEL BENNETT
(OF THE MIDDLE TEMPLE),
BARRISTER-AT-LAW.

London:
W. STEWART & CO.,
THE HOLBORN VIADUCT STEPS, E.C.

CONTENTS.

I. THE TWO PREMIERS.
II. YOUTH AND EARLY ASSOCIATIONS.
III. THE RISING HOPE OF THE TORY PARTY.
IV. PEEL'S LIEUTENANT.
V. MINISTER OF FINANCE.
VI. THE FRIEND OF HUMANITY.
VII. THE CRIMEAN WAR.
VIII. A PROSPEROUS REGIME.
IX. THE OTHER SIDE.
X. THE PRESENT SITUATION.

www.ingramcontent.com/pod-product-compliance
Lightning Source LLC
Chambersburg PA
CBHW032148230426
43672CB00011B/2485